MAR 11 2005

SCENE 17 - Goof enters gym thru door, broad shouldered, wears towel wrapped around head, bathrobe on. Removes three bathrobes, last one on coat hanger, and towel, is disclosed with narrow shoulders, etc.

18
18

22
21

MCU: Bashful, Sneezy and Happy.
Bashful: "LOOK OUT - SHE'S MOVIN'!"
Happy; "SHE'S WAKIN' UP."
Sneezy: "WHAT'LL WE DO?"

MLS: Group. Doc: "HIDE!" Group
scrambles under bed - Dopey last.

The Art of Walt

From Mickey Mouse to the Magic Kingdoms

REVISED AND EXPANDED EDITION

Christopher Finch

Harry N. Abrams, Inc., Publishers

For Willa, Milo & Romy Beckman, Milo Chamberlin,
Reeve Finch, Cerulean Ozarow, Griffin & Jasper Scott,
and Charlie & Benjamin Wasson

Editor: Andrea Danese
Designer: Russell Hassell
Photo Research: Samantha Topol
Production Manager: Maria Pia Gramaglia

Library of Congress Cataloging-in-Publication Data

Finch, Christopher.
   The art of Walt Disney: from Mickey Mouse to the Magic Kingdoms / by
Christopher Finch.— Rev. and expanded ed.
      p.   cm.
   Includes index.
   ISBN 0-8109-4964-4
   1. Disney, Walt, 1901–1966. 2. Walt Disney Productions. I. Title.

NC1766.U52D533 2004
384'.8'0979494—DC22

               2004010016

Printed and bound in China
10 9 8 7 6 5 4 3 2 1

Harry N. Abrams, Inc.
100 Fifth Avenue
New York, N.Y. 10011
www.abramsbooks.com

Abrams is a subsidiary of

LA MARTINIÈRE
GROUPE

Contents

Introduction

The Walt Disney Company occupies a unique place in the history of American popular culture. Among all major entertainment corporations, none is more marked by the imagination and persona of its founder.

More than eighty years ago, Walt Disney came to Los Angeles and with his brother Roy launched a tiny animation studio. Assisted by a feisty mouse, a dyspeptic duck, and many talented artists, he built that studio into an entertainment center that made his name world famous. He single-handedly developed the animated feature film – creating classics of the genre – then branched out into live-action films, television and other fields of entertainment. He rethought the amusement park, transforming it into the theme park, and dreamed of building a prototype city of the future.

Walt Disney achieved all this while, for much of his career, fending off financial disaster that was just a flop away. For all the precariousness of his position, Disney never wavered in his vision, and time and again he was vindicated by the success of enterprises that observers – including some of his closest advisors – had seen as follies.

So attuned was he to public taste that, almost forty years after his death, Walt Disney remains a powerful presence in the world of popular culture.

The entertainment empire he built has expanded and become more diversified. In the past two decades and more, since Michael Eisner and the late Frank Wells took over the corporation (with the crucial support of Walt's nephew, Roy E. Disney), The Walt Disney Company has enjoyed glittering successes, becoming one of Hollywood's most prosperous organizations. The revamped company is now a major player in every branch of entertainment, from the Broadway stage to network and cable television. Significantly, though, much of its strength still derives from the areas with which Walt Disney's name is most keenly associated, animated films and theme parks.

The story of Walt Disney's rise to fame, and the renaissance of the Disney organization under the guidance of Michael Eisner, are the twin subjects of this edition of *The Art of Walt Disney*, originally published over thirty years ago and now fully revised and updated for the second time.

When I completed the first version of *The Art of Walt Disney*, toward the end of 1972, I believed that the Disney Studio would continue to thrive in one form or another, and I had no doubt that the theme parks had a healthy future. The *raison d'être* for the book, however, was Disney's achievement in the field of animation. Everything else – no matter how remarkable in and of itself – grew out of that achievement, and it seemed, in the early seventies, that the Studio's great string of animated features was playing itself out.

The fate of Disney animation seemed to lie in the hands of a few veteran character animators and story artists who had been with Disney since the thirties and were, in the seventies, on the verge of retirement. True, there were gifted younger artists in the animation department, and the veterans had helped implement an ambitious training program (which has paid off handsomely), but it was hard to imagine then that the future held a full-fledged resurgence of Disney feature animation.

Yet this is exactly what we have seen in recent decades. Since the mid-eighties, Disney's feature animation department has produced a significant number of movies that deserve to be counted amongst the finest the genre has given us.

This is an extraordinary achievement, and much of the credit for it must go to the management team that has been in place since Michael Eisner became chairman, in 1984, of what was later renamed The Walt Disney Company. The Eisner team made sweeping changes so that the Studio could become fully competitive with industry giants like Warner Brothers and Paramount. The feature animation department, however, was a special case, left largely to its own devices and to the care of Roy Disney, the one man in the management team who fully understood animation.

Feature animation, therefore, was given an opportunity to make a place for itself in the new Disney firmament. Guided by department head Peter Schneider, a brilliant team of young veterans began to produce films that Walt Disney would have been proud of. They received solid support from Eisner, from Roy Disney, and from Studio chief Jeffrey Katzenberg, who, prior to his departure from the company in 1994, came to play an important role in shaping the future of Disney animation, involving himself in the creative process and encouraging the artists to set their sights high.

Unlike feature animation, the Disney theme parks were thriving when the new management team took over. EPCOT Center in particular was a success that should be credited to the interim management team, led by Card Walker, which guided the company for more than a decade after the deaths of first Walt Disney and then his brother Roy.

Michael Eisner and Frank Wells brought fresh energy to this already flourishing situation. Making use of the established corps of "Imagineers," many of whom had worked with Walt Disney, they set out to revivify the existing parks while at the same time developing new theme parks in Florida, Europe, and Japan (where Tokyo Disneyland had already opened in 1983).

Like the recent animated feature films, the Disney theme parks have been modernized in response to the taste of a new generation brought up in a world that has changed greatly since Disneyland Park opened its gates in 1955. The remarkable thing is that this has been achieved without in any way diluting the special character that has been drawing visitors to the theme parks for more than four decades.

Which brings me full circle to the assertion that today's Walt Disney Company is still powerfully stamped by its founder's vision and persona.

Who was the man behind the persona and what was he like?

Walt Disney was a celebrity before he was out of his twenties, and he stayed in the public eye for the remainder of his life, notably as the on-camera host of his own television show. Yet he remains an enigma. Even with his closest associates, he always held some aspects of his personality just out of reach.

Certain things are indisputable. He was a man who believed absolutely in his own instincts and abilities, an artist who would go to any lengths to ensure that a project was carried out exactly as he had conceived it. He surrounded himself with many talented men and women but always remained completely in control. Consider Walt Disney at any point in his career and it is difficult to avoid the feeling that a master plan was unfolding. That plan existed only in his head and remained unknowable until, piece by piece, it was given concrete form and grafted onto the mythology of our century.

Some reviewers of the first edition of this book objected to the assertion that Walt Disney was a great artist. A great entrepreneur, perhaps, they conceded, but how could he be considered an artist when he was dependent on the very evident talents of such immensely gifted animators as Ub Iwerks, Fred Moore, Art Babbitt, Bill Tytla, and the legendary Nine Old Men?

Iwerks, Moore, Babbitt, Tytla, and the rest deserve enormous credit for their brilliant contributions to the Disney oeuvre, but ultimately Walt Disney himself was the architect of all that was achieved in his name from 1923 until his death in 1966. He was not an outstanding draftsman and had given up animating by the time Mickey Mouse was created. (It was relevant to the expression of his genius, however, that he could turn his hand to every aspect of the making of an animated film, from drawing to operating a camera.) But he was the ultimate *auteur*. He had an astonishing command of the language of filmmaking, and beyond that he had an uncanny sense of how to shape a movie, and of how to squeeze the maximum emotional impact from a story.

Walt Disney's grasp of cinema was both intuitive and learned. He would have made an outstanding live-action director, but since he worked in the field of animation – where anything is possible, at least in theory – he developed an even broader vision than might otherwise have been the case. At the same time, his early experience as a producer of eight-minute cartoon comedies refined his sense of dramatic economy. In a Mickey Mouse cartoon or a Silly Symphony, not a single frame could be wasted. When he graduated to producing feature-length films, Disney remained as parsimonious as ever in terms of story-telling technique. In films like *Snow White and the Seven Dwarfs* and *Pinocchio,* nothing that was not essential to advancing the story or the delineation of character was allowed to slow the screen narrative.

Beyond that, Disney dared to do things that no one else had done. He was a visionary – but a visionary who had the common touch that enabled him to take the mass audience along with him into uncharted territory.

At the outset of his career, Walt Disney was often underestimated by his rivals and by unscrupulous impresarios. They recognized the caliber of the talents he surrounded himself with and assumed that if these talents could be lured away, the Disney Studio would collapse. In reality, the one man who made Walt Disney Productions so successful was Walt Disney himself.

Later, Disney was underestimated for other reasons. Since the values expressed in his movies and other enterprises are the deceptively simple values of the cartoon and the fairy tale, some observers have been fooled into presenting simplistic pictures of Walt Disney the man, and of what he stood for. Some have portrayed him as a naive genius – a natural rather than a cultivated talent – a notion that might help explain his popular appeal but that totally overlooks the subtlety, complexity, and refinement of vision in his best work.

Other commentators have ignored Walt Disney's gifts altogether and have presented him as an exploiter of talent with political views that verged on the despotic. It should be acknowledged that his record in the area of labor relations was far from unblemished, but it has never been convincingly demonstrated that he was an advocate of political authoritarianism, as has been suggested. (In one recent book that espoused this point of view, I counted more than thirty factual errors in a single chapter, which did little to encourage my trust in the author's more outrageous assertions.) It can accurately be said, I believe, that Walt Disney was sometimes guilty of high-handed paternalism toward his employees. Some artists thrived in this paternalistic atmosphere. Others – among them a handful of major talents – eventually became disenchanted and left the Studio.

So far as Disney's personal politics are concerned, they remain as mysterious as the man himself and would probably make a worthwhile – and possibly frustrating – subject of study for someone who was prepared to do some painstaking research. Doubtless Disney was subject to some of the misconceptions and prejudices that were common to most Americans of his generation. Having the common touch – the intuitive understanding of what the masses want – inevitably involves the popular artist with some of the questionable dogmas espoused by those same masses.

In any case, it must be emphasized again that Walt Disney was a complex man, not easily pinned down. To attempt to define him in terms of political cliché does a disservice to the intelligence of the reader. This is especially the case since Disney's sphere of influence was not the Republic that is governed from Washington; it was the Magic Kingdom that he ruled from Burbank.

There, Walt Disney's imagination was sovereign.

The sequence of recent animated films that began with *The Little Mermaid*, along with parallel developments in the Disney theme parks, is proof of the fact that the creative achievements of one man of genius can be sustained and built upon by a team of gifted individuals who have thoroughly immersed themselves in the master's imagination without surrendering their own sense of adventure and enterprise.

The word "team" is important here, because films like *Beauty and the Beast* and *Pocahontas* are brought into being by groups of artists who have learned how to interact creatively with their peers without sacrificing their own individuality. In certain respects, the way a Disney animated feature is created today is the *opposite* of the way *Snow White* was created. Although character suggestions were solicited from the outset, and concept art helped determine the look of the film, for all intents and purposes, *Snow White* took shape in one man's brain. It was then carried out by virtuoso artists, the way a well-rehearsed orchestra performs a composer's score. *Beauty and the Beast*, though it evolved with considerable guidance from Jeffrey Katzenberg, Roy Disney, Howard Ashman, Don Hahn, Kirk Wise, and Gary Trousdale – a leadership team within the greater creative team – was rooted in the contributions of scores of artists who helped shape the film at every stage. The musical analogy evoked is that of a very large jazz band with many soloists and group improvisers responding to the challenge presented by a handful of skilled arrangers and by a great precursor – Walt Disney.

The system evolves and responds to changing times. New technology comes into play. But still the end product remains consistent with Disney's original vision. The sense of continuity is apparent in the films and in the theme parks.

This edition of *The Art of Walt Disney* attempts to remain faithful to the 1973 original, while bringing the story up to date. In fact, the bulk of the material that was in that first edition remains intact in these pages, though some of it was revised at the time of the last major update, published in 1995, to bring the text in line with current research. That edition also added several new chapters dealing with the animation revival that had occurred under the Michael Eisner administration, recent live-action films, and the expansion of the theme parks.

This edition adds still more material, reflecting developments that have occurred during the past decade. It includes entirely new chapters devoted to the Pixar computer-generated films, to Disney's successful Broadway adventures, and to the new theme parks in Anaheim and Tokyo. In addition, there is greatly expanded coverage of traditional Disney animation, including such recent films as *Lilo & Stitch, Brother Bear,* and *Home on the Range.* Several other chapters have been revised and in some cases expanded. This version of *The Art of Walt Disney* also includes many new illustrations, bringing the Disney story up to the present.

I A New Art Form

1 Early Enterprises

Walter Elias Disney was born into a modest Chicago household on December 5, 1901. His birthplace, 1249 Tripp Avenue, was a small wood-frame structure of the type that can be found in the inner suburbs of any Midwestern city. His father, Elias Disney, was Canadian born and of Anglo-Irish descent. At this time Elias was a building contractor, and we may judge the success of that operation by the fact that Walt later described how his mother sometimes went out to the building site with the men, sawing and hammering planks. Mrs. Disney was the former Flora Call, an Ohio girl whose family had moved to Kansas in 1879. There the Call and Disney families became friends. When the Calls moved to Florida in 1884, Elias followed and bought a citrus plantation. Four years later he married Flora, who was by then teaching school. At the time of Walt's birth, there were already three children in the family – Herbert, Raymond, and Roy. Walt was to develop an especially close relationship with Roy, who was nearest to him in age, a relationship that was to be of great importance to both of them. Later a daughter – Ruth – was added to the family.

In 1906, Elias Disney decided to pull up his roots once again and moved his family to a forty-eight-acre farm outside Marceline, Missouri. Then as now, small farms did not offer an easy route to prosperity. Herbert and Raymond, both in their teens, had developed a taste for city life and soon returned to Chicago. Walt and Roy were, of course, expect-

Walt Disney's birthplace at 1249 Tripp Avenue, Chicago, built by his father, Elias Disney.

Below, from left: Walt Disney at the age of nine months; Roy Disney in 1913; Elias and Flora Disney in 1913; Walt Disney at the age of twelve ed to help their parents with the farm chores. It was an extremely hard life, but one which Walt later remembered with considerable affection.

It was on the farm that he began to draw. We may be sure that this was not encouraged by his parents, but he did make the first tentative steps toward his eventual career. Meanwhile, the farm operation was in trouble. In 1910, Elias sold the property with all its livestock and moved the family once again – this time to Kansas City, ninety-five miles southwest. There Elias bought a newspaper delivery business. Naturally, Walt and Roy were co-opted into contributing their services and found themselves getting up at 3:30 in the morning to meet the trucks of the *Kansas City Star*. Walt, then just nine years old, made his rounds every day, even in the depths of the Kansas City winter, which often brought several feet of snow. Roy, eight years his senior, would soon be in a position to escape this drudgery, but he maintained his close relationship with Walt, giving him good advice and finding ways for him to earn a little money (the work for their father was unpaid). The good advice included telling Walt that he need no longer stand for the beatings Elias was in the habit of administering.

The hard work continued, but Walt's interest in drawing persisted, as did a growing taste for theatrical expression. In a rare gesture of indulgence, Elias allowed Walt to enroll for Saturday morning classes at the Kansas City Art Institute (the elder Disney justified this on the grounds that the classes would be "educational"). Thus, at the age of fourteen, Walt acquired a smattering of formal art training. Just as important, in view of later developments, was Disney's relationship with one of his schoolmates, Walt Pfeiffer. Pfeiffer (in later years a Disney staffer, holding for a while the position of Studio manager) shared Disney's budding interest in the performing arts. They evolved a kind of juvenile vaudeville act – "The Two Walts" – and made occasional appearances at amateur nights in local theaters, even managing to win a few prizes.

Pfeiffer remembers that getting to these performances was not easy because of the strictness of Disney's parents. "Walt's dad always hated anything that had to do with entertainment. A lot of times, when we were fooling around, getting on amateur nights and things like that, I'd go down and sneak Walt out the window. We'd be real quiet and I don't think his dad ever missed him not being in the room. When we'd get through, we'd shove him back in the window and I'd go home. I'd always tell my folks where I was going because my dad encouraged me. He encouraged Walt too."

Pfeiffer recalls another incident that occurred when Disney was about twelve. "We went to Benton School, where J. M. Cottingham, the principal, ran the place like a king. One Lincoln's birthday, Walt came to school all dressed up like Lincoln. He had a shawl that I guess he got from his dad, he made a stovepipe hat out of cardboard, and he got a beard from some place downtown that had theatrical things to sell. He did this all on his own. When Cottingham saw him, he said, 'Walter, you look just like Lincoln. Why are you dressed this way?' Walt said, 'Well, it's his birthday and I want to give the Gettysburg Address.' He had

Left: "The Two Walts": Walt Pfeiffer, left, and Walt Disney pose in costumes they devised for one of their amateur night performances, c. 1915. Right: Walt Disney, center right, on an outing of Benton School students

memorized it. So he got up in front of his class and the kids thought this was terrific. Then Cottingham took him to each of the other classes and he repeated the performance."

We know too that Disney was fascinated by Charlie Chaplin and the other great silent comedians, so he must have managed to visit the movies from time to time. This first Kansas City period seems, for all its stringencies, to have provided the young Disney with ample opportunities for learning and entertainment.

In 1917, Elias decided upon another move. This time he returned to Chicago, where he purchased a part share in a small factory. Walt remained in Kansas City to finish out his school year (Roy was still there, working as a bank teller); then he spent the summer as a news butcher on the Santa Fe Railroad (news butchers hawked newspapers, fruit, candy, and soft drinks), a job which enabled him to see a little more of the country while feeding his enthusiasm for trains – an enthusiasm which would provide him with an important outlet later in life. In the fall, he joined the family in Chicago and enrolled at McKinley High School. Here he contributed drawings to the school paper and managed to get some further art instruction from a newspaper cartoonist named Leroy Gossett. World War I was in progress, and on June 22, 1917, Roy Disney enlisted in the Navy. Walt had dreams of enlisting too, but he was underage. He discovered that one could become a Red Cross ambulance driver at seventeen and, though still sixteen, managed to join up. (His

Left: Walt Disney with the cartoon-decorated ambulance he drove in France in 1919. Center: in his barracks in Neufchâtel, Disney set up a drawing board and continued cartooning. Right: back to civilian life, Disney soon found work in a Kansas City commercial art studio

mother, probably relieved that he would be driving an ambulance rather than handling a rifle, allowed him to falsify his birth date on the application.) He was sent to a staging post at Sound Beach, Connecticut, but the armistice was signed before he got any further. There was still a need for drivers in Europe, however, and he eventually found himself in France, assigned to a military canteen in Neufchâtel, where he soon established himself as the unit's unofficial artist, earning a few extra francs with such enterprises as painting fake medals onto leather jackets and camouflaging captured German helmets so that they could be passed off as snipers' helmets.

Disney returned to the United States in 1919. His father had a job waiting for him, but Walt was determined to make a career in commercial art. He headed for Kansas City and found work at a local studio where he made friends with another employee, Ubbe "Ub" Iwerks, a young man of Dutch descent who was to become the most important associate of his early career. Iwerks was a talented draftsman, and it soon occurred to them to go into business for themselves. They acquired desk space at the offices of a publication called *Restaurant News* and immediately achieved some modest success. But then Disney saw a newspaper advertisement for a job with an organization called Kansas City Slide Company (soon changed to Kansas City Film Ad). This company made what we would now call commercials for display in local movie theaters. They were, in fact, producing crude animated films. This new medium and the salary

The staff of Kansas City Film Ad Service, with Disney seated on the right-hand brick post. Ub Iwerks is standing seventh from the right

offered – forty dollars a week – appealed to Disney. He applied for the job and got it. Iwerks took over the business they had started, but within a few months he, too, joined Kansas City Film Ad.

Throughout the nineteenth century, scientists and inventors had intrigued the general public with a whole series of devices which could take a sequence of drawings and make them seem to move. Most of these were variants upon a simple machine which had been conceived almost simultaneously by Dr. Joseph Antoine Plateau of the University of Ghent and Dr. Simon Ritter von Stampfer of Vienna. (The inspiration for their experiments was a paper entitled "The Persistence of Vision with Regard to Moving Objects," which Peter Mark Roget presented to the British Royal Society in 1824.)

The Plateau–Stampfer device consisted of two disks mounted on a single shaft. The images to be viewed – they might portray a man running or a horse jumping – were attached in chronological sequence to the rim of the inner disk. When this disk was rotated, an observer looking through one of the slits cut into the rim of the outer disk would perceive an illusion of movement. This system was developed into the zoetrope, which remained a popular toy for many years.

Photography had meanwhile come to the public's attention in 1839, and its own more spectacular development paralleled that of these "wheel of life" novelties. In 1872, Eadweard Muybridge began his

While at McKinley High School in Chicago, Disney contributed numerous drawings to the school paper and, during his service in France, sent an illustrated letter to his former schoolmates eyes hold disregard for others? The door opened noisily—Marie stood in the bright glare of the hall lamp.

"I beg your pardon," she murmured, backing into the hall, "my friend used to rent this studio. I did not know she had moved."

The door was closing—in a moment she would be gone——

"Marie!"

The door reopened.

"Won't you please come in?"

Marie came in and upon his invitation demurely seated herself on the edge of the chair before the painting.

"Oh! You are drawing my picture, aren't you?"

Kenneth was one vast monument of suppressed emotion. Marie knew this very well, but her gaze was as innocent as a baby's when she turned. Her smile brought out dimples—two of them.

Was she playing with him? He did not care. She was at least worth another trial.

"I—I didn't wait to hear your reason for not marrying—that is not caring to marry me."

He was a very embarrassed young man.

Again she smiled.

"I haven't any reason now. You see I was afraid people would say that I married you for your money. I thought I couldn't stand that. But, do you know, I've been thinking it over and I can't see that it matters what people think. You'll know that it isn't so—so I think I will marry—Kenneth—Kenneth you're mussing my hair—Kenneth really—now—please—I haven't any powder with me and my nose—"

A very flushed young woman made her appearance.

"Kenneth," a pause, "by the way—I—I—haven't any friend who ever lived here. I looked you up and came on purpose to make you ask me again. Now—Ken—"

The End.

"Oh! You are drawing my picture, aren't you?"

famous photographic studies of animals and humans in motion. In 1887, aware of Muybridge's work, Thomas Edison began to experiment with the idea of motion pictures, which he thought of as a logical extension of and accompaniment to his phonograph. By 1889 he had built the first kinetoscope, a kind of peep-show viewer which held fifty feet of film, enough to run for about thirteen seconds. The machine made its commercial debut on April 14, 1894, at a kinetoscope parlor in New York City. Several of these machines were exported to Europe, leading a number of pioneers there to explore the possibilities opened up by this invention. In 1895, the brothers Louis and Auguste Lumière took out a patent on a device which successfully combined the principles of the kinetoscope with those of the magic lantern – which is to say that it was able to project moving pictures onto a screen. They called their machine the *cinematographe*. By the following year, Edison films were being shown on a more sophisticated projector built by Thomas Armat of Washington. The Armat machine, known as the vitascope, was the direct ancestor of the modern movie projector.

These sudden advances, from the kinetoscope onward, were made possible by the fact that, in 1889, George Eastman of Rochester, New York, had begun to manufacture flexible strips of photographic film using a nitrocellulose base. This film – far more convenient than anything available until that time – was designed specifically to meet the mechanical requirements of "roller photography" in the Eastman Kodak camera. It was also ideally suited to the needs of the men who sired the motion picture industry, and it followed naturally that movies evolved primarily in terms of the photographic image.

Eadweard Muybridge, *Figure Hopping*, 1887

It was not until 1906 that the first animated film was attempted. In that year J. Stuart Blackton, a commercial artist who later produced movies for Edison, conceived a little entertainment which he called *Humorous Phases of Funny Faces*. The level of animation achieved in this first effort was rudimentary. It did not capitalize so much on drawings seeming to move as on drawings seeming to complete themselves (though there was some primitive use of movement – a man might, for example, appear to wiggle his ears). The notion that it was possible to photograph drawings and make them appear to move did, however, spark the imaginations of one or two other innovators. In 1908, Winsor McCay put his comic-strip character Little Nemo into an animated film. Later he toured the vaudeville circuit with a cartoon titled *Gertie the Trained Dinosaur*. McCay appeared on stage as the film was projected, and the gimmick was that Gertie seemed to obey his commands, concluding her performance by "catching" an apple which he pretended to throw to her. McCay was a gifted draftsman and, viewed today, the animation in this movie seems surprisingly accomplished. (He had selected a dinosaur as his subject so that nobody could accuse him of tracing photographs.) Gertie was devised to fit in with a stage act, which may account for the fact that the story line, crude as it is, is well enough shaped so that the film can still be watched with pleasure.

McCay's success prompted several other producers to experiment with animation. In 1913, two series were launched – *Colonel Heeza Liar*, devised by J. R. Bray, and *Old Doc Yak*, created by Sidney Smith. Bray's series was the more popular of the two, in part because he made it more comfortable to watch by using a range of grays, rather than just black and white, thus reducing screen glare. Within a couple of years he had three major competitors: Paul Terry launched *Farmer Al Falfa*, Wallace Carlson entered the market with *Dreamy Dubb*, and Earl Hurd introduced *Bobby Bump*. Hurd is a key figure in the history of animation, for he invented the idea of painting the animated figures onto celluloid. Previous to this, everything – including the static background – had to be drawn anew for each frame of the picture. Now, only the moving characters required this attention. A single background could be placed under the sequence of celluloid sheets – "cels," as they came to be known – and remain there until the scene was changed. This system offered an enormous saving in time and money, and, although other methods persisted for a while, it was the one that became generally adopted throughout the industry.

By 1917, the International Feature Syndicate was releasing animated versions of popular newspaper cartoon strips, including *Bringing Up Father, The Katzenjammer Kids, Krazy Kat*, and *Silk Hat Harry*. That same year, Max Fleischer introduced his *Out of the Inkwell* series, in which live action was combined with animation.

At that time the industry was centered in New York City. One of several studios there was that of Raoul Barre, best known for his early work on the *Mutt and Jeff* series. Dick Huemer, later a Disney animator and story man, was, in 1916, a student at the Art Students League and

Diagram of a zoetrope

The photograph at left, taken in 1922, was probably intended to promote the young Disney's image as a filmmaker (the man with the gun is Walt himself). At right, we see him in another role, behind the camera

Disney, left, and an assistant filming on location

Disney at work in the Laugh-o-Grams office, 1922

living in the Bronx, where the Barre studio was located. He recalls seeing Barre's business sign on a door at the corner of Fordham Road and Webster Avenue.

"I had done a lot of illustrating, in yearbooks and things like that. One day, out of curiosity, I just walked upstairs and there was this plump little guy sitting there – a very genial character with a French accent. I told him I'd seen his sign and would like to be a cartoonist. He said, 'All right – go into the next room, they'll put you to work.' And that's how I got into the business. Because in those days, who knew about animated cartoons? I don't believe the name had even been coined yet."

The picture Huemer paints of the industry in those days is not one that suggests that *Snow White and the Seven Dwarfs* was barely two decades away.

"I'm afraid that we only did our cartoons to please ourselves. There was no story – we'd say 'Let's have a picture about building, it'll add up in the end.' Each guy sat at his desk with a pile of paper and did his animation, and when it was finished he handed it over and they would put it together. Enter left, exit right – that's what it amounted to. No definite plot line. Never. We were having fun. We'd laugh at each other's stuff, but when it ran in the theater – plop! Nothing. . . . Because we hadn't considered what the impact of what we were drawing would be. What were these old cartoons, anyway? There was no reality or life in them."

In these comments, Huemer is a little too hard on himself and his fellow pioneers. The movies they made possess, if nothing else, a certain period charm. It is undeniable, however, that they were very crude in terms of both animation and plot construction. As for character development, it didn't exist since characters were established in the most schematic of ways. They were recognizable because one had a big nose and another flat feet. Rough exaggeration of physical characteristics served as a substitute for personality.

This, then, was the state of the art when Disney joined the staff of Kansas City Film Ad.

The animation done at Kansas City Film Ad was, in fact, even cruder than that which was coming out of New York. It consisted mainly of stop-action photography of jointed cardboard figures – a technique that precluded any serious effort toward naturalism. Nonetheless, it provided Disney, still just eighteen years old, and Iwerks with the basic training they needed. Before long, Disney borrowed a camera and tried some animation on his own. The result was a little reel of topical gags – reminiscent in character of newspaper cartoons – which he managed to sell to the Newman Theater, a local movie house. A number of short "commercials" and illustrated jokes – known collectively as the Newman Laugh-O-Grams – were made for the theater. They dealt with such topics as shorter skirts and police corruption. Technically, they were very competent by the standards of the day, and, encouraged by this initial success, Disney managed to raise enough capital to leave Kansas City Film Ad and set up on his own, retaining Laugh-O-Grams as the company's name. It might be assumed that a young man just emerging from his teens would have been content to stick with familiar material, at least for a while, but Disney was ambitious and immediately started work on a series of updated fairy tales. Six of these were made: *Cinderella, The Four Musicians of Bremen, Goldie Locks and the Three Bears, Jack and the Beanstalk, Little Red Riding Hood,* and *Puss in Boots.* The Disney archives have prints of *The Four Musicians of Bremen* and *Puss in Boots,* and they provide clear evidence that Disney was not overestimating his ability when he entered production at this tender age. *Puss in Boots,* for example, is rather well animated, and the story displays a nice sense of humor (the fairy-tale atmosphere is updated so that, for instance, the King rides around in a chauffeur-driven convertible).

In the course of producing these short cartoons, Disney began to build up an able staff, which soon included, besides Iwerks, Rudolf Ising, Hugh and Walker Harman, Carmen "Max" Maxwell, and Red Lyon. Unfortunately, the Laugh-O-Grams were not selling (one sale was made but the purchaser went bankrupt after making a hundred dollar deposit), and the Disney production team was always having to look for alternate sources of income. They worked on a live-action short called *Martha* and, sponsored by a local dentist, even made a film on dental hygiene which combined live action and animation to get its didactic message across. Max Fleischer had been using this same combination in his *Out of the Inkwell* series. Since the live-action sections of the movies were relatively inexpensive to produce, the overall cost was reduced. At some time in 1923, Disney decided to try to save his Laugh-O-Grams venture by making just such a movie, in which a human heroine could cavort with cartoon characters. The film that resulted was *Alice's Wonderland.*

For his Alice, Disney chose a little girl named Virginia Davis, who had had some modeling experience with Kansas City Film Ad. The story begins as Alice explores the Laugh-O-Grams offices. She discovers Disney seated at his drawing board, on which a dog kennel has been sketched. Suddenly, a dog emerges from the kennel and, before she knows what has happened, Alice has become a part of the cartoon and finds herself involved with a variety of animals, including a quartet of lions who eventually chase her over a cliff (the surviving print is incomplete).

The effect of blending the real Alice with the cartoon characters was achieved by photographing Virginia Davis against a white background and then combining this film, in the printing process, with another strip on which the animation was shot. The technique worked well, but *Alice's Wonderland* exhausted Disney's remaining credit, and he was forced to close the studio.

He was not the type to be put off by a setback of this kind, however, and immediately planned to restart his career. Evidently he could not do this in Kansas City, and so, with very little hesitation, he made his move. We can assume that he considered the possibility of trying New York, which was still the center of the animation industry, but he chose Hollywood. There is reason to suppose that he considered abandoning animation and trying his luck with one of the major studios, most of

Top: the Laugh-O-Grams office, 1922; center: filming *Martha,* with Disney in the director's chair; bottom: Disney, at right, with friends at an artists' ball in Kansas City, 1922

The title frame from a Laugh-O-Grams
cartoon, c. 1922

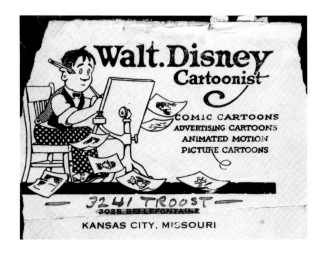

Walt Disney's letterhead, c. 1922

which were by now established in the pleasant foothills of the Santa
Monica Mountains. Another important influence was the fact that his
brother Roy was already in the West, recuperating in a veterans' hospital
from a bout with tuberculosis. In the summer of 1923 Walt Disney, aged
twenty-one, took a train to California, carrying *Alice's Wonderland* with
him as a sample.

On arriving in Los Angeles, Disney moved in with his uncle Robert
Disney at 4406 Kingswell Avenue. Walt began to look for a job and, in
his spare time, used his uncle's garage to build a stand for the animation
camera he had purchased (this would have been a conventional movie
camera converted to shoot stop-action).

Two months after his arrival, Margaret J. Winkler, a New York
distributor, commissioned a series of Alice Comedies which Disney would
produce. With Roy, Walt rented space in the rear of a small office occupied by Holly–Vermont Realty at 4651 Kingswell. They paid a rent of ten
dollars per month. On October 16, 1923, they signed their first contract
and were in business. The following January they increased their over-
head by another ten dollars a month, renting a vacant lot on Hollywood
Boulevard, about three blocks from the Studio (this lot was needed for
outdoor shooting on the Alice films). By February they had outgrown
their original studio space (the staff had grown to seven) and moved
into the adjoining store, at 4649 Kingswell, which they rented for thirty-
five dollars a month. A separate garage was rented for seven dollars
a month.

The initial contract called for one Alice Comedy a month. Virginia
Davis's parents had visions of her achieving Hollywood stardom, and
they brought her out to California so that she could continue to play the
lead. The first half dozen or so of the Alice Comedies featured a great
deal of live action which involved Virginia with other children in fairly
conventional comedy situations. Animation sequences were kept to a
bare minimum, since they cost more and took longer to produce. It
seems that Miss Winkler was not entirely satisfied with the results and
wanted to cancel the contract. The Disneys were not prepared to loosen
their tenuous grip on the future and persuaded Ub Iwerks to join them in
California. He arrived in July (Hugh Harman and Rudolf Ising followed
in June of 1925). Iwerks was just the man to streamline their productions. Soon they were able to increase the amount of animation included
in each film, and the series began to enjoy a modest success. Virginia
Davis was replaced, briefly, by a young lady named Dawn O'Day and
then by Margie Gay, who held the role for the remainder of the series.
Virginia Davis had had something of a post-Victorian image – her appeal
was that of a juvenile Mary Pickford – whereas Margie Gay was more
the flapper type, and this updating of Alice's image may have contributed
something to the increasing popularity of the series.

Further additions to the staff had to be made to accommodate Alice's
success, and one new employee was an Idaho girl named Lillian Bounds.
She often worked nights, and Walt would sometimes drive her home in
his car. A romance blossomed and, in July 1925, the pair was married.

Margie Gay poses with, left to right, Ham
Hamilton, Roy Disney, Hugh Harman,
Walt Disney, Rudy Ising, Ub Iwerks, and
Walker Harman

Margie Gay as Alice with animated friends
and, at top, with director Walt Disney

Clowning on the Alice set: Rudy Ising holding the hose; under the umbrella are Hugh Harman, Ub Iwerks, and Walt Disney

Early Alice Comedies involved a good deal of live-action filming. The original Alice, featured on this page, was Virginia Davis, whom Disney brought out from Kansas City to star in the series

Roy Disney had meanwhile married Edna Francis, his Kansas City sweetheart.

Another consequence of expansion was that the Studio was once again outgrowing its accommodations. On July 6, 1925, four hundred dollars was deposited to secure a lot at 2719 Hyperion Avenue, quite close to their existing premises (Hyperion lies just to the south of Griffith Park, not far from the present-day site of Dodger Stadium). A single-story building was erected there and this formed the nucleus of the plant which was to serve as the company's base for the next fifteen years (it was almost constantly being expanded). By 1927, it became evident that Disney had to find a replacement for the Alice movies if the Studio was to remain viable. By then the filmmakers were approaching the sixtieth episode, and the series was running out of steam. Apart from anything else, the use of live action placed severe restrictions on the artists' sense of fantasy, and Walt was anxious to get back to full animation. As the last of the Alice films were completed, work began on a new series which was to feature the adventures of Oswald the Lucky Rabbit.

By now Disney had completely abandoned his career as an animator to concentrate all his energies on the production side of the business. Animation could be left in the capable hands of Iwerks, Ising, and the Harman brothers, along with other newly signed draftsmen, such as Ham Hamilton and Friz Freleng. Disney was also recruiting apprentice animators, young men who showed some enthusiasm for the business. One of these was Les Clark.

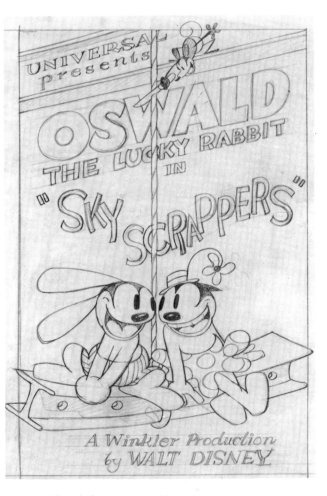

Sketch for an Oswald poster

The series of cartoons (opposite) that Disney built around Oswald the Lucky Rabbit was successful enough to attract merchandising tie-ins. The model sheet on the opposite page, top right, shows that Oswald anticipated some of the physical characteristics of Mickey Mouse. The page of story continuity sketches, bottom right, illustrates how cartoon stories were worked out in this period

Overleaf: Poster for an Alice Comedy, left, and original art by Hugh Harman and Carmen Maxwell for an Oswald poster, right

"I was working a part-time summer job at a lunch counter and confectionery store on Vermont and Kingswell," Clark recalled in 1972. "Walt and Roy used to come over there for lunch. While I was still in high school, I asked Walt for a job. He said, 'Bring some of your drawings in and let me see what they look like.' Well, I copied some cartoons out of *College Humor* and showed them to him. I told him I had copied them but he said I had a good line and invited me to start work the following Monday. So I graduated from high school on a Thursday and I went to work on Monday and I haven't been out of his employ since."

That was in 1927. What Clark did not know at the time was that the Studio was on the brink of a major crisis.

Most business crises are brought on by incompetence. The near catastrophe that the Disneys faced in 1927 resulted from the very opposite. The new cartoon series turned out to be very successful, making Oswald the Lucky Rabbit a desirable property.

Oswald was a likable little creature, all soft curves and energy. He had no voice, of course – this was still the silent era – but the adventures he found himself caught up in were, to judge by surviving examples, inventive and well constructed for the time. The Disney animators were becoming very skilled, and they took full advantage of the fact that they no longer had to compete with a live Alice. With Oswald, Disney equaled – and perhaps surpassed – the best products of his competitors. *The Mechanical Cow*, for instance, is chock-full of zany invention and surrealistic humor.

There was just one snag. Disney had signed a one-year contract with Charles Mintz, who had married Margaret Winkler in 1924 (their distribution outlet now tied in with Universal Pictures). The advertising announced "Oswald the Lucky Rabbit, created by Walt Disney," but – and this proved to be the fatal flaw in the contract – Oswald's name belonged to Mintz (who had, apparently, picked it out of a hat). As the first year moved to a successful conclusion, Walt Disney and his wife embarked for New York, where he expected to renegotiate the contract with provisions for a modest increase of income. He had kept in close contact with his distributor through George Winkler, Margaret's brother, who had made several visits to California, and there was no reason to suspect that anything was amiss. When Disney arrived in New York, however, the true reasons for Winkler's visits became painfully obvious.

Instead of offering an improved contract, Mintz actually proposed one which would entail a *reduction* of income for the Studio. This was clearly absurd, since Oswald had been very profitable. Obviously, Disney could not accept such a deal, and the reality of the situation became apparent. Mintz had decided to repossess Oswald. The character's name belonged to him, and his brother-in-law had persuaded several of Disney's best animators to take over production of the Oswald series. The motive was, of course, reduction of costs to the distributor. Mintz was the first of many people to underestimate Disney. He figured that if

Standing in front of their storefront studio, Walt and Roy Disney with, left to right, Walt's wife Lillian, Ruth Disney, and Roy's wife Edna

he could hire away Disney's best men, he would be getting the same product for a reduced outlay.

Disney was shocked and hurt. He had trusted Mintz, and he had trusted his employees. It is not hard to imagine the kinds of thoughts that must have run through his head as he and Lillian waited out the long, slow train ride back to California. He was disgusted but not, as the next few months would prove, discouraged. His team was depleted but it still included his two most important associates – his brother Roy and Ub Iwerks (who was, by then, a partner in the business). More important still, Walt Disney had faith in his own abilities. He had reached the age of twenty-six after touching many of the bases of hardship that had come to seem archetypal of America in the first quarter of this century. His personal creed must have included the notion that success does not come easily.

2 Mickey Mouse and Silly Symphonies

It seems appropriate that the birth of Mickey Mouse – a creature of mythic stature – should be shrouded in legend. Walt Disney is said to have conceived Mickey on the train, returning to Hollywood from his angry encounter with Mintz. There is no reason to suppose that this is not essentially true, but over the years this story became so polished by repetition that it began to lose its sense of reality and to take on the character of an official myth. A further dimension was added to the legend by the fact that Disney had managed to tame a mouse in his old Kansas City studio, a mouse that he had nicknamed Mortimer. The name Mortimer now became the first choice for his new character, but before the Mouse cartoons were released, the name was changed to Mickey (it seems that Mrs. Disney thought the name Mortimer was a little pompous for a cartoon animal, but pressure from potential distributors may also have had something to do with the switch).

What we can be reasonably sure of is that the Mickey Mouse who made his debut in New York City in 1928 resulted from a collaborative effort between Disney and Ub Iwerks. It seems probable that Iwerks, easily the best animator of the day, was largely responsible for defining Mickey's physical characteristics. Mickey did bear a family resemblance to Oswald, but Iwerks – presumably in close consultation with Disney – made the figure more compact. He was constructed from two large circles, one for the trunk and one for the head, to which were appended two smaller circles, representing ears, and rubber-hose arms and legs which terminated in plump hands (ungloved at this early stage) and large feet which gave him stability. He was also equipped with a long, skinny tail and short pants decorated with buttons fore and aft. The circular head was made expressive by the addition of a mischievous snout, a plum-shaped nose, and button eyes. He was designed for maximum ease of animation (it had been discovered that circular forms were simpler to animate effectively), but beyond that, Mickey's identity had a dimension which was quite new in cartoons. Certainly a character such as Felix the Cat was immediately recognizable, but he did not have a real personality. Mickey did have one, and an audience could identify with him in much the same way it would with a human performer.

The gift of personality was probably Disney's own contribution to Mickey. Iwerks made the whole thing possible through his skill as a draftsman, but it was Disney's control over the situations in which the Mouse found himself that allowed this personality to develop. Even at this early date, Disney had grasped the notion that cartoon characters should seem to think for themselves. In some ways he may even have viewed Mickey as his alter ego. He always maintained a special affection for the Mouse, a fact which suggests that he was intimately involved in every stage of its creation.

The Disney brothers had managed to save enough money to go ahead with the first Mickey Mouse cartoons even without a distributor, and work began almost at once. This was carried out in secret at first, since the Oswald contract had not yet completely expired. On October 23, 1927, a bombshell had hit the motion picture industry. Warner Brothers released *The Jazz Singer,* and the sound era became a reality. Lee DeForest had developed a practical sound system at least four years earlier, but the Hollywood production chiefs had fought shy of this new development. Now they had to confront it.

As the first Mouse cartoons went into production, the industry was still in chaos. One Disney cartoon, *Plane Crazy,* had been completed, and another, *The Gallopin' Gaucho,* was on the drawing boards before the decision was made – perhaps the most important decision that Disney ever made. He wanted Mickey to have real impact, and he saw that the future lay with sound. What he had in mind was a cartoon in which music, effects, and action would all be synchronized. Max and Dave Fleischer had already produced a cartoon which used a Lee DeForest sound track, but the track had been unsynchronized and the experiment had had little impact on the industry. Disney's plan was for something far more radical.

Wedding sound to animated drawings was not, he realized, something that could be approached casually. Where live actors were concerned, it might be enough for the audience to hear them speak – that seemed like a miracle after the decades of silence (the fact that sound pictures were quickly labeled "talkies" indicates just where the public's interest lay) – but Disney did not have the ready-made stars to whom he could return the gift of speech. He had to come up with a more imaginative solution.

When the great French director René Clair was first exposed to the

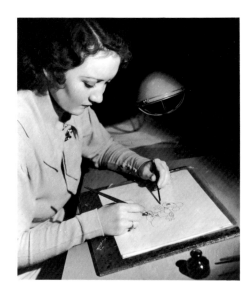

Mickey Mouse was originally drawn by Ub Iwerks, top, who was given credit in early publicity; center: an early poster. At bottom, Mickey is inked onto a cel

-Main Title-

Orchestra starts playing opening
verses of ' Steamboat Bill ',
as soon as title flashes on.

The orchestration can be so
arrainged that many variations
may be included before the title
fades out.

It would be best if the music
was arrainged so that the end of
a verse would end at the end of
the title...... and a new verse
start at beginning of the first
scene.

Scene # 1.
Opening effect of black foliage
passing by in front of camera
gradually getting thinner until
full scene is revealed

Action.......Old side'wheel river
steamboat paddleing down stream.
The two smoke stacks work up
and down alternately.... shooting
black chunks of smoke out as they
shoot up....smoke makes stacks
bulge out as it goes up and out.
(16 drawing cycle) 12 Ft. from
opening, the Three whistles on top
of cabin squat down before they
whistle tune ' TA--DA-DE-DA-DA---
DA-DA-'....2 Ft. of action after
whistle and cut.

Scene # 2.
Close up of Mickey in cabin of
wheel'house, keeping time to last
two measures of verse of ' steamboat Bill '. With gesture he starts
whistleing the chorus in perfect
time to music....his body keeping
time with every other beat while
his shoulders and foot keep time
with each beat. At the end of every
two measures he twirls wheel which
makes a ratchet sound as it spins.
He takes in breath at proper time
according to music. When he finishes
last measure he reaches up and pulls
on whistle cord above his head.
(Use FIFE to imitate his whistle)

The first page of the *Steamboat Willie* continuity
script. Disney kept this souvenir of his first major
breakthrough in his office

In *Steamboat Willie,* 1928, the first cartoon to feature a fully synchronized sound track, Mickey and Minnie transform the cargo of a riverboat – including livestock – into an orchestra

Plane Crazy, 1928, was the first Mickey Mouse vehicle to go into production, but it was not released until after the success of *Steamboat Willie*

The Gallopin' Gaucho was the second Mickey Mouse cartoon to be made, but, like *Plane Crazy,* it was produced as a silent film and not released until a sound track had been added

The Karnival Kid, 1929, used gags derived directly from earlier situations devised for Oswald

An early Mickey Mouse model sheet which shows the basic simplicity of his design

Scenes from *Mickey's Choo Choo*, 1929, and *The Fire Fighters*, 1930

Rough story ideas were often worked out in thumbnail sketches, as in this example by Wilfred Jackson

talking pictures, he quickly realized that there would be an enormous difference between mere "talkies" and those that used sound creatively. Walt Disney, prompted by circumstance and predisposed by temperament, was to become the first producer to find a genuinely creative way of using sound. Cartoon animals making noises might have offered something in the way of novelty, but novelties have a tendency to become clichés all too quickly. Evidently Disney was quite conscious of this danger. Animated creatures synchronized to a carefully structured sound track, he realized, would have far more impact. He and his team began to develop a third Mickey Mouse story, this one conceived specially for sound. Cartoons had always depended on action rather than verbal jokes (in the silent era one could not afford to break up a short sequence of animated gags with title cards), so Disney decided to preserve this emphasis on action while underpinning it with carefully timed sound effects and a strongly rhythmic music track.

Not that this was the easiest of things to achieve. To start with, no one at the Studio had any real knowledge of music theory, and there were also important technical problems to be solved. The artists had to proceed by trial and error. In their favor was the fact that Iwerks was something of a wizard with machinery and that almost everyone at the Studio knew something about practically everything within the animation field (specialization was still in the future; Walt Disney himself had a firsthand knowledge of every aspect of the business, from cameras to inking). A young animator named Wilfred Jackson played the harmonica and, since his mother was a music teacher, was familiar with the metronome, which, he suggested, might provide a means of relating a musical beat to the frames of film.

Les Clark, who was party to these early experiments, describes the system that was devised as follows:

"We worked with an exposure sheet on which every line was a single frame of action. We could break down the sound effects so that every eight frames we'd have an accent, or every sixteen frames, or every twelve frames. [Sound film runs through the projector at twenty-four frames a second.] And on that twelfth drawing, say, we'd accent whatever was happening – a hit on the head or a footstep or whatever it would be, to synchronize to the sound effect of the music."

By setting a metronome to correspond with the accents thus established in the action, a rough sound accompaniment could be improvised to the animation. One legendary evening, Disney and his coworkers presented a short sequence from *Steamboat Willie* – such was the title of the new cartoon – to an audience of wives and girlfriends. Roy Disney projected the film from outside a window (to eliminate motor noise) while his brother, along with Iwerks, Jackson, Clark, and a few others, improvised their sound accompaniment, live, in another room – all of them working carefully to the beat of the metronome. Jackson played his harmonica (the tune was probably "Steamboat Bill") while the others provided sound effects with cowbells, slide whistles, tin pans, and the like. This accompaniment was transmitted to the audience by way of a

In his early films Mickey often appeared as an entertainer. The examples shown here are, top to bottom, from *The Jazz Fool,* 1929; *Just Mickey,* 1930; and *Blue Rhythm,* 1931 crude loudspeaker system set up by Iwerks. The wives and girlfriends were only mildly impressed, but the performers were convinced that they had now found the answer.

By September 1928, a complete score had been committed to paper and Disney set out for New York to have it recorded. At that time, most recording devices were controlled by patents belonging to RCA and Western Electric, so it was necessary, first of all, to locate someone with "outlaw" sound equipment. Eventually, Disney came to terms with a man named Pat Powers, who operated a renegade sound system that gloried in the name Powers Cinephone. Walt wrote to Roy and Ub that Powers was a very much respected personage in the film business. "He is very shrewd and capable. He is careful and cautious." He might have added, had he known, that Powers was also somewhat notorious for his efforts to outflank producers in the sometimes informal business atmosphere that had prevailed earlier in the history of the film industry.

Disney hired Carl Edouwarde, who had led the pit orchestra at the Broadway Strand and worked for the Roxy chain, to provide a band and conduct the recording session. On September 14, Walt wrote to Roy and Ub: "We are using a seventeen-piece orchestra and three of the best trap drummers and effect men in town. They get ten dollars an hour for this work. It will take three hours to do it, plus the time the effect men put in today." Later in the same letter he says that there would be about thirty-five men on the job, but this may have included technicians. At all events, the first recording session was a disaster. Disney's team had developed a system of indicating – probably by flashes on the screen – the tempo to which the orchestra should play. Thus, the film could be projected and serve the same function as a metronome. Unfortunately, this system was a little crude, and Edouwarde did not feel inclined to have his tempo determined by such a coarse mechanical device. Disney was forced to cable California for more money and try again. Roy sent out enough money to proceed with a second session but not, it would seem, without some qualms. Walt, convinced that he had the problem licked, wrote back suggesting that he try to borrow another five thousand dollars so that they could be ready to go into full production. "I am firmly convinced," he insisted, "that it will be far cheaper in the long run to go into it in the proper manner. . . . Let's do things in the proper way and not try to save a penny here and there."

In the same letter (like the others, it was addressed to both Roy and Ub) he says, "We have all been working like the devil on the picture. . . . The orchestra leader and myself completely revised the Score . . . I finally got him to see it my way (he thinks he thought of the idea). The fact is that he just saw what I have been telling him for the last two weeks. . . . They are very clever in their line – but want too much beauty and too many Symphonic effects. . . . They think comedy music is low brow. . . . Believe me, I have had a tough fight getting them to come down to our level. . . . I wish you knew the whole story and I know you would sympathize with me. . . . I feel positive we have everything worked out perfect now."

One improvement was that instead of sticking with the crude flashing device that had been used at the first session, Disney had had the film reprinted with the addition of a bouncing ball system to indicate the accents as well as the beat, making it much easier for Edouwarde to follow. Fewer musicians were used at the second session, and everything went off without a hitch. *Steamboat Willie* now had a sound track and Mickey Mouse was ready for his debut.

Finding a distributor was not easy, however. Still in New York, Disney took his sound cartoon from screening room to screening room, but the industry remained in a state of confusion and the response he met with was discouraging. Eventually, Harry Reichenbach, then managing Manhattan's Colony Theater, saw *Steamboat Willie* and offered Disney a two-week run for the film. After some hesitation – he was hoping for a national distributor – Disney agreed. Reichenbach had made his reputation as a stop-at-nothing press agent and, when *Steamboat Willie* opened at the Colony on November 18, 1928, he saw to it that it received excellent coverage in the news media. This, combined with the fact that audiences roared with laughter at Mickey's adventures, encouraged the prestigious Roxy to book the movie. Pat Powers reentered the picture and offered to distribute Disney's cartoons on a States Rights basis (this was an old system of distribution that allowed an independent producer to bypass the major studios, which controlled most of the theaters at that time). The deal that Powers offered was not perfect, but it was the best offer Disney had received. He signed up for one year. He then busied himself with adding sound to *Plane Crazy* and *The Gallopin' Gaucho*. A fourth Mouse cartoon, *The Barn Dance,* was already animated, and work began on still another, *The Opry House.*

The Mickey Mouse who hit the movie houses in the late twenties was not quite the well-behaved character most of us are familiar with today. He was mischievous, to say the least, and even displayed a streak of cruelty (which soon disappeared), but from the very beginning he had that little germ of real personality, and this prevented him from seeming to be just another callously cruel cartoon animal. At times – when confronted by Pegleg Pete (the perennial villain who co-starred in both *Steamboat Willie* and *The Gallopin' Gaucho*) or when forced to defend Minnie's honor – he was even capable of heroic behavior. His heroism, however, was usually the heroism of the little man; it resembled the intermittent nobility of Charlie Chaplin's tramp. Chaplin undoubtedly provided Disney with one of his most important models, and we may say that Mickey and his gang provided for the sound era the kind of entertainment that Chaplin and the Mack Sennett comedians had provided for an earlier generation.

Since this *was* the sound era, Mickey had to have a voice. Several people, mostly from the Studio, had a shot at immortality as the Mouse's voice, but Disney was not satisfied with any of them. He knew just the kind of squeaky falsetto Mickey should have. He was also concerned, after his experience with Oswald, that no one should be able to steal his new creation. To help make sure of this, Disney became Mickey's voice

SCENE #3:

       Horse and cow in bathing suits. Horse puts his fingers in his mouth and whistles to attract the attention of Mickey and Minnie. Pantos, "watch me!" Runs out to left along a dock.

SCENE #5:

       Mickey uses Pluto for a pump to inflate the inner tube. Gag of Pluto letting go to bite at a flea, tube goes down, and Mickey bawls him out. Pluto gets back to work again, and when the tube is blown up, Mickey takes it, puts it on over his head, and runs down to the beach and into the water. The dog stops on the beach.

Typical gags from 1931 Mickey Mouse shorts:
The Beach Party, left, and *Mickey Cuts Up*

Scenes from *The Birthday Party,* 1931, top,
and two 1932 cartoons, *Barnyard Olympics*
and *The Grocery Boy*

This camera – adapted in the late twenties to shoot animation – was used for many decades

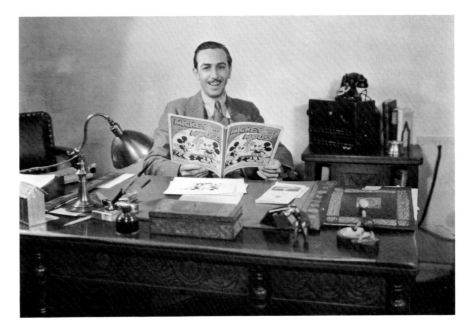

Walt Disney at his desk, c. 1931

In 1930, Carl Stalling, seen here at the piano, composed "Minnie's Yoo Hoo" as a theme song for Mickey. Seated alongside Stalling are Jack King and Ben Sharpsteen, two of the animators Disney had imported from New York. Standing, left to right, are Johnny Cannon, Walt Disney, Bert Gillett, Ub Iwerks, Wilfred Jackson, and Les Clark

SAME B.C. AS #41

(43)--(46)

This story sketch for *The Grocery Boy* shows how the scene is to be laid out. Different stages of the action are indicated in a single drawing

SCENE #43:

    Pluto drags Mickey into a pedestal holding a statue of Napoleon. The statue falls and lands over Mickey's head and shoulders. Pluto runs on out of scene with turkey.

Poster, 1932

JOSEPH M. SCHENCK
presents
WALT DISNEY'S
MICKEY MOUSE

"The WHOOPEE PARTY"
UNITED ARTISTS PICTURE

and continued to fill this role for twenty years.

Minnie was with Mickey from the very first. In *Steamboat Willie,* after Pete has chased Mickey from the bridge of the riverboat on which he is employed as a deckhand, Minnie is discovered on shore, about to miss the boat. The ship is already moving downstream when Mickey manages to snag Minnie's patched panties with a boat hook and haul her aboard. Later, on the deck, they cavort with the cargo of livestock, using the various animals as musical instruments on which to improvise "Turkey in the Straw."

This sequence is by far the most interesting in the movie in that it contains the seeds of much that was to come. It is also marked by a kind of humor Disney was later to abandon on grounds of taste. Mickey, for example, stretches a cat's tail so that it becomes a stringed instrument; the cat gives vocal expression to its displeasure at this misuse of its anatomy. A good deal of music and laughter is milked out of a cow's udder (later, the Hays Office was to insist that Disney cows be udderless and, indeed, it was actively suggested that they find some suitable form of apparel). Minnie cranks a goat's tail, transforming the unfortunate beast into a hurdy-gurdy, while Mickey plays xylophone riffs on a cow's teeth. (The xylophone was a much-used instrument in the sound tracks of these early shorts, providing good opportunities for visual puns; almost any more or less regular group of solid objects – the rib cage of a skeleton, for example – could double as a xylophone.)

We might note that the callous attitude displayed by Mickey and Minnie toward other animals made it quite clear that, although not human, these were not ordinary mice. They were creatures invested with special powers. They wore clothing and acted out roles that parodied the habits of men and women. In this respect they belonged to a tradition that goes back to Aesop and Aristophanes. Audiences were fascinated to see this tradition come to life on the screen, and if the gags were a little rough-and-ready, they were certainly effective. The way the action was tied to music and sound effects was unlike anything anyone had ever experienced before. *Steamboat Willie* was both a success and a major breakthrough for the animation industry.

Since *Plane Crazy* and *The Gallopin' Gaucho* were made as silent films and then had sound added to them, they are not so interesting from the technical point of view. *The Gallopin' Gaucho* has a plot that parodies Douglas Fairbanks melodramas (Mickey, in the Argentine, rescues Minnie from the clutches of Pegleg Pete). The animation and most of the situations are strongly reminiscent of some of the things in the Oswald series. *Plane Crazy,* the first Mouse cartoon produced, has considerably more to recommend it. The plot is topical. Mickey fancies himself a second Lindbergh (studying a picture of the aviator, he musses his hair and adopts a boyish grin), and, after some mishaps set in a barnyard, an automobile is converted into an airplane. Mickey offers to take Minnie for a spin. She climbs aboard, but before he can join her, the motor starts and the plane takes off on a crazy trajectory across the countryside, narrowly avoiding disastrous collisions with various items of livestock and a passing car. Mickey catches up with the plane just as it is about to become airborne. Once clear of the ground, Mickey attempts to engage Minnie in a passionate kiss. She takes umbrage at his advances and bails out, using her panties as a parachute. Back on the ground, Mickey laughs at her disarray and Minnie floors him with a horseshoe. *Plane Crazy* was animated in its entirety by one man – Ub Iwerks – making it something of a tour de force. The whole thing moves along at a lively pace, and parts of it still seem funny today.

When *Steamboat Willie* was released, Walt Disney was twenty-six years old. His operation was still a very small one by Hollywood standards, but he had his foot on the first, and perhaps even the second, rung of the ladder. Jack Cutting, later head of the Disney foreign department and responsible for such matters as the dubbing of Disney films into other languages, joined the Studio the following year and still remembers the atmosphere vividly.

"I had to leave the Otis Art Institute and look for a job. I had heard about a small cartoon studio near Glendale, so I went around to 2719 Hyperion without an appointment, walked in off the street with a few samples, and was hired that same day in August 1929. I had just turned twenty-one and most of the nineteen fellows on the staff were very young, with the exception of one or two – Roy must have been about thirty-five and the oldest on the staff was an animator named Burt Gillett, who may have been thirty-eight. I soon found being part of what was going on in that little studio very exciting. Walt was determined to develop the art of animation far beyond the level at which it was practiced in those days. He did it by being persuasive, by convincing everyone that his ideas and dreams for the future were exciting and worth believing in.

"During the early Mickey days, Walt was only taking fifty dollars home a week and Roy thirty-five. Some of us, like myself, who were just out of art school, were making eighteen dollars a week. We worked eight hours a day, six days a week, and we'd often come back nights to help get the work out. We didn't get paid overtime but that didn't matter if you were under the spell of the animated cartoon business, as I was in those days. I came to the Studio without any experience in animation. A few of the older members of the staff, whom Walt had imported from the East, were experienced animators and, of course, Ub Iwerks was the Studio's top animator at that time. When you came in green, like I did, you learned to do a bit of everything. We began by inking cels, then we were taught in-betweening; we would come back at night and Ub would explain the principles of animation to us. The Studio was very small and the atmosphere informal. Most of us had a key to the front door.

"If you were an animator's assistant, after you did in-between drawings for a scene you had to shoot a pencil drawing test. [In-betweens are the drawings used to fill in the gaps between the key drawings made by the animator. There must be an image for every frame, and the animator supplies perhaps just one in three or four. Pencil testing, a way of check-

What appears to be clowning probably had a serious purpose. The two dancers are trying out a pose for the benefit of other animators. Those involved are, left to right, Bert Gillett, Norm Ferguson, Ted Sears, Fred Moore, Gilles "Frenchy" de Trémaudan, Tom Palmer, Ben Sharpsteen, Walt Disney, and Jack King

This photo of the production staff was taken in 1932, after Disney had won an Academy Award – his first – for the creation of Mickey Mouse

Recording the sound track for *The Beach Party* at the Hyperion Avenue studio, 1931. At the microphone is Marcellite Garner, the voice of Minnie Mouse

ing out the animation on a scene before it is inked and painted onto the cels, was a Disney innovation.] After hand developing the test and putting it in a revolving drum to dry, you went back to the drawing board. When it was dry, you spliced it into a loop and ran it for the animator. We all had a chance to try our hands at different phases of the work."

Cutting recalls that Disney and Wilfred Jackson were both directing at the time he joined the Studio. Two shorts would be in production at any given time (they cost an average of about five thousand dollars apiece to make), and, in addition to supervising Jackson's work, Disney would always be working on ideas for new cartoons. From the beginning, gag conferences were held. Everyone on the production staff was expected to attend and invited to contribute jokes or other ideas that would enable the animators to get the most out of each story. Disney was also passionately interested in audience response, convinced that everyone at the Studio could learn a great deal about humor by studying the reactions of a group of laymen.

"When a picture was finished," Cutting reports, "Walt would take the first print from the laboratory to the Alexander Theater in Glendale and tip the projectionist to run it between the first and second shows. We all paid our way to get in and, directly after the cartoon was run, we would meet outside in front of the theater and Walt would evaluate the audience reaction and we would discuss why certain gags didn't go over and why others got such a big laugh."

The Disney brothers were working hard for their first modest success. An account book, written in Roy's hand, survives and indicates that Cutting's estimate of their take-home pay is quite accurate. Accurate, that is, except for the weeks when there was not enough cash to go around

In 1929, Disney launched a new series of
cartoons which he called Silly Symphonies.
The first was *The Skeleton Dance*, which
featured some imaginative animation by
Ub Iwerks set to a macabre score devised
by Carl Stalling

Silly Symphony poster, 1932

and the brothers' pay shrank to less than that of the lowliest apprentice animator.

A number of new Mickey Mouse cartoons appeared in 1929, sporting titles such as *The Karnival Kid, Mickey's Choo Choo,* and *The Jazz Fool* (this last a takeoff on Al Jolson). Within the space of a few months, Mickey acquired gloves, shoes, and a more endearing manner. There were other developments too. The sound tracks became increasingly sophisticated, and in most cases they were now recorded before the animators began work. This is to say, once a story line was established, a score was prepared to fit the action; it was recorded and the animators worked to the rhythms and accents contained in the sound track. This system permitted greater flexibility.

To handle the music side of the business, Disney called in an old acquaintance from Kansas City, Carl Stalling. Stalling had had years of experience in the theater pit, providing music for silent movies – a background which left him well equipped for his new career. Already the Disney team was becoming extremely adept in synchronizing sound and action, and several of the earliest Mickey Mouse pictures – *The Opry House,* for instance, and *The Jazz Fool* – took music as the main substance of the plot. The director always had a piano in his office so that, at story conferences, the composer could illustrate the melodic and rhythmic lines the animators would have to follow (for this reason, the director's room became known as the music room, a designation it retained for many years). Most of the music used was – like "Turkey in the Straw" – in the public domain, meaning that no royalties would have to be paid. Stalling was quite capable of producing original material, however, and soon came up with "Minnie's Yoo Hoo," which served for some time as Mickey's theme song (in the 1970s, it was revived as the signature tune of television's *The Mouse Factory*).

This emphasis on music led in 1929 to quite a new kind of animated film – the Silly Symphony.

It seems likely that some of the credit for the concept of the Silly Symphonies should go to Carl Stalling. An account of how the series came about was given by Wilfred Jackson in the magazine *Funny World* dated spring 1971. Talking of the Mickey Mouse cartoons, he recalled that there were often arguments between Disney and Stalling when "Walt would want more or less time for the action than could fit the musical phrase." The rest of the staff would sit in the next room, enjoying the whole thing but glad they weren't involved ("Walt could be pretty stiff"). Eventually a solution was arrived at. Walt decided that, so far as Mickey was concerned, the music must be made to fit the action, but that another series would be launched in which the action would be keyed to the music.

Stalling, interviewed in the same issue of *Funny World,* claims he was responsible for the idea of a series of musical cartoons. These were to be not merely illustrated songs, but films in which music and animation were combined to provide a totally new experience. The name Silly Symphonies was selected for the series, and work began on the first of them, *The Skeleton Dance*. (In the interview, Stalling indicates that the subject was his choice.)

The Skeleton Dance opens as cats, howling in a cemetery, are disturbed at midnight by four skeletons who emerge from their graves. The skeletons go through some fairly elaborate dance sequences and then, at dawn, scurry back to their resting places. The whole thing is set to suitably sepulchral music, a composition of Stalling's which utilized elements from Edvard Grieg's "March of the Dwarfs" (many film historians have erroneously reported that the music used is Camille Saint-Saëns's "Danse Macabre"). Despite the success of the Mickey Mouse shorts, theater owners were a little nervous of the reception that would be accorded this new kind of cartoon entertainment, and so *The Skeleton Dance* and its successors were released under the byline "Mickey Mouse Presents a Walt Disney Silly Symphony."

These first Symphonies were received well enough for the series to continue. Certainly they were very original in concept, but they now seem rather less interesting than the early Mouse shorts. Mickey gave his pictures a central core around which the action could develop. The Symphonies had no such core. Each of them was constructed around a rather generalized theme – *The Merry Dwarfs, Winter,* and *Spring* are typical early titles – which had to be stated before it could be explored; with the techniques available in 1929 and 1930, this was quite a challenge. In a Mouse cartoon, you had only to catch one glimpse of Mickey to know exactly what to expect, and this allowed the animators to take much more for granted.

For the first year or two of their existence, the Symphonies had little real focus. But we must emphasize just how significant it is that Disney instituted them and then persisted with them when it would have been far easier to exploit Mickey for all he was worth. Before long, the Symphonies would have an invaluable role to play in the development of the art of animation. We should lay to rest, too, the idea that the occasional classical music content of these cartoons showed Disney displaying pretensions toward high culture. All the evidence suggests that he saw himself as making motion picture entertainment for the masses. If he persisted with the Silly Symphonies, it was because he wanted to give his animators an opportunity to extend the range of subject matter they were dealing with. He was, as usual, looking to the future.

In 1930, another personnel crisis hit the Studio. Ub Iwerks and Carl Stalling quit the Disney operation.

The loss of Iwerks resulted directly from the fact that Disney's contract with Powers was due for renewal. It would seem that Powers had, at the beginning, thought of these cartoons as little more than a novelty that might help promote his Powers Cinephone system; but Mickey (and *The Skeleton Dance*, too, by dint of a successful run in New York) had proved that there was a real long-term potential for this kind of entertainment. Meanwhile, the Disneys had not been entirely happy in their relationship with Powers. For one thing, they had been unable to

From the very first, the Silly Symphonies touched a wide variety of subjects and moods. Examples illustrated here are, top to bottom, from *The Merry Dwarfs,* 1929; *Winter,* 1930; *The China Plate,* 1931; *Midnight in a Toy Shop,* 1930; and *Pioneer Days,* 1930

Silly Symphony posters, 1932

get detailed financial reports from him. His method of doing business consisted of sending sums of money from time to time – just enough to keep the Studio operating. Powers must have suspected that the Disneys might be disinclined to renew their contract, so behind their backs, he approached Ub Iwerks and offered him a series of his own. Iwerks accepted the offer. The distributor then confronted the Disneys with the *fait accompli* but promised to tear up the Iwerks contract if they would renegotiate. He made an offer of a guaranteed $2,500 a week, which must have sounded like a great deal of money, but the Disneys refused to sign and instead negotiated a distribution agreement with Columbia Pictures (Harry Cohn made the deal at the suggestion of director Frank Capra, who had been greatly impressed by the originality and vigor of Disney's cartoons). Iwerks found himself out on a limb. We can only guess at the acrimony that must have been stirred up by Powers's maneuverings, but the end result was that Iwerks sold out his partnership to the brothers for $2,920 and then, backed by Powers, set up his own studio. He produced, among other things, a series called Flip the Frog, which

Flowers and Trees, 1932, has a special place in the history of animation as the first cartoon to be made in full color. From this point on, all Silly Symphonies were produced in the Technicolor® process never attained any substantial success. Great as he was as an animator and technical innovator, Iwerks did not possess either the story sense or the business acumen of Walt Disney.

It should be acknowledged, however, that Iwerks had been an enormous asset to the Studio. His work on Mickey alone would have been enough to establish his importance, but he also contributed inventive work to practically all the early Disney cartoons. Not only were his drawings of absolute top quality, he also turned them out at a phenomenal rate – according to at least one source, as many as seven hundred a day. He had also been the resident technical genius, adapting most of the equipment used in the production of the early pictures. Next to Walt Disney himself, Ub Iwerks had been the most important single figure in the development of the Studio. Small wonder that Powers had figured he would not be an easy person to replace (like Charles Mintz before him, Powers was underestimating Disney's own importance).

Some ten years later, Iwerks returned to the Studio and reestablished himself there as a special-effects virtuoso, developing – among other things – the Xerox camera that was used in many Disney animated films and the traveling matte process that lent Mary Poppins some of her magic powers.

Stalling left at about the same time as Iwerks, mainly, it would seem, because he thought that without Iwerks the Studio had little future. He remained in the animation industry, eventually becoming musical director for Warner Brothers' Looney Tunes–Merry Melodies, an assignment that suited his talents perfectly.

Both these losses, then, were serious, but they do not seem to have caused Disney to so much as break his stride. He quickly replaced Stalling with Bert Lewis. Iwerks could not be replaced by any one man, so Disney coped with his loss by building up his stable of animators in two different ways: he brought in a number of apprentices and he imported experienced animators from New York. Certainly the Disney product did not seem to suffer. By the end of 1930, Mickey had become an international celebrity. Known in Italy as Topolino and as Miki Kuchi in Japan, the Mouse continued his adventures, saving Minnie

From 1932 to 1934 the Silly Symphonies evolved a new range of subtleties. Shown here are scenes from *Babes in the Woods, The Grasshopper and the Ants, Father Noah's Ark,* and *The Wise Little Hen* from immolation by fire and worse, confronting Pete in various exotic situations, and performing to audiences of exuberant animals whose taste in music ranged from ragtime to violin concertos. A simple-minded bloodhound made an appearance in a 1930 picture called *The Chain Gang* and developed, before long, into Mickey's faithful companion Pluto. As Mickey's career unfolded in the thirties, other characters, such as Horace Horsecollar and Clarabelle Cow, began to enjoy the status of co-stars, but their personalities offered relatively little for the animators to work with, and, as the pictures became more sophisticated, their roles became less significant and eventually vanished entirely.

By 1931, Mickey was important enough for *Time* magazine to devote a feature article to him. Another feature, printed in *Motion Picture Daily* (July 20, 1931), tells us that the production staff, including assistants, had grown to more than forty. Several of the animators – Dave Hand, Ben Sharpsteen, Rudy Zamora, Tom Palmer, and Jack King, for instance – had experience in New York studios, as had story men like Ted Sears and Bert Gillett. Other animators – such as Les Clark, Jack Cutting, Dick Lundy, Gilles "Frenchy" de Trémaudan, and Johnny Cannon – had learned their craft with Disney. Emil Flohri, a former newspaper cartoonist and art director, was painting backgrounds, and Frank Churchill had joined Bert Lewis in the music department (both of them, like Stalling, had received their training in theater pit orchestras during the silent era). Floyd Gottfredson was drawing the daily Mickey Mouse comic strip (and continued to do so until the 1970s) while Hazel Sewell, Lillian Disney's sister, headed up the ink and paint department. Wilfred Jackson was directing and contributing to story. Still listed as assistants were Webb Smith, soon to be an important member of the story team; Roy Williams, who later attained fame on television's *Mickey Mouse Club*; and Fred Moore, who would become one of the very best animators of his generation.

The New York animators were employed, to a large extent, in a stop-gap capacity. Their experience was needed by the Studio at that point, but their approach to animation differed somewhat from that which had been established by the Disney artists under Iwerk's tutelage. Les Clark

In 1933, Walt Disney produced *Three Little Pigs* – a cartoon which had an extraordinary impact on the American public. Its hit tune, "Who's Afraid of the Big Bad Wolf?" swept the nation. Many people saw this film as Disney's comment in fable form on the Depression era. Whatever his motives for making it, it did display a marked advance in terms of story-telling and character development

explains that Disney-trained animators usually worked from key pose to key pose – that is to say, they picked out the signal poses in any action, established those first, then filled in the gaps afterward. The New York animators had been trained to animate "straight-ahead" – in other words, they started at point *a* of any action and worked their way through to point *z*. The New York animators were very good at this (Clark recalls his amazement as he watched Zamora animate the flight of a butterfly by the straight-ahead method), but in the long run the key-pose style of animation was much more efficient and flexible. Apart from anything else, it fitted in perfectly with the Disney system of animating to music (key poses being made to correspond with rhythmic accents). Gradually, Disney-trained animators took over, but the experience of the New York imports was not wasted. Dave Hand, Ben Sharpsteen, and Jack King all had important careers ahead of them at the Studio as animation directors.

It is interesting to note that there was, by 1931, a full-fledged story department. This was not like any other story department because everything was worked out in visual terms (all the story men were competent draftsmen). At about this time, or shortly after, the first "storyboards" made their appearance. The storyboard was an important innovation. It is difficult to attribute its invention with any certainty to one person, but Disney himself always credited it to Webb Smith. Until then, stories had been worked out comic-strip fashion in notebooks or on loose sheets of paper (generally there would be three or six drawings to a page, sometimes accompanied by a written description of the action and dialogue notes). Smith, on his own or in collaboration with other people, hit upon the idea of making each of his drawings on a separate sheet of paper and pinning them all, in sequence, to a bulletin board. The story for an entire short could be accommodated on a single board, and thus the director, or anyone else concerned with the production, could see the plot of an entire movie spread out in front of him. If changes had to be made, drawings could be moved or taken down and replaced by others. The ideal system for developing cartoon stories, it quickly came into general use throughout the Studio and eventually throughout the industry. Employed more than ever today, this invaluable tool has been adopted not only by other animation studios but also by producers of live-action films and commercials.

Disney himself must have been delighted by this innovation. The storyboard enabled him to participate even more closely in the development of his cartoons, allowing him to walk into a music room and see at a glance exactly what needed to be done.

Dick Huemer was working for Charles Mintz at this time and he recalls that everyone in the industry figured that Disney must have some trick – a gimmick or secret of some kind – that made his films so superior.

"Whenever we met a guy like Ted Sears or Ben Sharpsteen, we'd say, 'Oh, come on now – what is it that Walt does that we don't do?' and they would simply say something like, 'He analyzes.' Analyzes! So do we – we think! But we didn't and Walt did. He did chew everything over, did prepare beautifully, so the director could just take it and give it to the animator and then look at it and correct it."

By the end of 1931, Disney's demand for constant improvement had driven the cost of a single cartoon to more than $13,000. The Studio was barely breaking even, and in 1932 another innovation drove costs still higher. In that year, Disney released a Silly Symphony called *Flowers and Trees*. This cartoon caused something of a sensation in the industry. It was in full color.

Technicolor® had introduced a two-strip system – it required two strips of film running through the camera – as early as 1929, but it had been used sparingly by the major studios which, with good reason, thought it had little more than novelty value. (Its chief limitation was that the color values were somewhat distorted.) By 1932, however, Technicolor had a three-strip system ready which offered far more accurate color reproduction, and Disney at once saw its advantages. *Flowers and Trees* had been partly made as a black-and-white film. This footage was scrapped and the whole thing was done again in color. It was premiered at Grauman's Chinese Theater in Hollywood along with Irving Thalberg's production of *Strange Interlude*.

By today's standards, *Flowers and Trees* is a strange mixture of charm and absurdity. A romance between two young trees is disrupted by a crabby tree stump who initiates a fire that threatens the whole forest. Birds puncture clouds so that rain falls and douses the fire. The stump is destroyed and the two young lovers are married, with a glowworm for a wedding ring, while neighboring flowers celebrate their nuptials. Whatever weaknesses or strengths this cartoon may have had were overshadowed by the fact that it was in color. Color made it a valuable property and, from that point on, all Silly Symphonies were fully chromatic. Walt Disney made an advantageous deal with Technicolor which gave him exclusive rights to the three-color process, as far as animation was concerned, for the next two years. For the time being, the Mickey Mouse cartoons continued to be in black and white – but the Symphonies took full advantage of the new possibilities. Almost at once they became more inventive. *Flowers and Trees* was followed by *King Neptune* and *Babes in the Woods,* both of which display tighter structure and livelier action than anything previously seen in this series.

One factor which contributed to their inventiveness was the addition to the staff, in 1932, of Albert Hurter. Hurter, a Swiss-born artist, had learned the art of animation at the Barre studio in New York. After spending some time in the Southwest (he was passionately devoted to the desert landscape), he set up a commercial art studio in Los Angeles and then, probably at the instigation of Ted Sears or one of the other New York exiles, joined the Disney staff. From the very beginning of this association Hurter had a special position at the Studio, Disney realizing that his gift was for producing what became known as "inspirational drawings." This is to say that he spent his time developing visual ideas for future projects and improvising on themes which might trigger the

Lullaby Land, 1933, top, presents a child's dream adventures in a landscape metamorphosed from the patchwork quilt that covers his bed. The following year, in *The Goddess of Spring,* center, Disney artists attempted to revive the myth of Pluto and Persephone. *Music Land,* 1935, bottom, offered a twist on the Romeo and Juliet story, in which the son of the King of the Isle of Jazz falls in love with the daughter of the Queen of the Land of Symphony

The layout drawing, opposite top, for *Old King Cole,* 1933, gives some idea of the detail that went into every scene of a Silly Symphony. Another layout drawing, opposite bottom, this one for *The Wise Little Hen,* 1934, illustrates the scene in which Donald Duck made his debut. He is discovered dancing a hornpipe on the deck of a somewhat decrepit barge, right note: Use a warm green on fan. Follow floor pattern on right and reverse. Try to get sampler feeling by imitating stitches as indicated. Color sampler as indicated on left and color center of hearts, with fine white separating line. Same around crosses. The lettering on box is not final, see me before doing lettering. *Horvath*

Sc 12

imaginations of story men or animators. Neptune's court in *King Neptune* and the gingerbread house in *Babes in the Woods* both reflect his influence. He had been trained in Europe and his drawings were imbued with the spirit of the gothic fairy tale. This added another dimension to the native American vigor of the Disney product. As the Studio continued to evolve toward more ambitious projects, Hurter's influence was felt more and more strongly.

In 1933, Hurter designed the settings and main characters for what turned out to be the greatest Disney success up to that time – the famous *Three Little Pigs*. It is hardly necessary to recapitulate here either the plot or the success of Frank Churchill's hit tune, "Who's Afraid of the Big Bad Wolf?" The movie was a smash. Theaters retained it week after week, and its impact reflects the fact that it went far beyond any of the earlier Symphonies in terms of plot and character development. The story line is so strong that social commentators have seen it as an archetypal parable about the Great Depression. (Disney insisted that it was intended as entertainment and nothing more, but the film had such a mythic ring to it that it invited interpretations of this sort.) The animation was excellent and the characters had a real existence of their own – something which, to that date, had been achieved only with Mickey and Minnie. Just one thing marred the movie. In one section, the Big Bad Wolf approached the brick home of the Practical Pig in the guise of a caricatured Jewish peddler. Humor at the expense of ethnic stereotypes was not uncommon in Hollywood at the time, but this gag represented a serious lapse in taste even by the elastic standards of the period. Later, when *Three Little Pigs* was rereleased, this section of the movie was revamped to eliminate the offensive element.

The following year, 1934, saw the production of several excellent Silly Symphonies, including *The Tortoise and the Hare, The Grasshopper and the Ants*, and *The Wise Little Hen* – all of which were moral fables and showed just how proficient the Studio had become at structuring a story and establishing character. *The Tortoise and the Hare* put Aesop into modern dress as the rakish hare loses his race to the tortoise against a milky landscape that is typical of these early color cartoons. This milkiness – at times it resembles smog – resulted from the fact that Emil Flohri mixed a great deal of white pigment with his paint and water. In *The Grasshopper and the Ants*, the grasshopper is a particularly well-established character (his theme song is "The World Owes Me a Living") keyed to the voice talent of Pinto Colvig. Colvig – a former circus clown – was a musician and a member of the gag team, but his greatest claim to fame is that he provided the voice of Goofy, who had had his first supporting role in a 1932 cartoon, *Mickey's Revue*.

The Wise Little Hen introduced another voice talent and a new character who, within a year, was to challenge Mickey as Disney's star attraction. This character was Donald Duck, and the man who provided him with a voice was Clarence "Ducky" Nash. Until Disney discovered him, Nash had worked for a milk company, entertaining children with his animal

A general view of the Hyperion Avenue studio, c. 1933

A group photograph taken at the Studio in the mid-thirties, about the time that staff expansion was picking up momentum

Walt looks on as Mary Moder, Pinto Colvig, and Dorothy Compton rehearse "Who's Afraid of the Big Bad Wolf?" Composer Frank Churchill is at the piano

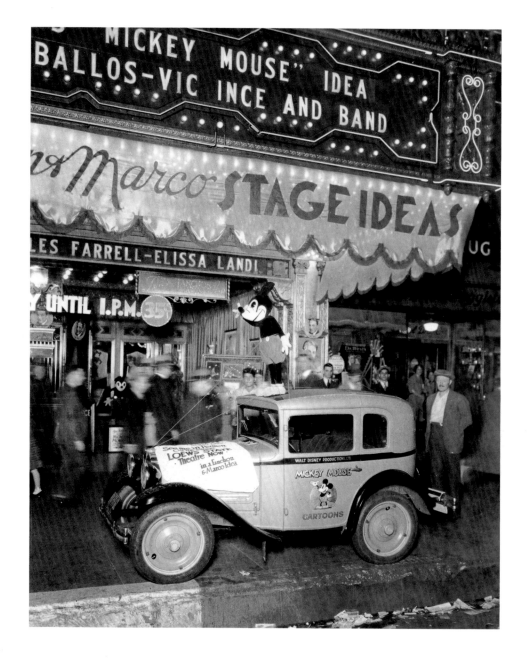

A promotional vehicle and theater marquees
advertising Mickey Mouse

imitations. One of these imitations evolved into Donald's ill-tempered
quack and made his voice known all over the world.

Donald Duck had a relatively modest role in his first screen appearance, making his debut as a dyspeptic creature, living on a ramshackle
houseboat, who feigned a bellyache every time the Wise Little Hen
asked him for assistance. (In this first incarnation he was drawn by Art
Babbitt and Dick Huemer, who had finally joined the Disney animation
staff.) Donald's bill was a little longer than it is today, but he had the
same voice, the same sailor suit, and the same irascible temperament.
He quickly made the jump to costarring roles in Mickey Mouse pictures
such as *Orphan's Benefit,* irritating everyone on the screen but endearing
himself to the audiences. Many animators found the Duck difficult to
work with, but two in particular – Dick Lundy and Fred Spencer – had a
way with him, and they must be given much of the credit for developing
him into a star.

We might remark at this point that the idea of animators being "cast" for certain characters was becoming quite common. Animators tend to think of themselves as actors who "perform" with their pencils, and, given this concept, it was only natural that some animators should have a better touch with certain roles and certain types of business than with others. Just as Ub Iwerks had given Mickey his initial impetus, so Donald found benefactors in Spencer and Lundy, and Pluto and Goofy began to develop as major characters largely because certain artists had strong feelings about them and the way they should behave. Pluto owed much of his evolving importance to Norm Ferguson. For a 1934 cartoon, *Playful Pluto,* Webb Smith devised a sequence in which Pluto becomes entangled with a sticky ribbon of flypaper. Ferguson took this sequence and turned it into a classic of comic animation. The man who had a real feeling for Goofy was Art Babbitt. Babbitt knew how to make the most out of any situation that the Goof might find himself in, and this led to more and better situations being invented for him. In this way the Goof developed from a bit player with a funny voice into the full-fledged idiot star of the mid-thirties.

Mickey, meanwhile, had become a national symbol, and as such he was expected to behave properly at all times. If he occasionally stepped out of line, any number of letters would arrive at the Studio from citizens and organizations who felt that the nation's moral well-being was in their

Lillian and Walt Disney at home with their pet chow

Walt and Mickey pose with Will Hays

hands. It was becoming harder and harder to find comic situations for Mickey that would not give offense in some quarter. Eventually, he would be pressured into the role of straight man, but the gradual change had not yet eroded the core of his personality, and the Mouse cartoons of the mid-thirties were consistently inventive while becoming increasingly sophisticated. The strides made by the Disney Studio between 1928 and 1934 were quite extraordinary. The story department came up with better and more fully developed ideas and the animators implemented them with increased skill. They had learned that for a character to seem real he had to have real weight – had to be seen to obey the laws of gravity (or to deliberately defy them if that was what the situation called for). This was not an easy thing to achieve. To take a single example, to make Goofy appear to have real weight, an animator like Art Babbitt had to understand exactly how gravity would affect the character's singular walk – part lope, part shuffle.

In Mickey's early days, he had expressed his reactions in terms of elabo-rate "takes" – throwing his whole body into a response so that there

Lunch at the Paramount commissary, 1934. Disney is seated with veteran animator Walter Lantz. Standing are Gary Cooper, left, and Walter Winchell

Disney's growing success abroad can be gauged from this French comic and this Bulgarian poster for a film presentation at the Royal Theater in Sofia

These stills from *Mickey's Surprise Party*, 1939, a commercial made for the National Biscuit Company, show that by the end of the decade Mickey and Minnie had developed a certain nonchalant sophistication and Pluto had come into his own

For *Playful Pluto*, 1934, Webb Smith devised and Norm Ferguson animated a scene in which Pluto becomes entangled with a strip of flypaper. A classic of its sort, this sequence demonstrates how Disney artists could take a simple situation and build on it in such a way that the humor arose directly from the personality of the character

Poster, 1933

In *Orphan's Benefit*, 1934, Donald Duck came into his own. His efforts to entertain a group of children are frustrated by the malicious behavior of the audience, which causes him to dissolve into helpless rage could be no doubt about the fact that he was surprised, angry, happy, or whatever. By the mid-thirties, Disney artists had learned how to convey a shift in mood by a subtle change of expression on a character's face or by an almost imperceptible alteration of physical attitude. And as the Disney team perfected its skills it continued to expand, drawing to itself talented young men who were attracted by the spectacular advances that had already been made.

One nonaesthetic factor made the Disney Studio especially attractive to young artists in the 1930s. The Great Depression was at its height, and there were not too many markets they could turn to. Ward Kimball's story is typical:

"I was going to art school in Santa Barbara and I thought I wanted to be a magazine illustrator. . . . This was the Depression and you had to make a little bread anywhere you could find it, so on Saturday mornings I would pick up four or five dollars at the local Safeway store. I'd have to get there by 5 A.M., rain or shine – or rather fog – and hack lettuce. . . . After I thawed out my fingers, I'd go back and paint showcards. . . . When I was through with this, about 9:30, I'd go across the street and up a block to the Fox Arlington Theater which, every Saturday morning, featured the original Mickey Mouse Club. . . . I was paid three dollars to rehearse and lead about ten kids who played instruments and did a short band march number at the beginning of the program. . . .

"About this time, I saw my first Disney color cartoon – *Father Noah's Ark,* a Silly Symphony – and I was amazed at the movement and the artwork. Rarely did you see a Technicolor live-action picture – maybe John McCormack singing partly in color – but here was this full-color *Father Noah's Ark.* Wow! I began to see that this was no ordinary, run-of-the-mill cartoon stuff. The Disney gags were funnier and there seemed to be one every few seconds. . . . The Disney cartoons had a realism that no others had – the giraffes ran like giraffes and the chipmunks and squirrels scampered like chipmunks and squirrels. Not only that, the faster animals caught and passed the slower ones – which I had never seen done before.

"Then along came *Three Little Pigs* with its hit tune which was played over and over on the radio. . . . Many of the other studios were reaching into their bag of old silents and rereleasing them with new sound tracks by people like Jelly Roll Morton and Fats Waller, to which they would add a few ratchets and honks and slide whistles – and that was supposed to be a sound cartoon – but Disney cartoons made a real honest attempt to integrate sound and picture.

"In 1934, when I'd been going to art school for two years and money was real tight, one of the instructors at school said, 'Kimball, you make a lot of funny drawings and it seems to me you ought to work for a man like Disney.'

"Well, to drive all the way to Los Angeles during the Depression was tough – gas was twelve cents a gallon. So my mother says, 'Okay – I'll take you into Los Angeles and bring you back just this once.' So I loaded my portfolio with paints and sketches. Well, nobody had ever come to

Gulliver Mickey, 1934, is one of several cartoons that make Mickey the hero of a children's classic

In this layout drawing for *Gulliver Mickey,* Mickey's dream self takes leave of his sleeping body

SCENE 3.   OHUH HELLO ROBIN... YA' FASCINATE ME!

Who Killed Cock Robin?, a Silly Symphony of 1935, gives the old nursery rhyme a new twist. Robin, below, it turns out, is not dead, but has merely been wounded by Cupid's arrow. The triumph of the cartoon is Jenny Wren, left, the object of Robin's passion, who is a thinly disguised caricature of Mae West. Even Walt Disney seems to have been satisfied with this polished and sophisticated little production, and it is said to have influenced him to go ahead with *Snow White and the Seven Dwarfs*

SCENE 2.

The Cookie Carnival, a Silly Symphony of 1935, is a bizarre little masterpiece full of humorous invention. As the title suggests, it concerns a holiday in Cookie Land, the high point of which is the election of a queen. In this variation of the Cinderella story, the prince is a poor hobo, right, and the heroine a heart-broken cookie who has been left out of the parade because she does not have a suitable costume. The action proceeds in a rapid-fire sequence of hilarious visual puns, and the witty, baroque imagery probably owes a great deal to the imagination of Albert Hurter

Broken Toys, another Silly Symphony of 1935, has W. C. Fields and other Hollywood characters appear in the guise of discarded dolls. The main plot involves a sailor doll who performs an emergency operation to restore the sight of a dainty little creature who has lost her eyes

Mickey's Service Station, 1935, was the last Mickey Mouse cartoon to be made in black and white. Pegleg Pete, the perennial villain, brings his car in for a checkup because he has been hearing a squeak. Mickey, Donald, and Goofy rip the car apart looking for the source of the offending noise. It turns out to be a cricket which has concealed itself in the vehicle, but our heroes do not discover this until the car is a wreck.

A typical enough plot, it affords all the main characters ample opportunity to display their usual foibles. Mickey is doggedly persistent in an ineffectual sort of way, Goofy is characteristically incompetent, and Donald's propensity for rage is tempered only by his latent cowardice

Generally recognized as one of the classics
of Disney animation, *The Band Concert*, 1935,
was the first Mickey Mouse cartoon to be
made in Technicolor. Mickey is discovered
in the park of a small Midwestern town,
directing an orchestra through a program of
popular classics. He embarks on a spirited
version of *The William Tell Overture,* but
events conspire to disrupt the performance.
Most troublesome is Donald Duck, in the
guise of a street vendor, who again and again
leads the orchestra astray by playing "Turkey
in the Straw" on an unending succession of
fifes which are concealed about his person.

As the orchestra approaches the storm
section of the overture, a more serious problem arises. A tornado, which seems to have
been conjured up by the music, approaches
the town. The twister picks up the entire
orchestra – along with Donald, a farm house,
and assorted vegetation – sending everyone
and everything spinning in the air. Mickey
holds the performance together by sheer
willpower, and the piece comes to a rousing
finale, with musicians hanging from trees
and anything else that has been left standing.

It is interesting that the disruptive Duck
plays Mickey's theme from *Steamboat Willie,*
suggesting that Donald has taken over the role
of mischief-maker from the Mouse

In the early thirties, Mickey and the other Disney characters were already being adapted for use in all kinds of merchandising operations. Dozens of companies manufactured items under license from the Studio. At least two were saved from bankruptcy by their Disney franchises

Disney's with a portfolio of his work before. So I come in and here I am, just turned twenty, and I come to the front office on Hyperion Avenue and ask for a job."

Kimball began work as a Disney apprentice on April 2, 1934. Within five years he would become one of the Studio's top animators.

The expansion of the Studio can be illustrated in another way. In 1929 and 1930, additions were made to the front, rear, and one side of the original structure on Hyperion Avenue. In 1931, a two-story animation building was erected. In four years, the Studio grew from 1,600 square feet of floor space to 20,000 square feet.

Mickey Mouse and Mary Pickford

3   Hyperion Days

On January 12, 1936, the *New York Times* published an interview head-lined "H. G. Wells in Close Up." The author of *The Invisible Man* had a few comments to make about the film industry. "Many do not realize that all Hollywood studios are so busy that they keep very much to them-selves. Consequently, Chaplin never visited the Disney studios. Imagine, Charlie and Walt Disney, those two geniuses, never met! I took Charlie there. Disney has the most marvelous machinery and does the most inter-esting experiments. Like Chaplin he is a good psychologist and both do the only thing in film today that remains international."

Four days after the *Times* story, on January 16, René Clair was reported by the *New York Journal* as saying that the outstanding figures in the movies at that time were Charlie Chaplin and Walt Disney. "The reason is," he explained, "that they have no outside interference. They act as their own producer, director, and even attend to their own stories and musical scores. Their artistry is sublime."

Two months later, on March 13, the *Tulsa Tribune* quoted Thornton Wilder as telling a lecture audience, "The two presiding geniuses of the movies are Walt Disney and Charlie Chaplin." Ten days after that, Mary Pickford told a reporter for the *Boston Post*, "There is only one Walt Disney. . . . He is the greatest producer the industry has ever turned out."

On May 25, the *New York Journal* carried some outspoken opinions expressed by the composer Jerome Kern. "Cartoonist Walt Disney," said

Left: Walt Disney with Will Rogers. Right: Disney with the Barrymores

Kern, "has made the 20th century's only important contribution to music. Disney has made use of music as language. In the synchronization of humorous episodes with humorous music, he has unquestionably given us the outstanding contribution of our time. In fact I would go so far as to say it is the only real contribution."

Harper's Bazaar, dated November 1 of that same year, printed an article titled "Boom Shot of Hollywood," by Janet Flanner, Paris correspondent for the *New Yorker*. "Certainly the sanest spot in Hollywood," she observed, "is that studio exclusively devoted to the creation of delicate deliriums and lovely lunacies – the fun factory of Mickey Mouse, Miss Minnie and Mr. Walt Disney, Incorporated. Visitors are rarely admitted. Withdrawn to a safe distance from the rest of the movie maelstrom, the Disney plant is remotely located in one of those endless suburban settings of Barcelona bungalows, pink roses and red filling stations that makes southern California so picturesque. The studio looks like a small municipal kindergarten with green grass for the children to keep off of and, on the roof, a gigantic glorious figure of Mickey to show them the best way. . . . With hysteria the seeming law for movie making, it's a wonder Mickey and Silly Symphonies succeed in this world at all, since the place where they're made is as sensible as a post office. Law and order reign there, without seeming unattractive, side by side with Minnie, Madam Clara Cluck, Donald Duck and Elmer the Elephant who, all Rabelaisian in spots but solidly moral at heart, are doubtless easier to get along with than the other big stars in the movie game."

Disney, then, did not lack for influential admirers, and the list could easily be extended. Arturo Toscanini, for example, saw *The Band*

Concert six times and invited its producer to visit Italy. Sergey Eisenstein, the greatest of Soviet directors, pronounced Mickey Mouse America's most original contribution to culture.

Mickey, though still a star, was rapidly becoming a symbol, representing some concept of comedy that was to all appearances universal. In 1934 Harold Butcher, New York correspondent for the *London Daily Herald,* had written, "After a quick trip around the world . . . I have returned to New York to say that Mickey Mouse has been with me most of the way. On the Pacific, in Japan and China, at Manchouli – suspended precariously between Siberia and Manchukuo . . ."

From England, in 1935, came the report that the Queen and the Duchess of York had selected Mickey Mouse chinaware as gifts for six hundred children. That same year, Mickey Mouse cartoons were used to test RCA's television system and the League of Nations voted its approval of Mickey.

The Disney merchandising operation was by now a multimillion-dollar enterprise. The *American Exporter* informed its readers that, "beside the 80 licensees in the U.S. who are manufacturing merchandise bearing the likeness of Mickey Mouse or some other of the Walt Disney characters, there are 15 in Canada, 40 in England, 80 on the European continent and 15 in Australia. Kay Kamen, Inc., representing Walt Disney Enterprises, has branch offices in Toronto, London, Paris, Copenhagen, Milan, Barcelona, Lisbon, and Sydney.

Disney with Stan Laurel and Oliver Hardy

"U.S. exporting manufacturers who are now exporting merchandise under Walt Disney license include Hickok belts, Lionel electric toys, Ingersoll watches, Dennison paper goods, Seiberling latex rubber dolls and Oak toy balloons.

"England is making a Mickey Mouse marmalade. Other products include cutlery, soap, playing cards, candy, bridge favors, wristwatches, toothbrushes, socks, shoes, garters, slippers, umbrellas, hot water bottles, lamps and sheets."

The same publication estimated that exports of Disney-licensed products would exceed $5,000,000 for 1935. The *New York Telegraph* reported that total sales were up to $35,000,000 a year. Cartier offered a diamond bracelet bearing the likeness of Mickey for a mere $1,150. More significantly, both Lionel trains and Ingersoll watches were virtually saved from bankruptcy by their Disney franchises (two million Mickey Mouse watches were sold in a single eight-week period).

Donald was by now seriously challenging Mickey's preeminence, and when the Studio announced his first birthday, the *New York Times* devoted a serious editorial to the growing popularity of the irascible duck, wondering if he might not replace Mickey in the affections of the public. Dozens of other papers echoed the question.

As for Disney himself, he was learning to field the questions that come with fame. Always he was suitably modest. "I do not draw, write music or contribute most of the gags and ideas seen in our pictures today," he told the *Times.* "My work is largely to supervise, to select and shape material, to coordinate and direct the efforts of our staff."

Thru the Mirror, 1936, is a witty improvisation on one of the Lewis Carroll themes that had fascinated Disney since the time of the Alice Comedies. Right: Dick Lundy's animation drawings for a sequence in which Mickey impersonates Fred Astaire clearly show how flexible Mickey's body had become

BOARDWALK

(Interior) 78

Moving Day, 1936, provides Goofy with some of his finest moments, pitting him against a piano with a mind of its own. This sequence, animated by Art Babbitt, is a sustained and inspired piece of nonsense. Comedy is distilled from the situation with a close regard for character that would have been unthinkable even two or three years earlier

Another reporter asked Disney how it felt to be a celebrity. "It feels fine," he replied, "when being a celebrity helps get a choice reservation for a football game. . . . As far as I can remember, being a celebrity has never helped me make a good picture, or a good shot in a polo game, or command the obedience of my daughter, or impress my wife. It doesn't even seem to help keep fleas off our dogs and, if being a celebrity won't give one an advantage over a couple of fleas, then I guess there can't be that much in being a celebrity after all."

So much for Disney the public figure, but what of Disney the man? How did his colleagues see him?

Jack Cutting recalls that Disney seemed mature beyond his years and, at times, very serious. "I always felt his personality was a little bit like a drop of mercury rolling around on a slab of marble because he changed moods so quickly. I believe this was because he was extremely sensitive. . . . He could grasp your ideas and interpret your thought rapidly. You didn't have to give Walt a five-page memo – he understood the point right away. . . .

"Although Walt could exude great charm if he was in the mood, he could also be dour and indifferent toward people – but this was usually

89

Moving Day also presents Mickey with a
number of problems, including a struggle with
a trunk that will not stay closed

Moose Hunters, 1937, presents Mickey,
Donald, and Goofy in a series of typically
disastrous confrontations with wildlife

SCENE 4
MICKEY AND PLUTO UP STAIRS. MICKEY: "OH BOY - RITZY STUFF, HUH?"

Mickey's Amateurs, 1937, offers a blend of entertainment and near catastrophe

Pluto co-starred in such movies as *The Beach Picnic* and *Society Dog Show,* both released in 1939. The top drawing is by Fred Moore

Above: *Mickey's Circus*, 1936, presented Mickey in a role that was a natural for him – the ringmaster. Right: a Fred Moore study for *Brave Little Tailor*, 1938. Bottom: a scene from *A Gentleman's Gentleman*, 1941. For a brief period during the early forties, Mickey was given ears that worked in perspective because he was preoccupied by problems. Sometimes you would pass him in the hall, say hello, and he would not even notice you. The next time he might greet you warmly and start talking about a new project he was excited about. You might not understand what he was talking about at first, because he didn't always give you a preamble on the subject. If you didn't pick up on his chain of thought quickly, he would sometimes look at you as though you were slow-witted, because when he was excited about an idea it was clear to him and he assumed it was to everyone else.

"The people who worked best with Walt were those who were stimulated by his enthusiasm. . . . More than once, when he was in a creative mood and ideas were popping out like skyrockets, I have suddenly seen him look as if he had been hit in the face with a bucket of cold water. The eyebrow would go up and suddenly reality was the mood in the room. Someone in the group was out of tune with the creative spirit he was generating. Then he would say it was difficult to work with so-and-so."

These creative moods were often exercised at the "sweatbox" sessions which were so essential a part of the Studio routine (the projection rooms at Hyperion Avenue were not air-conditioned – hence the name sweatbox). As soon as a sequence was animated and shot as a pencil test, it would be run in one of these projection rooms. Disney would be in attendance along with animators, story men, the director, and anyone else concerned. (Sometimes people from outside the production team would be invited in to give a layman's opinion.) The sequence under consideration would be subjected to an intense analysis in an effort to see if it could be improved in any way before it was sent off to the inking and painting department. Sometimes, instead of pencil tests, it would be a "Leica reel" that was under consideration. The Leica reel (another Disney innovation) provided a way of projecting story continuity drawings in synchronization with whatever part of the sound track had been prerecorded, thus giving at least a rough idea of how the final movie might look and sound. In any case, Disney would always lead these discussions and generally had valuable contributions to make.

"He always had the answers," says Dick Huemer. "He would go right to the middle of the problem and there would be this nugget that he'd pull out. Damnedest thing! You'd kick yourself and say, 'Why didn't I see it? There it is!' But he had an instinct for it, and I think the instinct was based on the fact that he always considered the common man's viewpoint. . . . Aside from his genius, he was just a down-to-earth guy."

Marc Davis is one of the many Disney artists who has emphasized his employer's readiness to gamble everything on an idea as one of the key factors in the growth of the Studio. "He was not afraid to risk every penny, go into hock, hire 150 people and wonder how he was going to meet the payroll. He did this all his life. He felt money is good only because of what you can do with it. Without him, I can't see animation having become much of a business because, for the most part, the other studios were either followers or they were just filling up programs. Almost anything they did that was half-way good was acceptable. But Walt was trying to make a little jewel out of each one of these things."

Studying penguins as an aid to animation: standing, left to right, Walt Disney, Albert Hurter, Leigh Harline, Frenchy de Trémaudan, Clyde Geronimi, Paul Hopkins (behind Geronimi), Hugh Hennesy, Art Babbitt, Norm Ferguson, and Bill Roberts. Seated, Dick Huemer and Wilfred Jackson

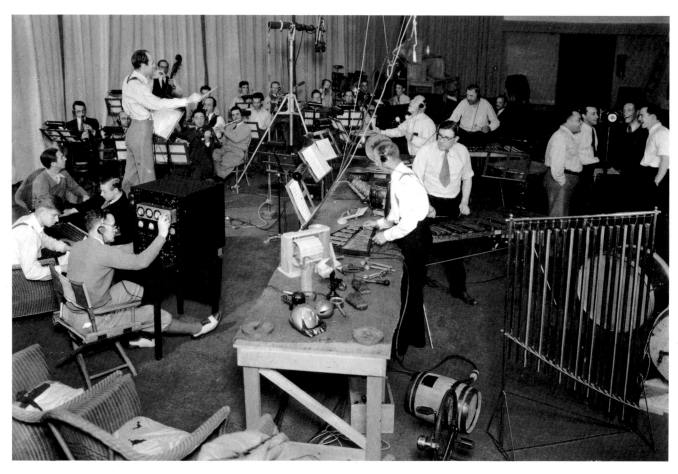

Frank Churchill conducts a recording session. Disney and Wilfred Jackson are seated at the extreme left. The clarinetist to Churchill's left is Pinto Colvig

Ted Sears

Disney listens as three members of his story team display their versatility: Webb Smith, piano; Ted Sears, violin; and Pinto Colvig

Jim Macdonald and Ed Forrest record sound effects

Of course, if you were a young and inexperienced animator you were not privy to the vital sweatbox conferences. "Word would dribble down to you," Frank Thomas remembers, "that someone had decided to do such-and-such to your scene. Milt Kahl and I once wrote a song – 'If I Should Die, Please Bury Me in Sweatbox Four' – because that's where all the big meetings were held and then we could find out what was going on."

Young artists joining the Studio usually started by learning to do in-between drawings. Ward Kimball remembers that the Studio was still a small place in those days. "The in-betweening department was down in the semibasement. . . . We called it the bullpen and in the summer you had to strip to the waist, it was so damn hot. . . . By five o'clock I was always exhausted. . . . I would get on a Big Red streetcar and, on those hot summer evenings, I sometimes would fall asleep leaning on the window and watching the loose screws twist in and out of the wooden window frames."

It was not every night, however, that an in-betweener could leave work at five o'clock. Apart from the overtime – which seems to have been plentiful – there were also art classes, which had become an integral part of the Studio schedule. As far back as 1931, Disney had decided that his artists would benefit from further training, and he arranged for some of them to take an evening class at the Chouinard Art School (Les Clark recalls that, since not all of them had cars, Disney himself would often drive them to school). The class these Disney artists attended was taught by a young man named Don Graham, who was soon to have an important role in the Disney organization. Graham remembers that for most of

Above: a pastel drawing for *Water Babies*, 1935. Opposite, top: a scene from *Cock of the Walk*, 1935, a Silly Symphony which includes clever parodies of Hollywood dance routines. Opposite, bottom: a story continuity sketch for *Toby Tortoise Returns*, the 1936 sequel to *The Tortoise and the Hare*

the 1931–32 school year he worked one night a week with a group of about fifteen Disney artists in his regular class.

"Walt, of course, picked up the tab. In the fall of 1932, Art Babbitt, one of the top animators at the Studio, convinced Walt that instead of sending his men across town to Chouinard, it would be far wiser to conduct classes at the Studio, where there could be more control of attendance.

"On November 15, 1932, the great Disney Art School was born in the old sound studio at Hyperion. First it was just two evenings a week, with some twenty or thirty men each evening. In a matter of three or four weeks, it became necessary to divide these classes. Phil Dike was called in and between us we worked these two evenings a week until 1934. During this period James Patrick, a talented young artist, was also employed for a few months as a teacher. The attendance during these two years averaged better than fifty men a session. . . .

"In 1934, the nature of the school changed its character completely. Dike was put in charge of the color coordination of all production work which went through Technicolor. . . . I was employed on a three-day and two-night basis. During the first year of this period I was trained in the sweatboxes under the direct critical eye of Walt and the directors. The evening school was put on a five-evenings-a-week schedule. Eugene Fleury and Palmer Schoppe filled in the evening schedule with me. A new training department was instituted in the daytime. . . .

"At about this time, Walt announced his intention of making *Snow White,* which implied a vast expansion of the animation department. Early in 1935, he came to me and said, 'I need three hundred artists – get

Above left: several Disney shorts exploited caricature, but Will Rogers had to be taken out of *Mickey's Polo Game,* 1936, after his death in a plane crash. Above right and opposite: *Mother Goose Goes Hollywood,* 1938, includes portraits of Groucho Marx, Katharine Hepburn, Laurel and Hardy, and W. C. Fields them.' And thus began a huge campaign of recruitment. Ads in all the newspapers up and down the West Coast, then on a national basis, and even opening up an office in the RCA building in New York City, where I spent three months looking at portfolios. . . .

"When the new training department was instituted, in 1934–35, the new employees were brought into the Studio in small groups, usually a dozen or so at a time. They were given from six to eight weeks to demonstrate their potential. . . . Usually I would work with them the first two weeks, every day, eight hours a day, utilizing a human model. Then their day would be devoted a half day to drawing, a half day to production problems. They were also encouraged to attend the evening school, which soon became extremely active, with a nightly attendance of about 150. Under George Drake's supervision, many authorities on various aspects of animation, drawing of characters, layout and background problems, et cetera, were called in to lecture and instruct."

Typical of the kind of instructional material used was a book assembled by Ted Sears and Fred Moore. This contained model sheets, indicating how the main characters should be drawn, photographs of humans and animals in action poses, and detailed analyses of the personalities of Mickey, Donald, Goofy, and Pluto. The following, written by Sears, is a typical example:

"Mickey is not a clown . . . he is neither silly nor dumb.

"His comedy depends entirely upon the situation he is placed in.

"His age varies with the situation . . . sometimes his character is that of a young boy, and at other times, as in the adventure type of picture, he appears quite grown up. . . .

A title card for the 1935 cartoon *On Ice*, top, and a background painting for *Mickey's Fire Brigade*, also released that year

Many fine artists – Charles Philippi, Hugh Hennesy, Tom Codrick, and others – made layout drawings for Disney during the thirties. Their work often displays a high standard of draftsmanship, as in these examples from *Thru the Mirror*, 1936

Mickey, Donald, and Goofy worked against
these spectacular backgrounds in a 1937 short,
Clock Cleaners

Pan shots – takes in which the camera moves
across a panoramic background – necessitated
elongated paintings like this one for *Three
Blind Mouseketeers*, 1936

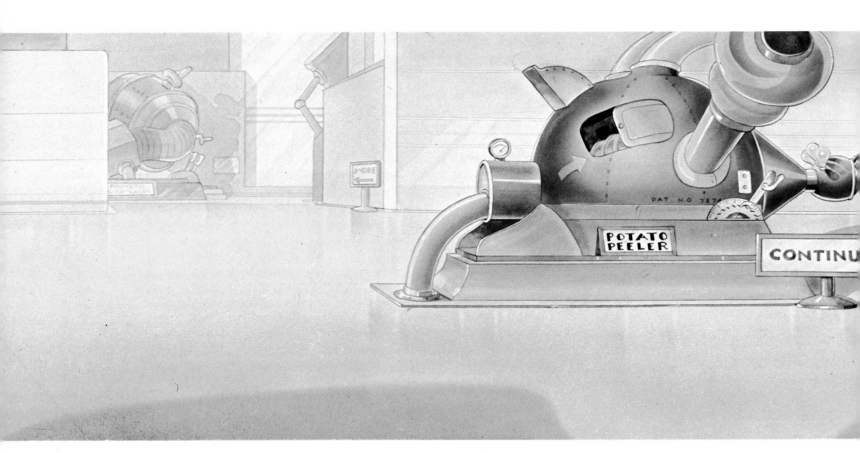

Background paintings for *Modern Inventions*,
above and opposite top, and for two other
1937 cartoons, *Pluto's Quinpuplets* and *Don
Donald*, the latter of which was Donald's
first solo vehicle

"Mickey is most amusing when in a serious predicament trying to accomplish some purpose under difficulties, or against time. . . . When Mickey is working under difficulties, the laughs occur at the climax of each small incident or action. They depend largely upon Mickey's expression, position, attitude, state of mind, etc., and the graphic way that these things are shown. . . .

"Mickey is seldom funny in a chase picture, as his character and expressions are usually lost."

Before giving hints on how to draw the Mouse, Fred Moore added his own thoughts on Mickey's personality:

"Mickey seems to be the average young boy of no particular age; living in a small town, clean living, fun loving, bashful around girls, polite and clever as he must be for the particular story. In some pictures he has a touch of Fred Astaire, in others of Charlie Chaplin, and some of Douglas Fairbanks, but in all of these there should be some of the young boy."

Moore's drawing hints include the following suggestions:

"The body to be drawn as somewhat pear-shaped, fairly short and plump. . . . The body should be pliable at all times. . . . If Mickey were taking a deep breath we would give him a chest. If he were sad, we would loosen chest and droop shoulders, etc. The body should be thought of as having a certain volume, so when it is stretched it should grow thinner. . . .

"The shoes are fairly large and bulky – a medium between hard and soft – flexible enough to help animation, but stiff enough to be shoes. . . . Mickey is cuter when drawn with small shoulders, with a suggestion of stomach and fanny – and I like him pigeon-toed."

Moore also added some suggestions to be kept in mind by the apprentice when drawing Minnie:

"Minnie seems cuter with her skirts high on her body – showing a large expanse of her lace panties. This skirt should be starched and not hang loose. . . . Her mouth could be smaller than Mickey's and maybe never open into so wide a smile, take, expression, etc. Her eyelids and eyelashes could help very much in keeping her feminine as well as the skirt swaying from the body on different poses, displaying pants. Carrying the little finger in an extended position also helps."

Clearly, these hints are rather elementary and were intended mainly for the recruits being processed by Don Graham's training program. The fact that so much critical attention was being lavished on these apprentices did not mean, however, that the senior animators were being ignored. Their work was always subject to the appraisal of Walt Disney himself. He had, sometime earlier, instituted the practice of issuing credit ratings on many of the cartoons. These would be sent to the director and to each of the animators. Individual scenes would be rated "A," "B Plus," and so on, and these ratings would be accompanied by extensive comments in which Disney indicated where and how he thought each sequence could have been improved.

In December 1935, ratings were issued for a Silly Symphony titled *Cock o' the Walk*. This film was directed by Ben Sharpsteen, to whom Disney addressed the following remarks:

Backgrounds for some 1938 shorts: *Polar Trappers,* above and opposite top, *Boat Builders,* far right center and bottom, and *Ferdinand the Bull*

Walt Kelly, of *Pogo* fame, was a Disney artist for several years. In the drawing above he portrays, left to right, an invented character, himself, Ward Kimball, and Fred Moore. Caricature was practically a way of life at the Studio. Center is T. Hee's version of Norm Ferguson. Right is Aurie Battaglia's caricature of layout artist Ken O'Connor

Paintings for a 1939 release, *Donald's Lucky Day,* and for *Pluto's Dream House,* 1940

"The direction is fine from a technical standpoint. Some of the technical scenes and setups were well planned but the direction of the action is very poor from a personality and interest-building angle. The main fault with the story lies with the director and the story men. Without a doubt the animators would have gotten a better result if the story had been properly worked out and if the director had taken the story and treated it from a fantastic comical angle . . . instead of having so many scenes that paralleled human actions."

The following are extracts from some of the comments aimed at animators who worked on this film:

"The actions, as they were given by the director, have been carried out, but the true spirit of the character of the hens is lacking. Instead of waddling, they run. There are certain things which, if handled properly, would have made the action typical of a humanized hen and would have expressed more personality and interest to the audience. . . .

"I would suggest that you concentrate more on caricature, with action; not merely the drawing of a character to look like something, but giving your character the movements and actions of the person you are trying to put over. Remember, every action should be based on what the character represents. . . .

"Something was started in this scene which is what we are striving for. This is doing things in the dance which humans are unable to do. I mean the pullet on the rooster's muscles and the juggling from side to

Donald's Nephews, 1938, introduced the indefatigable Huey, Dewey, and Louie

By the late thirties, Donald had all but eclipsed Mickey in popularity. Examples here are from two 1938 shorts, *Donald's Golf Game,* top, and *The Fox Hunt,* center. At bottom is one from the following year, *Donald's Cousin Gus*

After a cartoon was completed, story continuity drawings were stapled into books – often with surprising results. This group from *Fire Chief,* 1940, gives a marvelous sense of movement

side, but it was passed over before we had a chance to build it up into anything funny."

Seen today, *Cock of the Walk,* with its brilliant parodies of Busby Berkeley dance routines, seems one of the best cartoons of its period. In view of this, the severity of Disney's remarks seems extraordinary, but we must keep in mind the fact that he was trying to make each one of these films into a little jewel. He believed in pushing his animators as far as he would push himself. We should note, too, that by 1935 he was deeply involved in the planning of *Snow White* and was, therefore, very concerned with establishing the standards that would be required to make a success of his first animated feature.

Considering the level of activity maintained at the Studio, it is amazing that anyone found any time for leisure. In fact, a nearby vacant lot provided Disney employees with a suitable playing field for softball games, which, with volleyball, became popular lunchtime activities. Disney seldom joined in these sports but, apparently because of his friendship with Spencer Tracy, he did take up polo.

Jack Cutting, who played with him, recalls that he went about taking up polo by first finding out who at the Studio could ride a horse. He then hired Captain Gil Proctor, formerly a cavalry officer and a member of

Some idea of the complexity of making an animated film can be gathered from these "bar sheets," which govern the entire sound track of a movie, showing exactly where every accent should fall. At different times they have taken different forms, but this example is quite representative.

Above each bar, the film footage is noted, providing a convenient general reference. The three upper staves – E1, E2, E3 – are devoted to instructions for the three effects tracks. Immediately below these – D1 and D2 – are staves carrying the words to be spoken on the two dialogue tracks. A description of the action that will be seen on screen occupies the center section, along with scene numbers and other material, while the music is transcribed onto the lower half of each bar sheet

CU: Don looks down at chair; looks o.s. to right, goes into double take.

Donald's Vacation, 1940

Left, top: *Donald's Lucky Day*, 1939; bottom: *The Autograph Hound*, 1939

A 1939 cartoon, *Goofy and Wilbur,* above, was
the Goof's first solo outing. Later he starred in
a series of comic instructional films such as
The Art of Self Defense, 1941, top right, and
How to Swim, 1942

Goofy in *Mickey's Amateurs,* 1937

the Army polo team, to coach his recruits. After some reading and black-board instruction, they began to practice on a field in the San Fernando Valley. At first, practice was held two mornings a week, very early, so that everyone could be at the Studio by 8 A.M. In the summer there were further sessions after work and then serious competition on weekends. Initially, the play was between two Studio teams, but eventually Walt and Roy (who also played) bought a string of quality ponies and began to play with Tracy, Will Rogers, and other celebrities from the movie colony.

Aside from family life, polo seems to have been Disney's only form of recreation at that time. The Disney family, like the Disney Studio, was growing. By 1936, Disney had two daughters – Diane and Sharon.

Above left: the Studio polo teams: Walt Disney's in the light jerseys, Roy's in the dark. Above right: Walter Wanger, left and Walt Disney right, 1934 or 1935, at the old Riviera Polo Grounds. Below left: Spencer Tracy, Walt Disney, James Gleason, and Frank Borzage. Below right: Spencer Tracy and Walt Disney

II Feature Animation

4 Snow White: The First Feature

The initial success of Mickey Mouse and the Silly Symphonies did not satisfy Disney for long, and as early as 1934 he began to think seriously about making a feature-length animated film. Two important considerations prompted him to this line of thought. One was a question of simple economics, namely, that no matter how successful the short cartoons were, they could never make very much money. They might share billing with the main feature – they often did – but film rental was determined by running time, not popularity, so the revenue from these shorts would always be limited. Beyond this, Disney was anxious for an opportunity to work within an expanded format – a structure that would allow for more elaborate and leisurely character development, that would give him a chance to evolve more complex plot ideas and greater naturalism. In 1926, Max Fleischer had made a five-and-a-half-reel cartoon titled *Einstein's Theory of Relativity*, but nobody had made an animated feature that could compete on equal terms with live-action pictures, and most people in the industry thought that to do so successfully would be virtually impossible. After all, the reasoning went, the kind of cartoon antics that can make us laugh for seven or eight minutes would become very boring if we were exposed to them for seventy or eighty minutes at a time. Disney, as usual, was at least one jump ahead and had no intention of merely extending his established gag routines to fit into a larger format. He was planning to take a fairy story and bring it to the screen with a kind of magical realism that was beyond the reach of live-action movies.

As everyone knows, the story Disney chose for his first feature was *Snow White and the Seven Dwarfs*. (It may be recalled here that the first movie he had ever seen, on a newsboys' outing in Kansas City, was a silent version of *Snow White*.) At first he referred to his new project as the "Feature Symphony," and to some extent it was an extension of the Silly Symphony concept, music playing an important part in its structure. But it was much more besides. No one can say just when Disney began to think about *Snow White*, but by the summer of 1934 his ideas were beginning to take concrete form. An exploratory outline, dated August 9 of that year, includes the following discussion of the dwarfs:

> The names which follow each suggest a type of character and the names will immediately identify the character in the minds of the audience:

Before embarking on their first feature-length film, Disney artists needed experience in animating the human figure. A 1934 Silly Symphony, *The Goddess of Spring*, was designed to test their skills in this area. Meanwhile, rough versions of characters for *Snow White* began to appear at the Studio

Scrappy	Doleful	Crabby
Happy	Wistful	Daffy
Hoppy	Soulful	Tearful
Sleepy	Helpful	Graspy
Weepy	Bashful	Busy
Dirty	Awful	Dizzy
Cranky	Snoopy	Snappy
Sneezy	Goopy	Hotsy
Sneezy-Wheezy	Gabby	Jaunty
Hungry	Blabby	Puffy
Lazy	Silly	Strutty
Grumpy	Dippy	Biggy
Dumpy	Graceful	Biggy-Wiggy
Thrifty	Neurtsy	Biggo-Ego
Nifty	Gloomy	Jumpy
Shifty	Sappy	Chesty
Woeful	Flabby	

The same outline elaborates some of the possibilities seen for the dwarfs:

> SLEEPY: Sterling Holloway. Falls asleep in midst of excitement, in middle of sentence, and so forth . . .

> HOPPY-JUMPY: Portrayed by Joe Twerp, the highly excitable, nervous radio comic who gets his words mixed up (flews nashes ry bichfield). He is in constant fear of being goosed but is not goosed until last scene.

> BASHFUL: Portrayed by Buelow, a unique radio personality with a very funny bashful laugh, halting delivery and very funny way of misplacing the word "though" . . .

> HAPPY: Portrayed by Professor Diddleton D. Wurtle, whose wild Ben Turpin eyes are reinforced by one of the funniest tricks of speech in radio . . .

SNEEZY-WHEEZY – GASPY: Asthmatic inhalations and exhalations of every breath. . . . Dapper . . . nimble dancer – quick movements stopped in midair by embryonic sneeze. . . . Always trying nutty cures and diets . . .

BIGGY-WIGGY – BIGGO-EGO: Portrayed by Eddie Holden, in his character of Hipplewater. A pompous, oily-tongued know-it-all . . .

AWFUL: The most lovable and interesting of the dwarf characters. He steals the drinks and is very dirty . . .

As *Snow White* went into production, Disney artists were asked how they thought the dwarfs might look and behave. These sketches are representative of the suggestions they made

These ideas were probably dictated by Disney. Anyone familiar with *Snow White* will realize that the dwarfs were destined to go through many changes before they reached the screen, but we can see that certain characteristics were already beginning to take shape (it should be pointed out that not all the performers named in these descriptions contributed to the eventual movie – but they did provide Disney with a concise way of describing a personality). This early manuscript also lists a number of possible songs for the film – including "Some Day My Prince Will Come" – indicating that a good deal of thought had already been devoted to this aspect of the subject. The outline differs from the final version in a number of ways so that, for example, Snow White is envisaged passing through a whole sequence of enchanted places before the woodland animals lead her to the dwarfs' cottage. These include the Morass of Monsters and the Valley of the Dragons, which are self-explanatory, as well as Upsidedownland and Backwardland (where birds fly tail first and trees have their roots in the air) and the Sleep Valley ("vast poppy fields, slumbrous music from the wind soughing through the trees"). The Queen is described as being "stately, beautiful in the way of a Benda mask." We are told that she is cool and serene. Only in her emotional climaxes does she erupt to full fury (a note in parentheses urges study of Charles Laughton in *The Barretts of Wimpole Street*).

BASHFUL DWARF ALWAYS
TYING BEARD IN KNOTS—
SNOW WHITE UNTIES IT
FOR HIM—

Another outline, this one dated October 22, 1934, includes a complete breakdown of the cast of characters. We can see from this how quickly things were beginning to develop:

SNOW WHITE: Janet Gaynor type – 14 years old.

THE PRINCE: Doug Fairbanks type – 18 years old.

THE QUEEN: A mixture of Lady Macbeth and the Big Bad Wolf – Her beauty is sinister, mature, plenty of curves – She becomes ugly and menacing when scheming and mixing her poisons – Magic fluids transform her into an old witchlike hag – Her dialogue and action are overdramatic, verging on the ridiculous.

THE HUNTSMAN: A minor character – Big and tough – 40 years old – The Queen's trusted henchman but hasn't the heart to murder an innocent girl . . .

PRINCE'S HORSE: This gallant white charger understands but cannot talk – like Tom Mix's horse Tony – The Prince's pal.

MAGIC MIRROR: The Queen's unwilling slave – Its masklike face appears when invoked – It speaks in weird voice.

This outline also includes another set of descriptions of the dwarfs – not dissimilar to the earlier ones except that the names have become more settled. Already they include Happy, Sleepy, Doc, Bashful, and Grumpy. Sneezy has been temporarily ousted by Jumpy, and Dopey has yet to be christened.

By the fall of 1934, then, the cast was pretty well established in Disney's mind. A story team was being built up, and we may presume that Albert Hurter and Joe Grant were beginning to work on character design. Very soon, more detailed outlines began to circulate – mimeographed sheets that dealt with specific scenes and situations. These kept everyone in touch with progress and doubled as invitations to submit ideas and gags that would contribute to the development of the plot.

For the cartoon shorts Disney had introduced a bonus system whereby anyone suggesting a gag that was used in the picture received five dollars and anyone providing an idea that formed the basis for an entire cartoon received a hundred dollars. This system was adapted to the new situation, and an outline dated November 2, 1934, includes the notation, "We shall distribute, from time to time, various sequences and situations to be gagged up as the story develops. . . . The following sequences between Snow White and the dwarfs are now open for ALL POSSIBLE SUGGESTIONS AND GAGS."

Parts of the plot had already taken recognizable shape, as the following extracts show:

Snow White is going through the woods alone, discovers the home of the Seven Little Dwarfs, who are all away working in a mine – digging for gold and jewels. OPPORTUNITIES OFFER THEMSELVES HERE AS TO HOW SNOW WHITE MIGHT BE LED TO THE HOUSE

As ideas began to clarify, model sheets and articulated sculptures were prepared

BY BIRDS. *SUGGEST TYPE OF HOUSE YOU SEE THE DWARFS LIVING IN . . .*

Snow White proceeds to straighten up the house. We show her picking garments off the floor, making beds, washing the dishes. THE BIRDS MIGHT HELP. THEY COULD BRING IN FLOWERS AND VASES, CARRY OUT COBWEBS FROM THE CEILING OR RAFTERS. *SOME GOOD GAGS COULD BE USED HERE TO SHOW SNOW WHITE AND THE BIRDS BUSY FIXING UP THE HOUSE FOR THE DWARFS' RETURN . . .*

All props and the interior of the house want to be of a quaint, old-time nature, such as the dwarfs would have about them. The proportion of the dwarfs to Snow White is about one-half her size, so be governed by that in using utensils, chairs, tables, and so forth. . . .

The circular continues in this vein and ends with the reminder, "PLEASE DRAW UP ALL SUGGESTIONS AND GAGS *READY FOR COLLECTION THURSDAY, NOVEMBER 8, 1934.*"

On November 19, members of the production staff received a two-page memo which was headed, "Time and general sequences of *Snow White* as described by Walt." This gives a synopsis that conforms quite closely to the version that eventually appeared on screen, diverging from the final form mostly in that it includes several episodes that were later eliminated. That same day, another circular went out, accompanied by a letter from Disney which read, in part, as follows:

GAG OUTLINE sequence DWARFS DISCOVER SNOW WHITE.

Please read through the following outline carefully. . . . Study the gag action and dialogue possibilities of each section of this sequence and try hard to give some helpful suggestions. If you don't like any particular section of business, *please say so* and, at the same time, try to suggest something that might be better. . . . There are good gag possibilities through this sequence – let's see if we can't make the most of it.

Thanx, Walt

What followed was a series of notes and questions relating to how the dwarfs might react to finding Snow White asleep in their house. So far as one can gather, the response to these invitations was usually enthusiastic. Someone, for instance, might come up with a suggestion of possible dialogue for Doc ("You're a pot-bellied old Hop Toad." "He's a I'm a whose a belly potted old flop load – a hop todied old – a hop jellied pot pode – a jot jellied – a . . ."). Ideas were gathered and weeded out, then marshaled into some kind of usable structure. Within a matter of three or four months, *Snow White* had developed from the embryonic stage and was beginning to take shape as a viable endeavor.

The story at least was taking form. There was, however, a great deal more than story involved in a pioneering project of this kind. The Disney artists would be dealing with problems that neither they nor anyone else had confronted before.

There were, to start off with, several purely technical problems. All animation drawings up to this point had been made on sheets of paper measuring 9½ by 12 inches – layouts and backgrounds also being geared to these dimensions. The drawings were then traced and painted onto celluloid sheets of exactly the same size before being sent to the camera department, along with the appropriate backgrounds. The camera could be adjusted to photograph the entire setup – minus the margins – or a small part of it if a close-up effect was required. The area to be photographed was designated as the "field" (rectangles drawn on many of the layouts illustrated in this book are indications of field size). The size of the animation paper determined the largest possible field size, which was known as "five field." As soon as production of *Snow White* got under way, it became evident that this field size would be inadequate for much of the animation involved. A scene in which Snow White was to appear with all seven dwarfs, or with fifty animals, would – if they stuck with the old animation paper – mean that each character had to be drawn on a minute scale, making the animator's task extremely difficult, if not impossible. To overcome this problem, a new field size – "six-and-a-half" – was introduced, which meant that a complete new series of animation boards, sliding cel boards, checking boards, and inking and painting boards had to be designed, built, and installed; and animation cameras had to be adapted to shoot this new field size. Even so, certain long trucking shots demanded characters who would appear so small on the screen at some point that even this modification would be inadequate to the animator's needs. To get around this, a method of reducing drawings photographically was devised – a mechanical solution that allowed the artist to work on a convenient scale.

Another limitation that animation had run up against was its inability to produce a real illusion of depth. When a camera moved into a setup which consisted of a painted cel held tightly against a flat background, scale distortions were inevitable. Take, for example, a situation where a character stands in a meadow with mountains in the background. In reality, as one approaches that character, he will appear to become bigger, but the mountains will remain about the same size because they are so far away. When the camera moves in on a flat representation of the same scene, both the character and the mountains will appear to increase in size at exactly the same rate. In the short cartoons this had not presented a serious problem because such situations seldom arose, and when a little distortion did creep in it was not really noticeable in the context of quick-fire gags that were sweeping the audience along; but feature films required a much greater regard for naturalism. Flat backgrounds might still be adequate for most scenes, but from time to time a real illusion of depth would be necessary. William Garity, head of the camera department, was given the job of developing a multiplane camera – one that could shoot simultaneously several layers of action and background, layers that were separated in such a way as to produce an accurate sense of depth. (At about the same time, Ub Iwerks was working on a similar idea at his own studio.)

Albert Hurter's studies were vital to the concept of the story that began to emerge

The opening scenes of *Snow White* establish the movie's theme and atmosphere with great economy. The Wicked Queen, her magic mirror, the Prince, and Snow White herself – little better than a servant in her stepmother's palace (see overleaf) – are all introduced. The threat to the little princess's life is introduced without delay and made graphic by a close-up of the box in which her heart is to be placed

As Snow White flees into the forest, trees and fallen logs become monsters that seem to threaten her. The Disney artists tried to see the world through her frightened eyes, turning it into a nightmare

The Queen entrusts her huntsman with the task of murdering Snow White. Once in the forest, however, he is overcome by the princess's innocence and drops to his knees to beg her forgiveness. Clever use of shadows and camera angles adds to the drama of the scene

C.U. HUNTSMAN DRAWS KNIFE.

It is difficult to estimate exactly what kind of schedule Disney had in mind for the production of his first feature. The closing months of 1934 saw great progress in story planning, but was he ready to proceed at full speed? The indications are that the initial burst of energy was followed by a period of more cautious exploration. Technical problems could be solved – we can assume that that aspect of the project did not worry him unduly – but what about the animators? Were they ready to handle the demands that would be placed on them by a movie of this sort?

One serious consideration was that they had very little experience in animating the human form. Toward the end of 1934, several animators were put to work on a Silly Symphony titled *The Goddess of Spring,* which retold the Greek myth of Persephone. The character of Persephone – if not exactly a prototype – was certainly conceived with Snow White in mind. Because of Don Graham's art classes, Disney artists were now better equipped to deal with human anatomy, but animating a young woman still presented great difficulties. Les Clark, one of those assigned to this project, had his sister pose for him as an aid to drawing Persephone, but he was still disappointed with the results. Disney told him not to worry, that it was unreasonable to expect immediate success with so ambitious a project. The experiments continued.

The year 1935 saw a high point in the development of animated shorts at the Studio, and this must have provided the impetus to push *Snow White* into full production. The caricatures of Hollywood personalities in a cartoon titled *Broken Toys* were highly sophisticated, and Disney is said to have been particularly happy with the way in which Jenny Wren's character was established in *Who Killed Cock Robin?* These Silly Symphonies, and others like them, indicated that the time was ripe. Disney's veteran animators were coming into their prime and younger artists were catching up fast (soon Don Graham's recruiting system would bring many talented apprentices to the Studio). Character design was well advanced by now, and the animation team began to take shape. Dave Hand was assigned the task of supervising director (which meant he was the man responsible for seeing to it that Disney's instructions were carried out). Bill Cottrell, Wilfred Jackson, Ben Sharpsteen, Larry Morey, and Perce Pearce were named as sequence directors (each of them taking responsibility for specific sections of the movie) while Ham Luske, Bill Tytla, Fred Moore, and Norm Ferguson were made supervising animators (in charge of the quality of the actual animation). Then came the task of "casting" the artists.

Since animators think of themselves as actors with a pencil, the process of casting them for a production of this magnitude was a sensitive one. Moore, Tytla, Fred Spencer, and Frank Thomas were assigned to the dwarfs. (Moore's charm and Tytla's vigor would both be needed for these characters; Spencer had a sure touch with broad comedy and Thomas was one of the most promising of the younger artists.) The Queen as she first appears – an evil beauty – was given to Art Babbitt. After her transformation, she would be drawn by Ferguson. Three younger animators – Milt Kahl, Eric Larson, and Jim Algar – were put in charge of the animals who befriend Snow White. Snow White herself, the most difficult and crucial character of all, was consigned to Ham Luske and Grim Natwick. Luske specialized in character development and thus was a natural for the heroine. Natwick – who also drew the Prince – was a strong draftsman, chosen because of his ability to deal with the human figure.

Layout also presented new problems, and the layout team, headed by Hugh Hennesy and Charles Philippi, found itself confronted with a considerable challenge. Layout artists not only determine the spaces in which an animator must work, they are also in a sense responsible for deciding how the film will look when it reaches the screen. They take on many of the tasks which in a live-action movie would be handled by the art director, the director of photography, and the film editor. An animated film must, in effect, be cut in advance, since animation is so costly that the producer cannot afford to shoot extra footage. Every edit is determined at the layout stage (with the collaboration of the director and, sometimes, the story team). Camera angles and lighting are also determined in layout, as are final decisions about the character of the setting in which the action is to take place. This art direction aspect was especially important in *Snow White,* where it was necessary to maintain an atmosphere of fairy-tale quaintness. Much of the preliminary design work to this end – the bizarre furnishings of the dwarfs' cottage, for instance – was done by Albert Hurter, but it was the layout artists' responsibility to make these inventions work within the final context of the film. Color was an important consideration. In the interiors, it was keyed down to give them an aged look (Gustav Tenggren's elegant watercolor studies had an important influence on their eventual appearance). Everything had to be carefully designed so that the characters would read clearly against their backgrounds.

By the spring of 1936, production of *Snow White* was in full swing. Story conferences were being held almost every day and each scene was discussed and analyzed down to the last detail. Fortunately, a stenographer was present at all these meetings, so that a complete record exists. The following, for example, are extracts from a session dated Saturday, June 27, 1936. The transcript notes that it lasted from 8:45 A.M. to 1:00 P.M. and that those present were Walt Disney, Frank Churchill, Charles Philippi, Joe Grant, Bill Cottrell, Larry Morey, and Bob Kuwahara. The conference dealt with the sequence in which the Huntsman, having taken Snow White out into the woods, was supposed to kill her. The meeting began with Morey running through the continuity for the scene (we can imagine that the group was surrounded by storyboards) while Churchill played the musical score on the piano. Disney then led off the discussion:

"I feel that what Snow White says to the little bird should have a double meaning – such as, 'Are you a little orphan?' In other words, have the conversation with more contact to her present predicament. . . . She is stooped over [this little bird], which gives you a swell position for the knife in the back. Let the menace come in while she is still with the bird – just at that point, with some connection there where she kissed the

Adriana Caselotti, the voice of Snow White

bird and the bird perked up and flew away – it has a connection for the Huntsman to soften. It would be tying it together. Maybe instead of expressing the menace musically you ought to stay with her and let the menace come in. . . . The Huntsman comes along – he is a threat all during the thing – and Snow White is there with the little bird, which is very innocent – such a sweet girl as she to have picked up a little bird and then someone going to knife her. Get the contrast in there."

At this point, Philippi suggested that the little bird could start chattering and fly away – giving her a reason to turn around. Disney disagreed.

"That is too direct. I want the thought where she has kissed the bird and the Huntsman softens – that is a good contrast."

Disney wanted to develop the scene in such a way that it would show how the Huntsman loses his nerve.

"That is what we want to build. A shot of the bird flying away and the knife is right over her back and – just as she watches the bird go away – the knife drops . . . and she turns on around and looks and he immediately pleads with her. That would be better than a long bunch of dialogue. . . . You have your set-up there – the morning sun and Snow White dressed in her prettiest dress and being taken into the woods. . . . You know what to expect – you know that he is to kill her."

Clearly, the scene under discussion falls into the category of melodrama, but seldom had melodrama been subjected to the process of intensive refinement that we can see at work in these story conferences. If we consider *Snow White* from an artistic viewpoint, what is of special interest is not the fact that Disney selected melodrama as a storytelling form – evidently it was a genre he understood and felt was appropriate to the subject matter – but rather that he exposed it to this process of refinement. His overall approach was determined by his own predilections and by the taste of his prospective audience. What gave the film its impact was his obsessive drive for perfection.

Another typical conference was held on December 22, 1936, on the Hyperion sound stage. Twenty-nine people – mostly animators and animation directors – were present to discuss the dwarfs' personalities, but the main feature of this meeting – which lasted from 7:00 P.M. to 10:20 P.M. – was Disney's incredibly detailed shot-by-shot description of the movie, which seems to have been a virtuoso performance, as the following extract shows.

"We fade in on the sunset and hear the dwarfs coming home from the mine. They are marching home against the setting sun, singing the marching home song, which is the 'hiho' song that has a whistling chorus. We have a little sequence of these guys going over picturesque spots – mushrooms and roots of trees. There are little gag touches in there. We fade out on this sequence into the next sequence of Snow White, with a candle in her hand, and the animals following her upstairs. . . . She sees all these cute little beds, all seven, and she is pleased. These beds are hand carved and she reads the names on them, and she thinks they are little children. . . . Doc, Bashful, Grumpy, Dopey, Sneezy, Sleepy . . . and when she reads on

Snow White is befriended by woodland creatures who take her to the dwarfs' cottage. Assisted by the animals, Snow White cleans the cottage and then – exhausted by her experience – falls asleep across several of the dwarfs' beds

Overleaf: backgrounds were painted in low-keyed colors to emphasize the antique character of the cottage

to Sleepy she says, 'I am a little tired myself,' and lies there on three beds and tries them all out. The animals see her get in bed and cover her up with a sheet as she goes to bed. The rabbits and deer and all the animals get in these beds and settle down for a snooze. You hear the offstage dwarfs singing the marching home song, and the animals dash and look out the window. They immediately scram out of the bedroom, run down out of the house, and hide. They anticipate these dwarfs coming. Then we pick up with the guys coming home, on up to Fred Moore's sequence where they come up to the bedroom to attack this monster."

What we can learn from this meeting is that *Snow White* existed in Disney's head as a very real thing and that he was determined it should reach the screen just as he had conceived it. There can be no doubt as to who was in control. *Snow White* was a team effort, but it is still clearly the creation of one mind.

These meetings were the medium through which Disney exercised his control over the movie, and they permitted him to keep everything under close scrutiny. The musical score, for instance, which would be vital to the total impact of the film, was in the capable hands of Frank Churchill, Ollie Wallace, Leigh Harline, and Paul Smith, but Disney had his own ideas about how it should help move the action along – ideas that were strongly held and remarkably sophisticated. On February 16, 1937, during a discussion of the dwarfs' entertainment, he made the following remarks:

"It can still be good music and not follow the same pattern everybody in the country has followed. We still haven't hit it in any of these songs. . . . It's still that influence from the musicals they have been doing for years. Really, we should set a new pattern – a new way to use music – weave it into the story so somebody doesn't just burst into song."

By the time *Snow White* reached the screen, its songs were indeed integrated with the story in a fresh and original manner. The way this was done anticipates the ingenuity with which Richard Rodgers and Oscar Hammerstein II incorporated songs into the structure of *Oklahoma!*, which premiered in 1943. *Oklahoma!* was hailed as a breakthrough, but it seems that Disney was already moving toward the same goals several years earlier. With music, as with so many other things, Disney was not satisfied to do things the way they had always been done, and he did not want *Snow White* to be a mere imitation of live-action musical comedies. His attention to musical detail can be gauged by the attention he gave to the dwarfs' entertainment. For this sequence he insisted that the music be as bizarre as the characters of the dwarfs themselves, and he instigated experiments in which "legitimate" and "illegitimate" instruments were blended to sound like no orchestration that had ever been heard before. This sequence also involved yodeling, and various performers – described as Swiss, cowboys, and hillbillies – tested for it, but none came up to Disney's standards. Eventually, this problem was solved from within the Studio. Someone asked Jim Macdonald, the sound-effects man, to try out, and though he had never yodeled before, his understanding of music and the demands of the sound track enabled him to provide exactly what was needed.

Snow White was the only feature in which transparent colors were employed for the background paintings. Later, gouache became the usual medium

MCU: Doc at sorting table - tapping
diamonds - gets sour note - tosses
diamond away - o.s.song continues

MCU: Bashful, Sneezy and Happy.
Bashful: "LOOK OUT - SHE'S MOVIN'!"
Happy; "SHE'S WAKIN' UP."
Sneezy: "WHAT'LL WE DO?"

MLS: Group. Doc: "HIDE!" Group
scrambles under bed - Dopey last.

While Snow White sleeps, the dwarfs conclude
their day's work at the mine and head for
home. Mistaking the princess for a monster,
they are set to kill her, but – just in time –
they see that she is a girl and hide in confusion

At the mine, Dopey places two huge diamonds over his eyes like spectacles. The diamonds' facets create this frightening image

Snow White insists that the dwarfs wash up
before they eat. Grumpy, even more reluctant
than the others to submit to this humiliation,
undergoes a forced scrubbing

Voice talent was, of course, an important contributing factor to the success of the whole project. The most difficult voice to cast was the heroine herself, and Disney had a loudspeaker installed in his office so that he could hear singers auditioning on the sound stage without having to see them (he did not want his decision to be influenced by their looks). Finally, Adriana Caselotti – a young woman with some operatic training – was chosen.

Live actors were also filmed as an aid to animation. The problem with animating humans is that everyone instinctively knows how a man or woman moves, so that the least inaccuracy in the way they are drawn is immediately apparent. Nobody has ever seen a real-life Mickey Mouse or a real-life Dopey. Snow White, however – as well as the Prince and the Queen – presented a different kind of challenge. Years earlier, Max Fleischer had devised a method of filming live actors and using the results as a guide for his animators. This system, known as rotoscoping, yielded gestures and mannerisms that could never be invented. Now actors were brought to Hyperion Avenue (the performer cast as Snow White went on to achieve fame as the dancer Marge Champion), and they would act out a piece of "business" in front of the cameras – often under the direction of the animators themselves. This action would then be tranferred to a series of photostats which the animator could use for reference. The artist could, in fact, have simply traced the figures from the photostats, but this was seldom done because the characters had to be adapted in order to be consistent with the remainder of the animation. Instead, a kind of gentle caricature was employed, so that gestures and poses became slightly exaggerated. This system served the animators well, and they continued to use it in later movies.

The character of Snow White was an enormous challenge in many ways. Frank Thomas, recalling just one of the details that went into establishing her screen image, reports that when the cels came back from inking and painting, Snow White looked pale and anemic. "She had no color in her cheeks. So they tried painting color on there – which made her look like a clown. One of the girls said, 'Walt, can we try putting a little rouge on her cheeks?' He said, 'What do you mean?' So she took out her makeup kit and put some rouge on the cel and it looked keen. Walt said, 'Yeah, but how the hell are you going to get it in the same place every day? And on each drawing?' And the girl said, 'What do you think we've been doing all our lives?' He said, 'You mean to tell me you can put that in the same place on the girl's face no matter how she turns?' . . . They just knew where it ought to go and, without any kind of guide, they made Snow White up on each cel – so there's this lovely little tint on there. That's how much we cared."

Disney's perfectionism can be illustrated by another Frank Thomas story. As mentioned earlier, Thomas was assigned to work on the dwarfs, and one of his scenes called for Dopey to do a little hitch step to catch up with the others. "This was on the story board, not my idea. So I had him do a hitch step. Walt said, 'Hey, that's good – we ought to use that hitch step all through the picture.' Of course a lot of stuff had been

After supper, the dwarfs put on an entertainment. In a sequence animated by Fred Moore, Dopey experiences some difficulty while attempting to balance on Sneezy's shoulders

Grumpy says: "THE QUEEN! SHE'LL KILL HER!
WE'VE GOT TO SAVE HER"

Warned that the Queen (who has used magic
to transform herself into an old hag) has
reached her victim, the dwarfs set off to the
rescue. They are too late to save Snow White,
who has already bitten the poisoned apple,
but they pursue the Queen up into the mountains, where a storm is raging

The Queen attempts to send a boulder crashing down on the dwarfs, but lightning strikes the crag she is perched on and she is hurled to her death. The dwarfs return to the lifeless body of Snow White and sadly place her in a crystal casket. She remains there through a full cycle of the seasons until, finally, the Prince arrives to wake her with a kiss

At a Disney premiere: Marlene Dietrich, top, Judy Garland, center, and Charles Laughton with Elsa Lanchester

animated by then, so he called all the scenes back for hitch steps to be added. The guys came over to me and said, 'Was that goddamn hitch step your idea?' That kind of thing would often happen. You'd be well into a picture when a better idea would come along – and you'd back up and change everything that had been done."

Although much of the production work on *Snow White* was jammed into the final ten or twelve months, it was the result of more than three years of concentrated effort by Disney himself – three years in which he faced new problems almost daily. The whole venture was an enormous gamble from the very first. The industry was convinced that he had bitten off more than he could chew, and hints of impending disaster were commonplace both in the trade papers and the national press. During this period, the Studio staff expanded to more than one thousand, many of whom were directly involved in the feature project. Some names have been mentioned, but literally hundreds of other artists and technicians were involved in all kinds of capacities, from painting backgrounds to devising special effects. (How, for example, do you make a painted stream look like a stream or a painted rainstorm like the real thing?)

Finally, at a cost of close to $1,500,000, *Snow White* was completed. Four days before Christmas, 1937, it was premiered at the Carthay Circle Theater in Hollywood. The audience was studded with celebrities. It was the kind of opening of which Disney had always dreamed. The reviews were sensational. *Snow White* was an overnight success, justifying all of Disney's hopes for it and impressing itself on the imagination of the Western world.

Snow White is distinguished by two seemingly opposed characteristics: economy of construction and extravagance of invention. Disney's training in the field of cartoon shorts had taught him how to tell a story without wasting a single foot of film. There is nothing in *Snow White* that does not contribute either to developing character or to moving the plot forward. (Two fully animated scenes – the dwarfs eating soup and building a bed for Snow White – were deleted at the last moment as superfluous.) Yet this does not lead to a feeling of spareness, because crammed into this framework is a profusion of detail that is almost overwhelming. The fruits of three years' work by hundreds of talents are compressed into eighty-three minutes of action, imagery, music, and dialogue.

The songs are memorable and, like everything else, contribute to the movement of the story. As for the animation, the character of each dwarf is firmly established – each is a distinct individual. The development of the Queen is excellent, both before and after her transformation into the witchlike crone. The Huntsman is effective, and the birds and animals function well as a kind of Greek chorus. Snow White occasionally seems a little too much like a twentieth-century coed, but she has great charm and easily wins our sympathy. The only real failure is the Prince, who seems wooden and lacks character (Snow White deserves a better consort). Above all, the entire movie manages to sustain the ambience of timelessness which is so essential to the fairy-tale genre.

Shirley Temple presents Walt Disney with a special Academy Award incorporating one large and seven little Oscars for his production of *Snow White*

Some critics have found the film simplistic and therefore not worthy of serious consideration, but this approach is in itself simplistic. *Snow White* has the elemental quality of folklore – questions of right and wrong are understood in advance – which dictates a certain directness of approach that would be merely banal in most live-action pictures. But the character of animation is quite different from live action in that it permits virtually total control of every detail of every situation that may arise. Nothing need be left to chance, and in the case of *Snow White*, nothing was. Disney lavished such loving care on every aspect of the film that it took on an imaginative density which makes it quite extraordinary.

Other critics have charged that *Snow White* is excessively frightening – suggesting that it might have a harmful effect on children. In fact, many episodes in the fairy tales of Hans Christian Andersen and the Brothers Grimm are far more terrifying, and ultimately scariness is justified by the nature of the story. In the case of *Snow White*, without the Wicked Queen there is no story, and by definition the Wicked Queen must perform misdeeds that inspire fear.

Snow White and the Seven Dwarfs may have provided Walt Disney with his finest moment. There was an element of luck in Mickey's success (admittedly, Disney tended to make his own luck), but his first animated feature was a triumph of a different order. No happy accidents were involved. Disney walked into the project with his eyes wide open, knowing the risks involved and convinced that they were worth taking. *Snow White* was a conscious effort on his part to advance the art of animation to a new level of sophistication – a level that everyone else had thought was beyond reach.

5 Pinocchio

Snow White and the Seven Dwarfs may have provided Disney with his finest moment, but *Pinocchio* is probably his greatest film. It shares in all the qualities that made the first feature such a success and adds to them a technical brilliance that has never been surpassed.

Pinocchio opens with a stunningly effective shot – the camera pulling back from a large white star, panning across the tiled roofs of a sleepy European village, then closing in on the lighted window of Geppetto's cottage. It is the kind of shot that has become familiar enough in live-action movies since the advent of power-operated zoom lenses, but taken within the context of its own period, and within the history of animation, it is innovative and spectacular. Nor is it just a piece of flashy showmanship. It serves to capture our imagination and draw us into the atmosphere of the story before a single word has been spoken.

Disney's early success had resulted from his grasp of the potentials of the sound film. By the time of his first feature films, he had evolved a method of storytelling which relied primarily on visual means. Next to animation itself, camera movements provided his team with its chief narrative devices. Disney continued to make expert use of music and sound, but his greatest achievement was the creation of a visual language that was totally convincing and extremely flexible.

Some critics have suggested that this visual language is marred by being backward-looking – leaning heavily on the illustrational styles of the nineteenth century. This seems an unreasonable objection; given the subject matter of films like *Snow White* and *Pinocchio*, what idiom could have been more appropriate? Disney's obsession with naturalism seems anachronistic if one places him alongside Picasso (especially considering that the Spaniard was the senior by twenty years). At the same time, however, Picasso's fidelity to largely traditional media – such as the stretched canvas with its built-in limitations – might be considered anachronistic when compared to Disney's pioneering of the art of animation. Disney's great contribution was to break free of the static image. We might have seen interiors resembling Geppetto's workshop in old prints, but never before had we been able to penetrate these spaces and move about within them. Disney's imagination, the skill of his artists, and the technological magic of the motion picture camera made this possible.

The multiplane camera had seen only very limited use in *Snow White,* but *The Old Mill,* a short released in 1937, demonstrated its full potential, and it was employed extensively throughout *Pinocchio.* Disney now had the ability to produce a convincing illusion of depth. The only drawback was the expense involved in operating the multiplane. A single scene – in which the camera zooms down on the village with the school bells ringing and pigeons circling down and down until they are among the houses – cost $45,000 (equivalent to perhaps $300,000 today). The scene lasts for only a few seconds. To offset outlays of this kind, Disney technicians managed to create some simpler devices, which they used whenever they would not detract from the quality of the film. One sequence, for example, shows a steamer crossing an expanse of calm ocean. It was made by pulling a single cel, on which the boat was painted, across a background, with smoke effects trailing behind it and distortion glass over the water. Disney was immensely proud of this scene because it was so simple – yet so effective that at the premiere it received a round of applause.

More often than not, however, Disney's quest for perfection led to more rather than less expense. Figaro the kitten had a highlight airbrushed onto him on every single cel he appeared in. Most producers would have looked on this as unnecessary, even absurd. Disney thought it might improve his film, so he did it. The result of this attitude was an animated movie of unprecedented lavishness.

As has been seen, *Snow White* evolved rather gradually. With the experience of this one feature behind him, Disney seems to have felt that he need not be quite so cautious, and production of *Pinocchio* was put into top gear. Things did not work out according to plan, however, and after six months he called a halt to the project and put everyone on new assignments until the problems had been ironed out.

The primary dilemma centered on the character of Pinocchio himself. Should he be treated as a puppet or as a small boy? Until this issue was settled, very little could be done. Book illustrations of the story tended to show Pinocchio as essentially puppetlike, and this seems to have influenced

Walt Disney in action: a sequence of photographs taken at a *Pinocchio* story conference

Geppetto's workshop

PINOCCHIO

One of Gustav Tenggren's watercolor studies
for *Pinocchio*

Some of Albert Hurter's early sketches
for *Pinocchio*

Many models were made to guide the animators. Live-action footage was shot for the same purpose; the example shown here was used as an aid for a sequence featuring the Fox and the Cat

At the beginning of *Pinocchio*, the Blue
Fairy brings the hero to life and appoints
Jiminy Cricket to be his conscience

This panoramic background was painted for
the opening of *Pinocchio*

Jiminy Cricket in Geppetto's workshop

the animators' first efforts. Frank Thomas, Milt Kahl, and Ollie Johnston were assigned to the character, and they animated about 150 feet of film, using the speeded-up voice of Ted Sears as a sound track. Disney was not happy with the results. After further experimentation, they went ahead with a more boylike version of Pinocchio (except in the scenes, animated by Thomas, where he is still on strings) and found a child's voice which fitted with this interpretation. A further snag was Jiminy Cricket's personality, which became more and more important as the story developed, until he had usurped many of the functions originally intended for Pinocchio. The nominal hero of the film was soon reduced to speaking dialogue that did not go far beyond "Why?" and "Why not?" He was a total naive – the Blue Fairy had brought him to life and he had the innocence of a baby. The animators had to show that everything was a completely new experience for him, and this had to be evident in every movement he made. The success of the film hung on their ability to handle this formidable task.

Jiminy Cricket, drawn by Ward Kimball, Woolie Reitherman, and Don Towsley, presented another kind of challenge. Being a very small character (his physical size contrasts with the importance of his role in the film), he was difficult to animate except in close-ups. The artists rose to the occasion, making him so expansive a character that he seems larger than life. In contrast to the Cricket stands one of the villains of the piece, the puppet master Stromboli. Animated by Bill Tytla, Stromboli is an enormous, muscular presence who fills the screen with his infamy. His every gesture is a threat. Tytla, as we have remarked, was an

Geppetto, delighted with his new son, sends Pinocchio off to school. Before he gets there, however, Pinocchio is sidetracked by the Fox and the Cat, who persuade him that the theater offers more glamour. Soon he finds himself co-opted into Stromboli's puppet troupe

Stromboli, animated by Bill Tytla, is
perhaps the greatest of Disney villains –
totally consumed by rage and evil

Stromboli shuts Pinocchio in a wooden cage. The Blue Fairy rescues him, but not before he tells her a series of lies – only to discover that, with each lie, his nose grows longer and longer, eventually sprouting branches and leaves

Succumbing to temptation once more, Pinocchio, accompanied by the jaded street urchin Lampwick, finds himself on Pleasure Island. The image of Lampwick eating the ultimate club sandwich did not appear in the released version of the film

exceptionally gifted animator, and this was an ideal assignment for him. It is probable that no one else could have built this character to the same point of menace. Stromboli is a man whose anger combines with physical strength to keep him in a constant state of explosive agitation. (At the premiere, W. C. Fields was heard to say, "He moves too much," but Fields was noted as a harsh critic.)

Perhaps more likable, but in the villains' camp nonetheless, are the Fox and the Cat, who are slyly determined to lead Pinocchio astray for the sake of a fast buck. Animated by Norm Ferguson and John Lounsbery, these characters – like Stromboli – seem to be in constant motion, but it is motion less governed by rage. The cunning of the Fox and the stupidity of the Cat turn them into a kind of vaudeville team that keeps moving to hold the attention of the audience. The Fox knows just when to throw a knowing glance and the Cat is a malicious dolt with an instinct for mischief. Neither is subject to the eruptions of sheer evil that determine Stromboli's personality. They are self-made villains. He is a force of nature.

Geppetto, handled largely by Art Babbitt, is the least interesting of the main characters. He is asked to function on a single, fundamentally

Pinocchio and Lampwick engage in an orgy of self-indulgence which comes to a sudden end when the two revelers discover they are turning into donkeys sentimental emotional level, thus presenting the animators with very little challenge. Fred Moore was luckier in his assignment, treating Lampwick, the cocky street kid, as something of a self-caricature. Monstro the whale is suitably fearsome, and two small creatures, Figaro the kitten and Cleo the goldfish, add a touch of charm to the proceedings. Live-action footage was shot as an assist to the animation of several characters, notably the Blue Fairy, whose brief appearances are very effective.

Once again, Albert Hurter's influence is felt throughout the film, both in terms of character design and in the profusion of quaint detail that crowds the background of almost every scene. Gustav Tenggren contributed many line-and-wash studies which greatly affect the look of the movie. The multiplane camera and the visual complexity of the film as a whole presented the layout team with great opportunities which they eagerly seized. Under the direction of Charles Philippi and Hugh Hennesy, with important contributions by Ken Anderson, the art of layout was carried to new heights of inventiveness. Many of the layout drawings are extremely beautiful, and the same can be said of the background paintings. For *Snow White*, backgrounds had been painted mainly with transparent washes, but in the case of *Pinocchio*, while something that resembles a classic watercolor technique is adhered to, opaque pigment came into general use. For multiplane shots, all but the bottom layer was painted onto glass, and oil paint was used for this purpose.

Many character models, some fashioned from clay and some from wood, were made to assist the animators. The artist could refer to these models, turning them so that they could see at a moment's notice just how Jiminy Cricket, for example, would look from any angle (in this respect the models served a purpose similar to that of the live-action footage, and they could be used for characters who could not be shot in

Chastened by his experiences, Pinocchio sets out to find Geppetto – a search which takes him under the sea

Eventually Pinocchio and Geppetto are
reunited in the belly of Monstro the whale

Escaping from the whale, who gives furious
chase, Pinocchio is washed ashore, seemingly
dead. But he recovers, and, having proved
himself brave, truthful, and unselfish, is soon
changed into a real boy by the Blue Fairy.
Joyfully, Figaro the kitten dives into the fish-
bowl and kisses Cleo the goldfish

Jiminy Cricket and the whale's eye

The layout drawings for *Pinocchio* were made with great attention to detail. Often more than one artist worked on a single layout, the first making an outline drawing, and another adding the tonal rendering. Although never intended for public display, many of these drawings are very beautiful

live action). The special effects in *Pinocchio* are particularly striking – live-action rain is incorporated into one scene – and it is impossible to overlook the effectiveness of the musical score, highlighted by such songs as "Give a Little Whistle" and "When You Wish upon a Star" – both composed by Leigh Harline with lyrics by Ned Washington.

The plot of *Pinocchio* required extensive adaptation to make it suitable for the screen – far more radical changes being made than had been necessary for *Snow White*. Once again Disney was charged with frightening children, but compared with Carlo Collodi's original, his version of *Pinocchio* is quite restrained. He kept just enough of the element of horror to make the story effective. Certainly, the scene in which Pinocchio's nose grows longer as a result of each of his lies triggers a deep response, as does the sequence in which he and Lampwick are transformed into donkeys.

Although the reviewers welcomed it with enthusiasm, *Pinocchio* was not an immediate box-office success. The film was released in February 1940, five months after the outbreak of war in Europe, and it may be that the public was not in the mood for a fable of this sort. Not that *Pinocchio* was a frivolous movie. On the contrary, despite the happy ending, it presents the blackest vision of any animated feature produced during Walt Disney's lifetime. It is also Walt Disney's masterpiece.

Pinocchio was not the only thing on Disney's mind during the period from 1938 to 1940. Two more major film projects – *Fantasia* and *Bambi* – were already under way, and, in addition to this and a full schedule of short cartoons, Disney had decided to build a new studio. On August 31, 1938, a deposit was made on a fifty-one-acre site in Burbank, near the Los Angeles River, in the same general area as the Columbia Ranch and the studios of Warner Brothers and Universal Films. New buildings, designed by Kem Weber, a leading Los Angeles architect of his generation, were erected and others were brought from Hyperion Avenue. The move to Burbank began in August 1939 and was completed by the following spring.

Background paintings, opposite and overleaf,
followed the letter and spirit of the layout
drawings, above, adding the dimension of color

The atmosphere of *Pinocchio* owed a great
deal to the effectiveness of the background
paintings

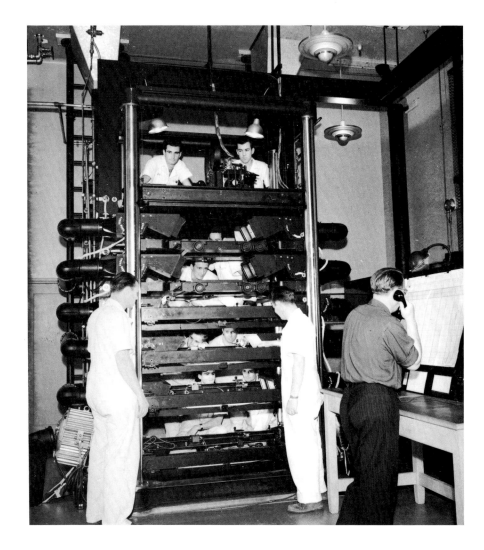

Operating the multiplane camera crane. The technician at the upper left is Card Walker, who later became president of Walt Disney Productions

When the new studio was nearly ready, Walt Disney took his father on a tour of the premises. According to legend, Elias, the former carpenter and contractor, was evidently a little disturbed by what he saw. "Walter – what can it be used for?" he asked. His son, taken aback, said, "It's a studio – where I work." Elias persisted: "No, Walter, what can it be used for?" Suddenly, it dawned on Walt that what his father wanted to know was what the property could be used for if the studio failed. "Now this would make a perfect hospital," said Walt, improvising. For the rest of the tour, the Studio became a hospital. The master filmmaker showed his father where the operating rooms could go, extemporizing upon the advantages of the wide corridors and the advanced air-conditioning system. His father left a happy man.

Elias's worries were not entirely unfounded. In April of 1940 Walt had found himself so short of operating capital he had been forced to offer stock to the public for the first time; thus, an artistic high in his career corresponded with an economic low.

Completely sure of himself, however, Disney refused to cut back on his ambitious production schedule.

6 Fantasia: The Grand Experiment

The new emphasis on feature film production did not mean that Disney had lost his special affection for Mickey Mouse, but Mickey was losing ground to Donald and this prompted Disney, in 1938, to plan a comeback for him. The vehicle he chose for this purpose was *The Sorcerer's Apprentice,* an ancient fairy-tale motif which Goethe had employed as the basis for a very popular poem; Disney's immediate inspiration was Paul Dukas's orchestral work of the same title, written in 1897. This popular piece of program music seemed to provide an ideal score for the Mickey project. Its running time made for a film about twice the length of the average cartoon short, thus allowing for leisurely storytelling and substantive character development. Anxious to lend his production as much prestige as possible, Disney sought the services of Leopold Stokowski. Stokowski, maestro of the Philadelphia Orchestra, had long admired Disney's work and was delighted to make himself available. In fact, he involved himself so intensely in the project that it soon began to develop into something far more ambitious.

The idea that evolved was for a full-length feature film which would take the form of a concert of orchestral pieces conducted by Stokowski and illustrated by the Disney artists. Eventually, in November 1940, it would be released under the title *Fantasia,* but for the time being it was referred to as "the Concert Feature."

The first thing to be decided upon was the program of music that would form the basis of this film. While Stokowski was instrumental in the process of selection, the final choice would have to be dictated by visual considerations, and therefore it was imperative that Studio artists be involved from the first. Disney called in Joe Grant and Dick Huemer (he knew that Huemer was an opera buff and that Grant's experience in character design would be invaluable) and had them listen to hundreds of pieces of music in order to evaluate them in terms of their potential as a basis for animation. It had been decided that a narrator would be needed to link the various episodes of the film, and Deems Taylor, known to millions as music commentator on the Metropolitan Opera radio broadcasts, was chosen for this role and to assist in the process of selection. The field was narrowed down to a dozen or so possible compositions, and Grant and Huemer began to investigate the story potential inherent in each of these.

Eventually, the film was broken down into seven main parts, the first being an introduction which culminated with Stokowski's orchestral arrangement of Bach's *Toccata and Fugue in D Minor.* Next came excerpts from Tchaikovsky's *Nutcracker Suite;* then came *The Sorcerer's Apprentice,* followed by Stravinsky's *Rite of Spring.* The fifth piece was Beethoven's Sixth Symphony, the "Pastoral." Then came "Dance of the Hours" from Amilcare Ponchielli's opera *La Gioconda.* The final selection combined Mussorgsky's *Night on Bald Mountain* with Schubert's "Ave Maria."

It has sometimes been suggested that in making *Fantasia* Disney was courting the intellectual community, but this does not seem consistent with his character or his goals. There is every reason to believe that he

Deems Taylor, wearing glasses, and Leopold Stokowski at the Studio. With Disney, they discuss the storyboard for *The Sorcerer's Apprentice* and inspect the multiplane camera. In the right-hand photograph, they visit the ink and paint department

Left: shooting live action for *Fantasia;* center: Stokowski in the Disney paint laboratory; right: dummy musicians used for silhouettes in the film are loaded onto a truck

was always careful to keep the mass movie audience in mind. If intellectuals praised his work, that was an added bonus, nothing more. With the exception of the Stravinsky piece, all of the final selections for *Fantasia* fell into the category of popular classics – tunes with which many people would be familiar. In this respect, *Fantasia* is reminiscent of some of the Silly Symphonies.

Disney did not have pretensions toward high culture. Nor did he claim any extensive knowledge of classical music, though, according to his daughter Diane, he enjoyed it tremendously. He certainly understood fully how music could be integrated into his movies. Everything he produced from *Steamboat Willie* on supports this. *Fantasia* should not be seen as a totally new development – a play for cultural respectability – but as a culmination of everything that had gone before.

Nonetheless, the concert character of the movie and the fact that Stokowski and Deems Taylor were associated with it raised certain expectations, and Disney went to great lengths to live up to them. He planned the film for a special wide screen but had to abandon this scheme for financial reasons. He also developed a sound system utilizing seven tracks and thirty speakers, which anticipated stereophonic sound and even some of the characteristics of Dolby sound. Stokowski himself handled the sound mixing for this multitrack system, and the results were, to judge by contemporary accounts, quite spectacular. Unhappily, the system was prohibitively expensive and was installed only in a few first-run theaters. For general distribution, the sound was remixed for more conventional equipment.

The film opens with a brief introductory section in which Deems Taylor sets the scene; then the *Toccata and Fugue* begins. Visually, this segment provided a field day for the Disney effects department (as did a later interlude which introduced the sound track as a character). When *Fantasia* was in production, more than sixty people worked for the effects department, and they were given the task of interpreting the patterns of Bach's music in terms of abstract and semiabstract forms. This was a new area of experimentation for them, and, under the circumstances, they did a creditable job. Their notion of abstraction owed more to Art Deco design motifs than to modern painting, but it is consistently inventive. The main criticism that can be made is that whereas the music is very formal and rigorous, the animation is rather lighthearted and stylized, emphasizing the melodic highlights of Bach's themes rather than the harmonic richness. Quasi-surrealistic images are used at times when a more strictly abstract interpretation might have been more appropriate.

Despite its flaws, this opening section of the movie does command one's attention and was a bold attempt to do something that had not been done before.

The *Nutcracker Suite* is ballet music, and Disney's artists treated the section of the film it underpins as a kind of animated dance sequence. The first two movements of the suite were dropped and the order of the others rearranged so that a continuous story could be constructed, leading off with "Dance of the Sugar Plum Fairy." Dragonfly sprites dart among flowers, touching them with wands so that they sparkle with

Hundreds of pastel studies were made of the *Toccata and Fugue* segment of *Fantasia* and for the "sound track" interlude, both of which used abstract forms to illustrate musical ideas tiny beads of dew. Buds open and more fairies are awakened. The atmosphere is one of great delicacy. (Airbrush work and special transparent paints contribute greatly to the sense of lightness.)

The next movement, "Chinese Dance" – animated with great wit, principally by Art Babbitt – is one of the high spots of the movie. A group of humorously choreographed mushrooms moves through a solemn routine with almost ritualistic movements. One, smaller than the rest, has great difficulty following the steps of its associates.

"Dance of the Flutes" follows, with blossoms drifting down to the surface of a stream, where they are transformed into tiny ballerinas. A breeze picks them up and sends them skimming out across the surface of the water and among the branches of overhanging trees, until they are swept over a cascade and vanish from sight.

As the fourth movement, "Arab Dance," opens, bubbles rise to the surface from the spot where the blossoms vanished. The camera fades into the depth of the stream and there, among a forest of water plants, exotic fish – some gold and some black – perform an aqua ballet. As the sequence ends, the light fails and bubbles again begin to rise to the surface.

A thistle in the form of a Cossack bursts from the largest bubble and "Russian Dance" begins. More thistles join in, whirling with orchids that resemble girls in peasant costume. Music and dancing become faster and faster, then freeze to a final tableau.

This segment concludes with "Waltz of the Flowers." Autumn fairies move among the trees, touching leaves which take on their fall colors and drift with the wind. The fairies touch milkweed pods which burst,

Disney artists transformed Tchaikovsky's *Nutcracker Suite* into a nature ballet featuring spectacular effects animation and delicate airbrush work releasing their seeds, which become yet another kind of dancer, complete with bouffant skirts and sleek black hair. Frost sprites appear and skate across the surface of the stream, transforming it to ice as snow begins to fall, covering the landscape.

A technical tour de force, the *Nutcracker Suite* section succeeds admirably within its own terms, allowing the effects department to display its skills and making imaginative use of multiplane shots. It features some extraordinary animation and picks up on the romantic flavor that had colored so many of the Silly Symphonies, transforming that sensibility into something substantial enough to provide a base for bravura performances by all concerned.

Disney had planned *The Sorcerer's Apprentice* as a spectacular showcase for Mickey, and it became exactly that, the whole project being developed with great care and attention to detail. Under Jim Algar's direction, nothing was left to chance. Story sketches were made in full color, and some of the Studio's top animators were put on this assignment (Bill Tytla, for example, and Les Clark, who had been drawing Mickey for ten years).

Mickey is portrayed as a young magician, the disciple of a great Wizard who, bored for the moment with his own powers, leaves Mickey in charge of the subterranean cavern where he practices his arcane craft. Mickey has been ordered to fill the large water vat in the cavern, but the ambitious apprentice discovers that the Wizard has left his magic hat behind and decides to take advantage of this. Donning the hat, he brings a broom to life and directs it to carry the water. The broom marches to the well, fills a wooden pail with water, and starts on its appointed task. Satisfied with the success of the spell, Mickey settles down in the Wizard's chair to take a snooze. Soon he is dreaming that he is high above the earth, far out in space. His powers have become so great that he can control the paths of stars and planets, and comets change their course at his bidding. Next he is standing on top of a towering crag, conducting the waves of the ocean. With a gesture worthy of Stokowski, he beckons to the breakers to smash against the base of a rock. He repeats the gesture and waves break over the top of the crag, drenching the dreaming apprentice and startling him from his reverie.

He awakens to find that the cavern is awash. The broom is following his instructions with too great a zeal and has already brought thousands of gallons of water from the well, threatening to cause a disastrous flood. Mickey orders it to stop, but his magic powers have vanished, and the broom mechanically continues its task. In desperation, Mickey attacks it with an axe, only to see the broom split into many brooms, all of which continue with dogged perseverance, sweeping him aside and swamping the cavern. The water gets deeper and deeper. Furniture is afloat. Mickey seeks safety on a gigantic book of spells, which is soon sucked into an iridescent whirlpool. The apprentice seems on the point of losing his life when, suddenly, the Wizard appears at the top of the stairway. A single gesture from him and the waters subside. Everything returns to normal. Mickey, chastened, is left to clean up the mess.

The Sorcerer's Apprentice presents Mickey as
a neophyte magician dabbling with spells he
cannot control

As *The Sorcerer's Apprentice* moves toward its climax, Mickey finds himself quite literally out of his depth

With this story, Mickey had certainly come a long way from *Steamboat Willie*. The fantasy of controlling the universe is not something that one would have suspected of Minnie's old sweetheart, not even of the conductor in *The Band Concert*. Yet one of the things that has always given Mickey's personality a certain depth was his true-to-life tendency to indulge in fantasy (and, more often than not, his fantasies would clash with some pressing reality). The Mickey of *The Sorcerer's Apprentice* is the same old Mickey, but the circumstances he finds himself in encourage him to indulge in more grandiose dreams. The magnitude of his fantasy and the absurdity of the reality with which he finds himself in conflict enable us to learn something more about Mickey's psychology. As a magician he is a failure, but he succeeds in something much more important – for the first time he becomes a fully rounded, three-dimensional character.

Although told in an amusing way, *The Sorcerer's Apprentice* presents psychological ideas that are very basic to the human condition. Technically, like everything else in *Fantasia*, the segment is superb.

Rite of Spring heralds an abrupt change in mood. Disney saw Stravinsky's ballet music as providing the score for nothing less than a portrayal of the creation of the world (and certainly the insistent rhythms are suggestive of primeval forces). In later years, Stravinsky expressed displeasure

The Sorcerer's Apprentice presents Mickey at his most Chaplinesque. The mindless robotlike force of the brooms and pails is reminiscent of the production-line machinery in *Modern Times*

with the way his music had been used, but this seems to relate mostly to alterations in the orchestration that may have been made without his permission; there is no reason to suppose that he was dissatisfied with Disney's overall concept. He visited the studio and saw the storyboards that had been prepared. Photographs taken during the visit suggest that he was not unhappy with them.

This segment begins with visions of a time when the earth was still a molten mass, and it carries the story of evolution to the point at which the dinosaurs disappeared from the face of the planet. Millions of years are telescoped into a few minutes. We see mountain ranges thrown up by gigantic volcanic convulsions; then primitive forms of marine life emerge from the oceans and learn to live on dry land. Later, huge reptiles roam the surface of the earth and engage in titanic battles to the death. Eventually, a massive drought turns whole continents into deserts.

Unfortunately, all this is not too convincing on the screen. The formation of the earth is treated imaginatively by the effects department, and the emergence of life in the sea is handled with delicacy; after that, however, the story becomes crudely melodramatic. Dinosaurs are transformed into ham actors. When they fight, theatrical lighting is used, as though the action would not seem dramatic enough by itself. The music overpowers the imagery, which finally seems far too schematic.

The next segment, set to the "Pastoral" symphony, is difficult to judge objectively. It has considerable charm, yet its visual character seems to have very little to do with the true nature of Beethoven's music.

This can be explained in part by the fact that the Arcadian scenes which make up this segment were originally intended for a much lighter piece of music – an excerpt from Gabriel Pierné's *Cydalise*. The rhythms of the Pierné selection proved to be too persistent to support the subject matter (the animators needed some pauses and legato passages). Disney decided to switch to the Beethoven work – apparently against Stokowski's better judgment.

Visually, this segment owes a great deal to the stylized decorative and illustrative idioms of the thirties – it passes before the viewer like an animated mural for some fashionable restaurant. The backgrounds are extremely elegant and pleasing (Art Riley, Claude Coats, and Ray Huffine must share credit with the layout team of Ken Anderson and Hugh Hennesy), combining gently curving forms with an innovative use of color.

The best scene comes near the beginning, when flying horses resembling giant butterflies glide in above the lake before settling on the surface of the water. This has a wonderful sense of poetry which only animation could supply. Much of the action concerns flirtations between centaurs and centaurettes. The former – a hybrid species combining football players and cart horses – seem rather clumsy, but the centaurettes, styled by Fred Moore, display a certain adolescent charm, looking like high school coeds who have undergone some unlikely transformation.

Good comic interludes are provided by Ward Kimball's Bacchus and his drunken unicorn-mule. Toward the end, Zeus, aided by Vulcan, stages

In *Fantasia*, Stravinsky's *Rite of Spring* is used to underscore the story of the earth's prehistory, including the age of the giant reptiles a thunderstorm for his own amusement. Night falls and Artemis appears in the sky to launch an arrow of fire from the bow of light formed by the new moon.

It is difficult to give an adequate idea of Disney's interpretation of "Dance of the Hours," but we might begin by saying that it is possibly the best – and certainly the funniest – segment of the movie. The animators, who included John Lounsbery, Howard Swift, and Hugh Fraser, were given the task of developing a parody of classical ballet featuring hippos, elephants, ostriches, and alligators. The result is hilarious. A hippo in a negligible tutu does pirouettes as though she weighed no more than a feather. Alligators swoop down from behind pillars, the inherent menace of their species amplified by choreographic fantasy and clever camera angles. Elephants hide timidly behind flimsy architectural elements, and ostriches perform entrechats with an inspired absence of grace. Gravity and reason are denied in a triumph of insanity. Directed by T. Hee and laid out by Ken O'Connor, "Dance of the Hours" is a classic of comic animation.

Fantasia concludes with *Night on Bald Mountain* and "Ave Maria." As technical achievements they are extraordinary, but emotionally they are unsatisfying. The concept of this segment is a simple contrast of good and evil. To Mussorgsky's dramatic music, witches ride demonic steeds and tormented spirits rise from the grave to join the Devil on top of a jagged, rocky peak. The special effects in these sequences are excellent, and Bill Tytla's Devil is realized with enormous vigor. At dawn, the ghosts return to their resting places and, to the strains of "Ave Maria," a procession moves slowly toward a Gothic chapel.

Most of the great monuments of Christianity – whether Chartres Cathedral or the King James Version of the Bible – were the products of years of patient labor. To expect the Studio artists to come up with something even remotely comparable while working to specifications and under deadline pressure is unfair; yet anything less in this area does not seem worth attempting.

Fantasia is a film with great merits and great faults. Structurally, it owes very little to anything that preceded it in the history of the cinema, and Disney deserves great credit for breaking so boldly with precedent. His artists deserve praise for some of the finest animation that has ever reached the screen.

It has been said that *Fantasia* was ahead of its time, and in certain respects this is true (the popularity that the film continues to enjoy bears this out). In other ways, it was very much of its time. For the most part, its imagery belongs essentially to the pre–World War II era, as does Deems Taylor's commentary.

The film has had many critics. Frank Lloyd Wright visited the Studio while it was in production. Invited to lecture the staff as part of the art education program, he was shown sections of the movie and was out-

A pastel drawing for the "Pastoral" segment. Such pre-production studies are sometimes referred to as "concept art"

From the top down: Disney and Igor Stravinsky discuss the score of the composer's *Rite of Spring;* Disney and sequence director T. Hee (in shirtsleeves) with Stravinsky and choreographer George Balanchine; Julian Huxley inspects a *Fantasia* model, watched by Disney and astronomer Dr. Edwin Hubbel; members of Associated American Artists visit the Studio – left to right, George Biddle, Reeves Lewinthal, Thomas Hart Benton, Ernest Fiene, Grant Wood, and George Schreiber

Early studies for the "Pastoral" segment of *Fantasia* betray influences reaching back to the nineteenth-century Symbolist movement (see overleaf)

The version of the "Pastoral" segment that reached the screen owed a good deal to Art Deco idioms

"Dance of the Hours," as interpreted by the
Disney artists, became a hilarious parody of
classical ballet

FOLDER Dance of the hours 205 ①

Fantasia concludes with *Night on Bald Mountain* and "Ave Maria," a presentation of the conflict between Good and Evil

spoken in his dislike for it. It was absurd, in his opinion, to illustrate music. He felt that Disney should take a long vacation and reconsider his position.

If we try to assess *Fantasia* objectively, we find that two segments – *The Sorcerer's Apprentice* and the animal ballet of "Dance of the Hours" – have a universal appeal. Each of the other segments has merits of one kind or another, but they are not held together by the aesthetic coherence that is evident in *Snow White* and *Pinocchio*. The viewer is asked to make too many taste adjustments during the course of the movie for it to be a complete success.

Nonetheless, *Fantasia* is an amazing piece of filmmaking, one that will continue to fascinate audiences. For all its faults, there have been few movies in the entire history of cinema to compare with it in terms of boldness of concept and brilliance of execution.

Top: artists Art Riley, left, and Ray Huffine at work on *Fantasia* backgrounds. Center: Retta Scott, an animator who worked on the "Pastoral" segment. Bottom: working on study for *Rite of Spring*, Woolie Reitherman consults a model of a dinosaur

7 Dumbo and Bambi

Cinematically, *Snow White, Pinocchio,* and *Fantasia* were blockbusters. The two features that followed – *Dumbo* and *Bambi* – were a little different in character. *Bambi,* except for its final climactic scenes, is a rather low-keyed movie. The Disney artists took great pains to establish the tranquillity that – according to the scenario, at least – prevails in the forest under normal conditions. This led to a lyrical approach which is quite distinctive and separates *Bambi* from all other Disney movies. *Dumbo* is a delightfully unpretentious picture, relying almost entirely on charm and humor rather than on spectacular effects.

   Like *Pinocchio, Fantasia* did not have a great financial success at the time of its first release, and *Dumbo* was conceived as a way of recouping some of those losses. It was made for a fraction of the cost of the two preceding releases, yet its earning potential would prove to be at least equal to theirs. Multiplane shots and other expensive effects were kept to the bare minimum that would assure good production values, and the story was told as simply and directly as possible, with the emphasis placed on humorous character development. In many respects, this represented a shift back to the spirit of the cartoon shorts. After the demands of the first three features, *Dumbo* was practically a vacation for the Disney artists, and they clearly enjoyed themselves on this project. It is probably the most spontaneous animated feature that the Studio has ever produced. Audiences responded well to it, and the film brought in much-needed revenue (only the fact that it was released just two months before Pearl Harbor prevented it from having an even greater impact).

Dumbo is the story of a baby elephant who discovers that he can fly. Adapted for the screen by Joe Grant and Dick Huemer, the film has a number of highlights. The circus parade and the scenes with Dumbo and the clowns have a splashy vigor spiced with the kind of knockabout humor that benefited greatly from the expertise of the veteran animators. The older elephants, caricatured as gossipy women, feature fine animation by Bill Tytla and John Lounsbery. Perhaps the most original sequence of the movie is the one in which Dumbo and his friend Timothy Mouse get drunk and see pink elephants – brilliantly animated by Hicks Lokey and Howard Swift. This leads directly to the scenes in which Dumbo learns that he can fly, a discovery which is prompted by the raucous encouragement of Ward Kimball's quartet of hipster crows.

Disney's own involvement with *Dumbo* seems to have been less than it was with the earlier features. This is not to say that he was uninterested in the project – he was, of course, involved in the important story conferences, and all decisions were still subject to his approval – but he was not aiming for a new plateau of achievement in this film and clearly felt that much responsibility could be delegated to members of his staff.

All was not well at the Studio, however. Along with continuing financial difficulties, Disney found himself confronted by labor unrest. By 1941, unionization was firmly established in most of the other Hollywood studios, but it had not yet made inroads into the animation industry.

This is not the place to discuss the pros and cons of the dispute that led to picket lines going up outside the Studio, but the strike itself cannot be ignored since it did have a significant effect on future productions. In retrospect, it seems inevitable that some kind of unionization would have come about sooner or later, but Walt Disney refused to accept this. The strike was a bitter one and left deep wounds. As a direct or indirect result of it the Studio lost some excellent animators, as well as much of the freewheeling atmosphere that had typified it in the thirties. The Age of Innocence was over.

By coincidence, the theme of *Bambi* focuses on the passing of a state of innocence (man invades the forest, bringing terror and destruction to the animals who live there). Disney had begun preparatory work on *Bambi* as early as 1937, before the release of *Snow White,* but for various reasons it did not reach movie theaters until 1942. By its very nature, it was a project that could not be rushed, and the Studio's economic problems impeded the progress of the production. Disney's strongly held ideas about how *Bambi* should be made dictated that the film would have to be very expensive, and rather than cut back on production values, he waited until he was able to make the movie that he wanted. While *Fantasia* was eating up the company's resources, *Bambi* was cut back to a skeleton crew and did not return to full production until *Fantasia* was finished.

The prevailing mood of this film (until the climax, at least) is one of

Top: Joe Grant and Dick Huemer at work on the script of *Dumbo.* Center and bottom: while researching Dumbo, Disney artists spent time sketching at the Cole Brothers' Circus

Some of the most inventive animation for *Dumbo* was done by Ward Kimball, who drew the hipster crows lyricism. Humor is blended with the lyricism, but it is humor of a very gentle variety and does not interrupt the mood. The forest becomes a character in the movie, every bit as important as any of the animals. Its response to weather (as in the raindrop sequence with its effective use of multiplane shots) and to season (as in the autumn montage) is as much a part of the story as any of the things that happen to Bambi and his friends. Much of the credit for this should go to Tyrus Wong, who keyed the background styling.

Great emphasis was placed on naturalism in the making of *Bambi*. Special art classes – an extension of the existing training program – were instituted so that Rico LeBrun could instruct the animators in the finer points of drawing animals. Real deer were kept on the lot as models for the artists. Books of photographic studies and innumerable model sheets were compiled, along with analyses of animal action and thousands of feet of live-action material to be used for reference.

The *Bambi* unit departed from the usual Disney procedure of casting specific animators for specific characters. This time the film was simply broken down into sequences and scenes, and any artist might be asked to draw any character. Because of this, the art classes and other aids had a special importance.

Technically, *Bambi* had a great deal to commend it. Much patient work went into it, and we might single out the contributions of the art direction team, headed by Tom Codrick, and the animation of Frank Thomas, Milt Kahl, Ollie Johnston, Eric Larson, and Retta Scott. But, for all the effort and skill, *Bambi* is ultimately unsatisfying – especially by the standards Disney had set for himself in his earlier features. The artists cannot be faulted. The problem lies with the interpretation of the story, perhaps with the story itself. In earlier Disney films – both shorts and features – the fact that animals take on human characteristics and have human voices is not disturbing since they exist in a world of their own which is governed by its own rules (as we have already noted, this links them to a tradition that has its roots in Aesop and Aristophanes). We are not surprised, for instance, when Pinocchio is seduced from the straight and narrow by a fox and a cat, for they are clearly caricatures of human types and the story unfolds in a fantastic dimension which we recognize as a metaphor for reality rather than as a naturalistic portrayal. Even the animals and birds in *Snow White* do not disturb us by their intelligent behavior. Within the framework of the fairy tale, it seems quite acceptable, and only relatively small demands are made on them – they are not even asked to speak. Prior to *Bambi*, Disney's use of humanized animals had always been within the limits of established idioms.

Bambi, however, is something quite different. This film aims for a kind of naturalism which falls outside the borders of fantasy and fairy tale – yet it presents an owl on friendly terms with baby rabbits who, in the real forest, would be his victims, and we are asked to believe in deer that speak the language and share the emotions of the humans who are supposed to be their enemies. It is very difficult to reconcile these contradictions.

Voice talents involved in the making of *Dumbo* included Sterling Holloway, left, who played Ol' Doc Stork, and Verna Felton as one of the gossipy elephants

Dumbo – opposite and overleaf – follows the career of a young elephant from the night he is delivered by stork at the winter quarters of the circus to the day he learns he can fly and to his "arrival" as a national celebrity

Circus clowns in *Dumbo*

At the end of the film, the circus train carries Dumbo over the mountains and to the bright lights of the big city

Preparatory work for *Bambi* included elaborate studies of animals in action

In *Bambi*, Disney artists aimed for a degree of naturalism quite unprecedented in the history of the animated film

Background treatments for *Bambi* were
conceived to sustain a lyrical mood

Bambi and his father in the snow

The most sympathetic characters are those, like Thumper the rabbit and Flower the skunk, who are used mostly for humorous relief. They seem to belong to the Disney mainstream and work well in those terms.

Yet despite its shortcomings, *Bambi* is an important movie. Along with the four preceding feature films and the short cartoons of the thirties, it gave the Studio a tremendous reservoir of idioms and techniques. The Disney artists could now handle everything from the broad stylization of Mickey or the Goof to the naturalism of Faline. They had learned how to create any atmosphere they might need, and the multiplane camera allowed them to use space in new and complicated ways. The Disney paint laboratory had developed hundreds of new colors to extend the possibilities of animation in still another way.

Bambi also marked the end of an era. The expansion that began in the early thirties reached a peak and leveled off about 1940. By the time *Bambi* reached the screen, the armed forces were already depleting the Studio's ranks. Unionization precluded the possibility of ever building the staff to the level of the early forties, and, in any case, the economic conditions that made so many artists available in the thirties were a thing of the past. This did not mean that Disney animation had no future – obviously, this was far from being true – but it is fair to say that the initial momentum was spent. For a while, the Studio would have to coast – capitalizing on its past achievements, working well within its capabilities, experimenting a little, and waiting for energies to be restored.

From the top down: special classes for *Bambi* artists were conducted by Rico LeBrun; animators Ollie Johnston, left, Milt Kahl, center, and Frank Thomas, right, pose with Peter Behn, the voice of Thumper; Frank Thomas sketches Faline

8 Interruptions and Innovations

America's entry into World War II had an almost immediate effect on Walt Disney Productions. In December 1941, part of the Studio was commandeered as quarters for an antiaircraft unit which stayed for several months. Before long, someone in the Navy realized that animation could be of great value in the presentation of training material. The Studio began to receive contracts from military and government agencies that led to the production of such titles as *Aircraft Carrier Landing Signals, Food Will Win the War, Automotive Electricity for Military Vehicles, Basic Map Reading,* and *Fundamentals of Artillery Weapons.* Since these productions had to be made as inexpensively as possible, extensive and clever use was made of "limited animation" techniques, in which camera movements and other simple devices were substituted for fully drawn animation. A more ambitious project was *Victory Through Air Power,* a feature-length film presenting the strategic bombing theories of Major Alexander de Seversky, made at Disney's expense but utilizing some of the techniques devised for the government-backed shorts.

Throughout the war period, Disney continued to produce short cartoons featuring Donald, Pluto, and Goofy (Mickey Mouse shorts were temporarily discontinued in 1942). Some of these were geared to the war effort or served a propaganda purpose. *Victory Vehicles,* for example, used Goofy to encourage Americans to conserve rubber and gasoline while *Der Fuehrer's Face* takes the form of a nightmare in which Donald imagines himself to be a worker in Nazi Germany. A still more extraordinary propaganda film, *Education for Death*, employed broad satire and powerful graphics to suggest that Germany's children had been schooled and disciplined into becoming a ruthless military machine.

The two most important commercial releases of the period – *Saludos Amigos* and *The Three Caballeros* – were themselves indirect products of the war. With Europe in turmoil, the Latin American market became increasingly important to American industry, including Hollywood, and it was with government sponsorship that Disney and a team of artists from the Studio traveled in 1941 to Argentina, Peru, Chile, and Brazil. Each of these nations provided the background for an animated short, and these episodes were then connected with documentary footage of the tour to create a "package" film released in 1943 as *Saludos Amigos*.

Perhaps the most interesting character to emerge from this mélange was José Carioca, the energetic, samba-loving parrot who would reappear two years later in *The Three Caballeros*, another package film featuring José, along with Donald and a Mexican rooster called Panchito, who sports a large sombrero and an itchy trigger finger.

The package film was not an ideal format for Disney artists, but it was a way of putting together feature-length releases at a time when wartime shortages and economic pressures made it impractical to produce full-length animated features. Some of these pressures continued after the war, and three more package films were released – *Make Mine Music* (1946), *Fun and Fancy Free* (1947), and *Melody Time* (1948). The first and third of these made use of the musical talents of recording artists such as Benny Goodman, Ethel Smith, and the Andrews Sisters, featuring them in animated segments that were sometimes comedic, sometimes semiabstract in a way that was reminiscent of *Fantasia*. *Fun and Fancy Free* featured just two animated story sections – "Bongo" and "Mickey and the Beanstalk" – though Jiminy Cricket was used in the introduction and incorporated into the linking live-action sequences.

For economic reasons, the Studio was coming to rely more and more upon live action and upon live-action/animation hybrids such as *Song of the South*, released in 1946. Although human actors carry the main body of the film's narrative, three Brer Rabbit stories are included as cartoon inserts and represent the best Disney animation of this period. In several scenes, live action and animation were combined very effectively.

By 1949, the Studio was almost ready to return to true feature animation. That year saw the release of *The Adventures of Ichabod and Mr. Toad*, which was still technically a package film but consisted of just two longish "featurettes" – more substantial than those in *Fun and Fancy Free* – linked only by the fact that the hero of each segment is prone to disaster. The "Toad" episode is based on Kenneth Grahame's *The Wind in the Willows* and is enlivened by fine character animation and some imaginative art direction. Unfortunately, the story is too compressed for any of the personalities to be fully explored. All of the action is there but not the leisurely pace of the original (it seems that Disney had intended the story to serve as the basis for a feature-length film but was forced to settle for this compromise version).

Walt Disney in Argentina

Der Fuehrer's Face, 1943, took the form of a nightmare in which Donald Duck found himself working in a Nazi munitions factory

During World War II, Disney characters were often used to illustrate matters of public interest. In *Victory Vehicles*, 1943, opposite, Goofy urged people to save scrap metal and gasoline

The 1943 package film *Saludos Amigos*
included the story of Pedro the mail plane and
introduced Donald's friend José Carioca

"After You've Gone" is a segment of the 1946 package film *Make Mine Music*

227

The animated portions of *Song of the South*, 1946, left, brought the animals of the Uncle Remus stories to life

Released in 1949, *The Adventures of Ichabod and Mr. Toad*, opposite, combined screen adaptations of two famous stories

The tale of Ichabod, based on Washington Irving's *The Legend of Sleepy Hollow,* is narrated by Bing Crosby. For the most part, it is presented in a rather pedestrian manner, but the final sequence, in which Ichabod Crane is pursued by the Headless Horseman, is outstanding, with the drama building to a fine pitch of excitement. *The Adventures of Ichabod and Mr. Toad* fell short of being a great movie, but it was a significant step toward regaining past glories.

The Studio was still producing short cartoons for theatrical release. (It continued to do so until 1956.) Donald and Goofy were now the biggest stars, each benefiting from character traits that made him easy to write for. Mickey made occasional appearances, but usually as a straight man, and Pluto continued to find himself in situations that derived from Webb Smith's 1934 flypaper gag. Important newcomers were Chip and Dale, highly territorial chipmunks who knew how to make Donald's life miserable. Besides these "character" cartoons, there were also occasional one-shot shorts like *Morris the Midget Moose* (1950) and *Susie the Little Blue Coupe* (1952), which went some way toward replacing the Silly Symphonies. Several skilled directors – Jack King, Jack Hannah, Bill Roberts, and Jack Kinney – specialized in short cartoons during this period, as did some first-rate animators, such as Bill Justice, John Sibley, and Bob Carlson.

On occasion, short subjects were accorded rather special treatment, as was the case with *Toot, Whistle, Plunk, and Boom* (1953). A highly stylized history of music, devised by Ward Kimball, this was the first CinemaScope® cartoon ever produced. A similar subject from the same year, *Adventures in Music: Melody,* was an experiment in 3-D animation.

Meanwhile, in 1950, Walt Disney released his first true animated feature since 1942. This was *Cinderella* – a project that had been in development for several years – and it was a success both at the box office and as a piece of imaginative filmmaking.

In spirit, it harks back to *Snow White and the Seven Dwarfs,* though with an added frosting of surface glamour and a greater reliance on gag routines. Cinderella, her stepmother, and the Prince are treated somewhat naturalistically while the ugly stepsisters, the Fairy Godmother, the King, and the Duke are essentially caricatures, but they all work well together. The animal characters are excellent. Lucifer the cat is a splendid villain, and the mice are consistently entertaining.

The backgrounds are less distinctive than those which added so much to *Snow White* and *Pinocchio,* but they are more than adequate, establishing a kind of French Provincial look. The well-constructed story consists of two parallel plots – one concerned with the human characters and the other with the animals – linked only by Cinderella herself. Songs in the film include "A Dream Is a Wish Your Heart Makes," "Bibbidi-Bobbidi-Boo," and "So This Is Love."

Cinderella succeeds because it remains faithful to the spirit of the original fairy tale while embroidering it with the kind of business that Disney understood better than anybody else. The next feature, *Alice in*

Much fine work went into the short cartoons of the forties, as in these examples of backgrounds from Donald Duck and Pluto vehicles

Left: *Slide Donald Slide*, 1949. Top: the 1950 short *Motor Mania* is one of several that take an ironic look at the habits of the American driver. Center: *Two Chips and a Miss*, 1952, a typical outing for Chip and Dale. Bottom: *Toot, Whistle, Plunk, and Boom*, 1953, is an experimental short made in Cinemascope

Wonderland (1951), failed because it neither captured the unique atmosphere of Lewis Carroll's story nor displayed the authoritative Disney touch except in a few isolated scenes. Given the fact that the *Alice* shorts had provided him with his first success, it's hardly surprising that Disney had long cherished the idea of adapting the *Alice* books, first mentioning the idea while *Snow White* was in production. He worked at the idea intermittently for years, but it was no easy matter to translate Carroll's highly intellectual verbal humor into visual terms.

The movie has occasional moments of sharp surrealistic invention – the Mad Hatter's tea party is a memorable sequence – but for the most part it is a confusing hodgepodge of disparate story elements and stylistic inconsistencies. Carroll's fictional world is dislocated by inversions of reason but held together by the insane persistence of his own preposterous logic. Disney responded to the nonsense element in the *Alice* books but found no adequate cinematic equivalent for Carroll's erudite word games. Disappointed with the film, he blamed its failure on the heroine's "lack of heart."

Peter Pan, released in 1953, is an altogether more satisfactory picture – which incidentally provided a demonstration of just how expert the Disney animators had become at handling the human form. As in *Cinderella*, naturalism and caricature were skillfully blended.

Unlike *Alice*, Sir James Barrie's play adapted very well to the screen. If the movie has a weakness, it derives from the fact that there are too many characters to permit all of them to be developed adequately in the seventy-seven minute running time. The Lost Boys, for example, are potentially as interesting as the Seven Dwarfs, but they are individualized only in the crudest of ways. Even Peter and Wendy are a little sketchy. Captain Hook, meanwhile, emerges as a well-defined personality, and Tinker Bell, though her petulance becomes irritating, has an insistent presence.

Character development apart, the movie has a satisfying narrative flow, well-handled comedy routines, and more than its fair share of genuine magic moments in which the art of animation makes the impossible possible. The flying sequences are handled with great panache, permitting the viewer to imagine the excitement of defying gravity.

Peter Pan is not a masterpiece, but it is an enjoyable piece of entertainment that only the Disney Studio could have made. If Disney had had a problem making the overly inquisitive Alice believable, he had no such difficulty identifying with Barrie's boy who refused to grow up.

The year 1955 saw the release of *Lady and the Tramp*, Disney's first animated feature in CinemaScope. It was innovative in another way, too. Set in the recent past, the film deals with a kind of milieu Disney feature animation had not addressed until then – something rather close to our everyday world. (*Dumbo* had been set in the present, but the circus environment introduced an exotic element.) *Lady and the Tramp* unfolds in the suburbs of a medium-sized American city in the early years of the century, a setting compounded from vernacular elements that are still familiar today.

CinemaScope itself presented a challenge, especially to the layout artists. With a conventional aspect ratio, it is easy enough for a single

Cinderella was Disney's first true animated feature since *Bambi*. Released in 1950, it recaptured much of the spirit of the early features, modified by a new lightness of touch and an emphasis on surface glamour (see also overleaf)

Cinderella's Fairy Godmother prepares her for the ball

Disney's version of *Peter Pan*, 1953, is a
generally entertaining interpretation of Sir
James Barrie's stage classic

Released in 1951, *Alice in Wonderland* had some brilliant
visual touches but failed to capture the flavor of Lewis
Carroll's story

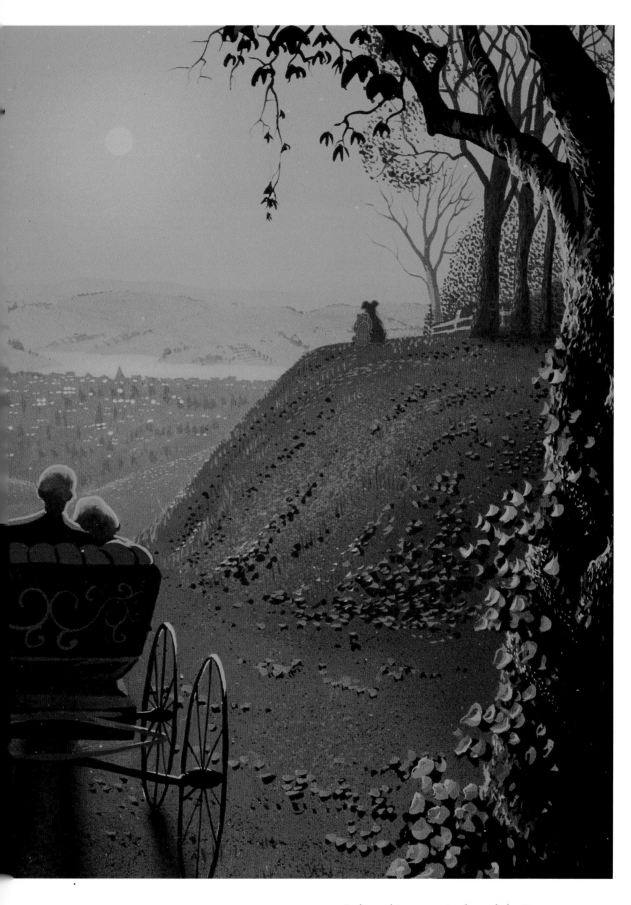

Released in 1955, *Lady and the Tramp* was
the first animated feature made in CinemaScope.
More significantly, it broke new ground in terms
of subject matter, setting a more informal tone
for future Disney movies

character to activate the whole screen, and characters can be closely grouped, which makes them easy to handle. CinemaScope provides a sense of space, but the stretched-out format makes it difficult for a single character to dominate the screen, and groups must be well spread out to keep the screen from seeming bare. Longer takes become necessary since the constant jump-cutting that is the norm in animated films would seem busy and annoying.

The Disney team overcame these difficulties remarkably well, and the animators did a fine job of grafting human personas onto the principal canine characters without losing the nuances of dog behavior that were necessary if the story was to be convincing. There are some well-executed action scenes – Tramp killing the rat comes to mind – and the movie introduced some memorable songs, including "Bella Notte" and "He's a Tramp." *Lady and the Tramp* and *Cinderella* were the strongest Disney animated features of the 1950s.

Lady and the Tramp was followed by another wide-screen feature – one that began with high hopes and ended in near disaster.

Sleeping Beauty was conceived as the most spectacular of Walt Disney's postwar productions. The artist Eyvind Earle was called in to devise background stylings somewhat remotely based on medieval tapestries and early Renaissance paintings, and the characters were designed to blend with these settings. Much care was lavished on planning scenes to make the fullest possible use of the Technirama® 70mm format. The multiplane camera would also be extensively used.

Unfortunately, *Sleeping Beauty* went into production at a time when Disney was preoccupied with both live-action films and also with his major project of the 1950s – Disneyland. Despite his ambitious plans for *Sleeping Beauty,* he seems to have had a difficult time immersing himself in the subject. As always, nothing could proceed without his approval, but because of his other concerns he often neglected the movie for weeks at a time. *Sleeping Beauty* took six years to complete. It finally reached theaters in January of 1959 and was greeted with almost universal disappointment.

The film has its good moments. The evil fairy, Maleficent, is one of Marc Davis's finest creations, and there is some splendid effects animation toward the climax, as the Prince fights his way to the castle. Against this must be set the fact that the hero and heroine are the merest of ciphers who often seem to become lost against the overelaborate and overstylized backgrounds. The Technirama format led to some static scenes, but a more serious problem was the fact that Disney did not succeed in transforming the story in the way he had metamorphosed *Snow White* and *Cinderella. Sleeping Beauty* refused to submit to his genius for recreating archetypal stories. While it was in production, his genius was at work elsewhere.

As far as animation was concerned, new formats like CinemaScope and Technirama 70 proved to be more trouble than they were worth. *One*

An *Alice in Wonderland* story conference: Winston Hibler, Ted Sears, Walt Disney, and Ed Penner.

Recording the voice track for *Alice in Wonderland:* Jerry Colonna, Kathryn Beaumont, and Ed Wynn

Six years in the making, *Sleeping Beauty*, 1959, marked a temporary return to the world of the fairy tale. Unfortunately, its highly stylized treatment tended to slow the action and interfere with character development

Hundred and One Dalmatians, released in 1961, made use of a technical innovation that would have a more lasting impact. Ub Iwerks, now in charge of special processes at the Studio, had been experimenting with Xerox photography as an aid to animation and by 1959 had modified a Xerox camera to transfer animators' drawings directly to cels, thus eliminating the inking process and preserving much of the spontaneity of the pencil line. This saved time and money and had a major effect on the way Disney animation would look for the next thirty years since the style of everything else had to match the style the system imposed on the cels so there would be no clash between, for example, characters and backgrounds. The new look would be graphic and linear, quite different from the tonal renderings so typical of the early features. (Eventually, the system was modified and made somewhat more flexible by the introduction of color xerography.)

One Hundred and One Dalmatians was an all-Xerox feature, with the old inking method being resorted to only in a few instances where a colored line was needed. In fact, the film would have been difficult to make without the Xerox camera. There are scenes in which literally dozens of puppies fill the screen – each of them liberally spotted – and to animate these scenes using traditional methods would have been a herculean task. The Xerox camera allowed the artists to circumvent the problem by animating one small group of puppies, then using the camera to repeat their actions, making sure, of course, that the repeat was not too mechanical.

Beyond that, the new technique made the animators' task easier and permitted them to concentrate on the real substance of the film – character development and story. Set in England, in the present, the movie starts a little slowly but comes vividly to life when Cruella De Vil – another of Marc Davis's delicious delinquents – enters the picture. The pace picks up and never flags as the story builds steadily to its climax.

As in *Lady and the Tramp,* the dogs and other animals are presented as human surrogates and work well as such. Some of the most interesting animation in the movie, however, was reserved for the humans, who were

One Hundred and One Dalmatians, 1961, was the first feature to use the Xerox camera – a device which gave the backgrounds a more linear and graphic quality and helped preserve the spontaneity of the animator's drawings. This film provides fast-moving entertainment and many good touches, including "quotations" from old Disney cartoons (seen on television), and Cruella De Vil, who is perhaps the best villainess in Disney's postwar movies

Released in 1963, *The Sword in the Stone*
brought to the screen Disney's version of the
boyhood of King Arthur

drawn with a looseness new to Disney features. Elbows and knees are not always where they should be according to anatomy books, but everything works. Cruella is especially memorable, her face a blend of death mask and fashion plate, perfectly expressing her character, which is at the same time evil and laughable.

With *One Hundred and One Dalmatians*, the Studio recovered much of its old assurance and arrived at a new idiom. A good deal of the credit for this should go to Ken Anderson, who was responsible for production design, and to Bill Peet, who developed the story. Interestingly, Walt Disney is said to have strongly disliked the look of the movie. The public approved and made *One Hundred and One Dalmatians* a resounding commercial success.

By the early sixties, the animation staff had been pared down to a fraction of what it had been in the heyday of *Pinocchio* and *Fantasia*. Increasingly, Disney relied on the group he referred to as "the nine old men": Frank Thomas, Ollie Johnston, Milt Kahl, Eric Larson, Marc Davis, Woolie Reitherman, John Lounsbery, Ward Kimball, and Les Clark. These veterans were the key animators, but their ranks were depleted when Davis, a brilliant draftsman, switched his attention to designing for Disneyland and Reitherman began to concentrate on directing. As the staff settled into a new rhythm, a policy emerged of having one feature-length movie ready for release every three or four years, with occasional special projects.

The next animated feature was not one of the Studio's better efforts. Released in December 1963, *The Sword in the Stone* presents the boyhood of King Arthur, concentrating on his education at the hands of Merlin the Magician. The film totally misses the tone of T. H. White's story, and while there are some amusing set pieces and the animation is as accomplished as ever, character development is weak. Merlin, instead of being awesome, is presented as a bungling nincompoop, thus destroying the essence of the plot.

The Jungle Book, which appeared four years later, was an altogether more satisfactory production. Based on Rudyard Kipling's tales about Mowgli, a human child brought up in the jungles of India, the movie took liberties with the original, but these were amply justified by the end results.

Part of the success of *The Jungle Book* derived from the skillful casting of voice talent. Voices for the animated features had always been chosen with care, but – with a couple of exceptions – voice talent had not played a major role in defining character. It would be easy enough to imagine Geppetto or Pinocchio with slightly different voices (though Cliff Edwards's Jiminy Cricket is another matter). In the shorts, by contrast, characters like Goofy, Donald, and Mickey himself were inseparable from the voice talents (Pinto Colvig, Clarence Nash, and Walt Disney, respectively) who had helped shape them.

The Jungle Book was the first animated feature in which, across the board, the voice talents were more than just appropriate. Phil Harris, George Sanders, Sterling Holloway, Louis Prima, Verna Felton, Pat

Voice talents – including George Sanders, Phil Harris, Louis Prima, Sterling Holloway, and Sebastian Cabot – played an important part in the production of *The Jungle Book*, 1967. This adaptation of Kipling's stories also features some of the best animation of the postwar period

O'Malley, and Sebastian Cabot were chosen to speak for the creatures of Kipling's jungle – all of them actors whose voices had very distinct personalities that would influence the approach the animators would have to take.

The two greatest successes of the film are Baloo the bear, whose voice belonged to Phil Harris, and Shere Khan the tiger, played by George Sanders. Harris knew how to dominate a recording session, improvising on the "script" supplied by the storyboards and building the character into something that felt real and alive. The animators had the challenge of entering this character and making him perform on the screen.

The typical Disney villain is menacing and comic at the same time. We must sense that he is a real threat, but unless we can laugh at him too, he could destroy the mood of the whole film. Shere Khan is a tiger stalking an innocent boy – not the usual stuff of humor – but Sanders's delivery, sinister and affected at the same time, had just the right edge to it. One regrets only that Shere Khan did not have more screen time.

The Jungle Book proved to be Walt Disney's last animated film. In the late fall of 1966, a routine medical exam revealed that Disney – a heavy smoker – was suffering from advanced lung cancer. One lung was removed, but six weeks later, on December 15, he died in his room at St. Joseph's Hospital in Burbank, directly across the street from the Studio. He was sixty-five years old.

The Jungle Book was not quite finished, but Disney had already left his mark on it through the influence of his story sense and his attention to production values. Combining first-rate animation, fine background paintings (styled by Al Dempster), lively songs, and crisp direction – as well as the voice talents already noted – *The Jungle Book* would be one of the best of the Studio's postwar films, a fitting memorial to the man who had virtually invented the animated feature.

9 The End of an Era

Before he died, Walt Disney had given the go-ahead – on the strength of a board of drawings by production designer Ken Anderson – for the next animated feature, which appeared, in 1970, as *The Aristocats*. This film blends the vernacular style of *One Hundred and One Dalmatians* with *The Jungle Book*'s developments in voice characterization, and the result is a frothy comedy that has enjoyed considerable popularity.

An aristocratic cat named Duchess (her voice supplied by Eva Gabor) and her three kittens become the objects of the evil designs of their mistress's butler. Stranded in the French countryside, they are befriended by an alley cat named O'Malley (Phil Harris again). The film follows their adventures as they make their way back to Paris, only to be confronted once more by the black-hearted majordomo. This time the villain gets his just deserts and Duchess and O'Malley live happily ever after.

The plot is full of amusing incidents and is enlivened by some well-established secondary characters, who include the country dogs Napoleon and Lafayette (Pat Buttram and George Lindsey) and a delightful pair of English geese (the voices of Carole Shelley and Monica Evans).

Winnie the Pooh and the Honey Tree (1966) and *Winnie the Pooh and the Blustery Day* (1968) are a pair of admirable featurettes made during this same period. (The first appeared while Walt Disney was still alive, and he had approved the idea of the sequel.) Apart from the unnecessary Americanizing of some of A. A. Milne's characters, the Disney artists

Starring Tigger, Eeyore and, of course, Pooh
Bear, *Winnie the Pooh and the Blustery Day,*
1968, is a charming featurette-length adaptation of an A. A. Milne story (see overleaf)

Scenes from *The Aristocats,* 1970,
which featured a villainous butler and
strong comic relief

dealt very capably with the difficult task of translating the original Christopher Robin stories to the screen. The second film is especially good, with imaginative animation of the book itself. (Wind and rain threaten to blow or wash the words from the pages.) Most of the characters are very well conceived, with Tigger perhaps the outstanding success.

Winnie the Pooh and Tigger Too (1974) and *Winnie the Pooh and a Day for Eeyore* (1983) were later additions to the series. The 1974 film maintained the standards of the first two adventures. The animation for the fourth episode in the series was not done at the Studio but was farmed out to another animation house, with mediocre results.

Following *The Aristocats,* it was decided that the animation department should tackle a classic story as its next feature. Ken Anderson suggested a new treatment of the Robin Hood legend, and the idea was received with enthusiasm. As soon as a broad outline of the script had been established, a remarkable array of voice talent was assembled. Peter Ustinov was signed to play Prince John, a vain and insecure lion who is the comic villain of the piece. Terry-Thomas was cast as his obsequious sidekick, Sir Hiss, a snake. Other voice assignments included Phil Harris as Little John, Andy Devine as Friar Tuck, Roger Miller as Allan-a-Dale, and Brian Bedford as Robin Hood.

Robin Hood, released in 1973, is distinguished by much fine character animation on the part of veterans like Milt Kahl, Frank Thomas, Ollie Johnston, and John Lounsbery, backed up by Don Bluth and other talented newcomers. Its weakness, perhaps, is that it is a film that places *too* much faith in the powers of character animation to carry the day on its own. Compared with earlier Disney treatments of classics, it is weak in the area of art direction and production values. More important, it does nothing of any real originality with the Robin Hood legend.

Ken Anderson said at the time that the idea of doing *Robin Hood* with animals was in part the result of a desire to recall the spirit of the animated segments of *Song of the South.* "It's the kind of thing we do best," he argued, and the rest of the animation staff was in general agreement.

A *Robin Hood* story conference with, left to right, writer Larry Clemmons, director Woolie Reitherman, art director Ken Anderson, and animator Frank Thomas

A scene from *Robin Hood*, 1973

There is no doubt that one of the things Disney animation does do best is to use animals as human surrogates. In order for this to be fully effective, however, it must be done within the context of a powerful allegory, and this version of *Robin Hood* is almost entirely lacking in allegorical power. Rather, it uses first-rate character animation to enliven conventional situation-comedy gags. It is not a bad film, but it does not live up to the potential of the subject.

It was almost four years before another animated feature appeared, and this time it was *The Rescuers*, based on stories by Margery Sharp. The plot involves Bianca and Bernard (the voices of Eva Gabor and Bob Newhart), a pair of noble-spirited mice who set out to rescue a young orphan from the clutches of a suitably avaricious villain named Madame Medusa (Geraldine Page).

The Rescuers is not one of the Studio's great animated allegories either, but it is a lively entertainment full of colorful characters and situations. It lacks a powerful central theme, but it does have villainous deeds, sadistic crocodiles, a souped-up "swampmobile," a grouchy albatross named Orville in the charter-flight business, a dragonfly called Evinrude, some hungry bats, hidden treasure, the Louisiana bayous, and a benevolent society that meets in the basement of the United Nations building. In short, the Disney animation staff was given a chance to have fun, and everybody concerned made the most of the opportunity.

The Rescuers was a transitional movie in that it was still made under the guidance of the old guard – Woolie Reitherman, Ollie Johnston, Frank Thomas, Milt Kahl, Ken Anderson, Larry Clemmons, John Lounsbery, Eric Larson – but it was the first feature to display a significant influence from the next generation of Disney artists. The list of character animators includes names like Ron Clements, Glen Keane, and Andy Gaskill, who would have important roles to play in the Disney animation renaissance of the eighties and nineties.

This changing of the guard was even more in evidence by the time *The Fox and the Hound* (1981) went into production. Woolie Reitherman was still there, as producer, and the project was very much his to the extent that he had championed the Daniel P. Mannix novel that the movie is based on. (One of Reitherman's sons had once raised a pet fox.) Larry Clemmons was on hand as dean of the story team, and Frank Thomas and Ollie Johnston did much of the developmental animation for the main characters. Most of the animation, however, was done by a youthful team that included Clements, Keane, and John Musker. Others listed in the credits for this movie were Don Hahn (assistant director) and Burny Mattinson (story), both of whom, like the three artists listed above, would contribute to the coming animation renaissance.

The Fox and the Hound tells the story of Tod, a fox, and Copper, a hound, who become childhood friends but grow up to find themselves face-to-face with the conventional prejudices of the adult world – a world in which foxes and hounds are not supposed to get along. The grown Tod (the voice of Mickey Rooney) is ready to overlook these prejudices.

Based on stories by Margery Sharp, *The Rescuers*, 1977, is a lively adventure yarn which once again benefits greatly from the voice talents employed, notably Eva Gabor (Miss Bianca), Bob Newhart (Bernard), and Geraldine Page (Madame Medusa)

The Fox and the Hound, 1981, was a transitional
movie in that – despite important contributions
from studio veterans, especially at the planning
stage – it was carried out largely by younger
artists, some of whom would be key figures in
the Disney renaissance of the eighties and nineties.
Among the most gifted of the newcomers was
Glen Keane, who animated the bear in a
memorable fight sequence that was one of the
highlights of the movie

Copper (Kurt Russell) has serious doubts about maintaining the friendship. For a while, he grudgingly protects Tod from fox-hating hunter Amos Slade and his best hound Chief. Later, believing that Tod is responsible for Chief being wounded, Copper turns against his former friend. Only when Tod saves Copper and Slade from a bear does Copper embrace the friendship without equivocation.

The movie is full of solid characters, including Tod's mate Vixey (Sandy Duncan) and his mentor, an owl named Big Mama (Pearl Bailey). It is also enlivened by some strong action footage, notably the climactic fight between Tod and the bear. Brought to life by Glen Keane, the bear was a splendid achievement, one that gave notice that this was a young animator to be reckoned with.

Like most of the best Disney animated features, *The Fox and the Hound* also has a strong theme, rooted in the durability of true friendship and the blight of prejudice. Unfortunately, the theme is weakened because the relationship between Tod and Copper remains somewhat one-sided. Under Amos Slade's evil influence, Copper is so mindlessly obedient that the audience is left with the feeling that friendship is almost *forced* on him by Tod's selfless act – though in the end this misgiving is mitigated when Copper saves Tod's life with a selfless act of his own.

If the theme is not resolved as satisfactorily as it might have been, however, *The Fox and the Hound* is still an entertaining film, slight by the standards of some of its predecessors, but accomplished in what might be described as middle-period Disney feature animation style – the style that began with the animated episodes of *Song of the South,* evolved in the fifties, and prevailed for three decades during which time Disney animation was dominated by a handful of great character animators. *The Fox and the Hound* was a vehicle for the new generation of Disney artists, but they were still working in the shadow of their elders.

They needed to escape this formidable shadow. In the classics of the thirties and forties, Walt Disney had made bold use of camera movements, effects animation, and other technical devices, to enhance dramatic situations and advance the story. The films of the fifties, sixties, and seventies were different in that they were predicated, almost exclusively, upon the character animator's ability to breathe life into heroes like Peter Pan and Mowgli, heroines like Cinderella and Bianca, comic characters like Gus and Jaq (the mice in *Cinderella*), and villains like Cruella De Vil and Shere Khan. The other weapons in the animation armory were assigned to backup roles.

There were two principal reasons for this. An animated film could be made for less money if the production avoided expensive setups and elaborate effects. More important, the nine old men and the younger animators they trained had become extremely good at what they did. If creating believable human characters for *Snow White* had been a seemingly insurmountable challenge, by the fifties it was still a challenge but one that was approached with more than a decade of experience and acquired virtuosity.

Amos Slade's shack: one of the settings used
for *The Fox and the Hound*

It was almost as if the lead actors in the Disney repertory company –
the key character animators – had set out to demonstrate that they could
perform elaborate dramas on a bare stage if necessary. Scenery was
provided, but, as time went by, it became less and less significant to the
way the story was told. (*Sleeping Beauty* is the one big exception to this
rule, and in that instance the art direction almost suffocated the story.)

Not to put too fine a point on it, the animated features of the middle
period never reached the creative heights attained by *Snow White* or
Pinocchio, yet the least of them provides matchless examples of character
animation. Artists like Milt Kahl, Ollie Johnston, Frank Thomas, and
Marc Davis were to animation what Spencer Tracy or Charles Laughton
were to screen acting. Ward Kimball was animation's Ernie Kovacs. Eric
Larson was not only a superb animator but also as important a teaching
figure, in his field, as Lee Strasberg was in his.

These were the men who inspired and trained the new generation of
animators that began to come into its own in the early eighties. (A training program had been in place at the Studio since the early seventies.)

These younger animators were all too aware of the great skill of the men whose mantles they were assuming. They wanted to prove themselves worthy successors. At the same time, though, they wanted to show that they were capable of breaking the mold and creating something original.

They were looking for a major challenge, and they received it when Ron Miller – Walt Disney's son-in-law, who had become head of production – gave the go-ahead for *The Black Cauldron*, to be based on the five Lloyd Alexander books that make up his popular Chronicles of Prydain cycle.

At a time when there was a great interest in sword and sorcery fiction, this must have seemed like a good idea. The award-winning Alexander books had been very successful with a certain readership, offering exactly the blend of gothic creepiness, supernatural high jinks, cryptomythology, antic chivalry, chimeric violence, and pseudo-Celtic names that keeps young adult males glued to the pages of thick paperbacks with blond heroines, fierce dwarfs, and heavily muscled warriors on the cover.

In retrospect, however, this may have been exactly the kind of material the Disney animators should have stayed away from. To begin with, the subject matter may have had great appeal for that specific group, but it did not have the kind of broad appeal that would make it attractive to younger children or females of any age – important components of the audience for animated features. The plot was calculated to capture the imagination of young males, a category that included most key members of *The Black Cauldron*'s production team. The story team and the animators had little problem – at first, anyway – in immersing themselves in the adventures of Taran and Eilonwy as they pitted themselves against the evil forces of the Horned King. Free of the supervision of the generation of the nine old men, the new Disney artists were making a movie entirely for themselves.

That may have been where their problems started. By the time they ended, the Studio was under new management.

10　New Beginnings

At the time *The Black Cauldron* went into production, the Studio was desperately seeking a sense of direction and purpose that would permit it to thrive in the eighties. To compete with other studios, such as Warner Brothers, Paramount, Columbia, and Universal, it needed to reach segments of the market that Disney had not yet tapped.

It had been realized for some time that the Disney name could be a liability where certain types of films were concerned. Disney products had become identified almost exclusively with the family market, and that meant that young adults, in the fifteen to twenty-five age range, tended to stay away from movies with the Disney name attached to them, believing that they were strictly for children. Since the young adult category comprises more regular filmgoers than any other age group, it was important for the financial health of the Studio to reach out to it.

This problem was most pressing in the area of live-action films (see chapter 13), but the sense of demoralization that goes hand in hand with lack of direction was felt in the animation department as well, especially because this was a time of change in key personnel. The emerging generation was coming into its own but had not yet elected its leaders. Partly because of this, Don Bluth – among the most talented of the younger animators – had quit Disney in 1979 to form his own studio. There had been other departures, too.

In this context, *The Black Cauldron* was perhaps an overly ambitious production for the new generation to take on. In any case, the early enthusiasm for the project soon dissolved into bickering and backbiting. Production was divided up among several units, some of which hardly communicated with certain others as individuals battled for power. One result of this was that there was no clear directorial vision, and the finished movie lacked narrative and visual cohesion.

As difficult as it was, the period of *The Black Cauldron* brought some brilliant new talent to the Studio – young artists such as Andreas Deja and Ruben Aquino (who would become key animators in the renaissance of the eighties), and Tim Burton (who would go on to direct and/or produce such movies as *Beetlejuice, Batman, The Nightmare Before Christmas,* and *Ed Wood*).

Much of the new talent was coming out of the California Institute of the Arts, a school located in the hills near Los Angeles that had been partially built with money bequeathed by Walt Disney. Its animation department – with senior Disney animators serving as teachers and advisers – now nurtured budding artists, some on Disney fellowships, who often went on to the in-Studio training program. (CalArts is also home to pro-grams intended to train artists for other branches of the film industry, as well as to one of the most prestigious fine arts departments in the country.)

Not all of the young artists coming to the Studio, from CalArts and elsewhere, were character animators. There were also effects animators, layout artists, and background painters, and this led to something of a rebirth of these departments, which is evident on-screen in *The Black Cauldron*. Imaginative effects and carefully constructed camera moves were used to carry the action forward, and the backgrounds were the best since *The Jungle Book*.

All this showed a nostalgia for the glory days of *Snow White* and *Pinocchio*. Unfortunately, that nostalgia was not reflected in story sense and overall vision. The production dragged on for years and seemed to become more confused with each passing day. As it finally limped toward a conclusion, the mood of uncertainty escalated, and the Studio was plunged into a state of turmoil, with various management and shareholder groups battling for control of the company. Eventually, in the fall of 1984, a new corporate team took the reins, with Michael Eisner (former president of Paramount Pictures) as chairman and Frank Wells (former vice chairman of Warner Brothers) as president of what would soon be renamed The Walt Disney Company. Eisner and Wells would prove to be a formidable team. Wells was a sound businessman, highly regarded on Wall Street and throughout the entertainment industry – a secure individual who preferred the respect of his peers to public acclaim. Eisner, on the other hand, would prove himself to be a creative and intuitive executive with a flair for publicity, able to provide the Disney organization with something it had lacked since Walt's death: visible leadership.

This was by far the biggest break with continuity in the company's history, but it was by no means a severing of ties with the Disney family since the new leadership had the strong backing of Roy E. Disney – son

Concept art for *The Black Cauldron*, 1985

A critical and commercial disaster, *The Black Cauldron* is a film that most of those involved with its making would like to forget. Despite its very evident shortcomings as a narrative, however, *The Black Cauldron* did display a high level of ambition that signaled the aspirations of the new generation of Disney animators of Roy O. Disney and nephew of Walt – whose large block of shares had been used to tip the scales in favor of the Eisner/Wells team.

"Roy gave two conditions for his support," says Eisner. "One was that the company should not be broken up, which had been a threat of the early eighties, and the other was that we should give animation a fair shake."

The new executive team was voted in at a meeting of the board on September 24, 1984. Later that day, a celebration was held at the Lakeside Country Club, a stone's throw from the Studio, and during the proceedings, Eisner asked Roy Disney (who would assume the title of vice chairman) what role he would like to play in the company's future.

"Well," Disney recalls replying, "why not give me the animation department? I'll bet I'm the only guy around here who knows anything about it."

While Roy Disney had no hands-on experience in animation, he was a skilled filmmaker, and animation was in his blood. When he was a child, the Studio had been his second home. He had trained as a film editor – working on the *Dragnet* television series and on Disney's True-Life Adventures – before going on to produce nature movies and television movies of his own. He had grown up watching legendary animators like Fred Moore, Ward Kimball, and Norm Ferguson at work, and he had listened to his uncle discuss and describe upcoming projects with Walt's habitual enthusiasm and dramatic flair. Roy Disney knew a good deal about the possibilities of animated film and about the resilience of the Disney tradition.

Most people in and around the feature animation department believe very strongly that Roy Disney deserves credit for saving Disney animation from possible extinction. Certainly, he took control of the department when it was at its artistic and commercial nadir, nursed it back to health, and helped boost it to new creative heights. Had he not stepped forward at the critical moment, it is conceivable that executives whose backgrounds were exclusively in live-action films might eventually have decided that the animation department was a costly luxury the Studio could no longer afford.

"Roy was the hero," says producer Don Hahn. "Without him there might never have been *Beauty and the Beast* or *Aladdin*. He believed in animation, he understood it, and he fought for it."

Disney himself admits to having had some early doubts about the wisdom of his choice.

"The first thing I did," he recalls, "was to run the production reel of *The Black Cauldron*, which was close to being finished. I had heard there were problems, of course, but I wasn't prepared for what I saw. I looked at it and knew we were in deep trouble. There were bits that worked on their own, but they didn't hang together. The story got lost partway into the movie, and the movie was dark in an unrelieved kind of way, without the kind of light relief that's needed to make the bad guys palatable."

One of Michael Eisner's first executive acts had been to appoint Jeffrey Katzenberg – former head of production at Paramount – to the position of chairman of Walt Disney Pictures. It would be Katzenberg's responsibility, in tandem with Roy Disney, to determine the future of feature animation.

Top: When Michael Eisner became chairman of the Walt Disney Company, he set about reorganizing the Studio and transformed it into an entertainment industry giant. Center: As president of the Walt Disney Company, Frank Wells proved to be a skillful financial strategist, helping to lay the groundwork for the company's growth in the 1980s and 1990s. Bottom: Jeffrey Katzenberg played a key role in the renaissance of Disney feature animation during his decade as studio head

Like Disney, Katzenberg screened the production reel of *The Black Cauldron* and, like Disney, he was horrified by what he saw. Drawing on his experience with live-action movies, he announced that he would take the expensive production (it had cost about twenty-five million dollars at that point) into the editing room and recut it. Katzenberg did not realize (or perhaps care) that such a notion was looked on as sacrilege in animation circles. As explained in chapter 2, an animated movie is laid out on storyboards and preedited by layout artists and scene planners before animation ever begins. The idea that an executive would have the effrontery to *cut* a Disney animated feature seemed almost scandalous, and it appeared to augur badly for the future of the department. If the new regime was capable of committing such crimes against the nature of the medium, how could it be expected to support animation in the future?

In reality, it was the animation department that had created the monster. Katzenberg was merely trying to save what he could of a sizable investment in the only way he knew how.

"We had to get in there with a scalpel," he says. "I know this was very disturbing for some people, and I understood this, but I was not imposing my personal values on what [the animators] should or shouldn't be doing. I was responding to what I saw as our responsibility to the consumers – to the members of the public who vote at the box office."

Katzenberg managed to trim two or three minutes from the film, but it was too late to alter the overall conception.

Filmed in 70mm and released in the summer of 1985, *The Black Cauldron* received generally unfavorable reviews and did poor business. It does have its admirers, but few of them come from among the ranks of the artists who worked on the movie, most of whom look back on the production as a fiasco they would rather forget. It is difficult to find much to defend in the ineptness of the storytelling. The Horned King is a decidedly two-dimensional villain. There is little consistency about the character design, and the movie is weighed down by an excess of quasi-mythological claptrap. That said, however, it remains a watershed in the Disney canon if only because it represents an elevation of ambition on the part of the young animation artists.

The new regime did not close down the animation department, but it did move the animators out of the hallowed 1940 Animation Building, where most of the classics had been produced, and into a cavernous industrial structure several miles away in Glendale. (In time, the department would come to occupy several buildings in the industrial complex that was already home to the Imagineers of the Disney theme parks.)

"It seemed like a kind of warning," says Andreas Deja. "The old Animation Building was being turned over to live-action production. That was a signal that live action was to be the Studio's bread and butter. We were being sent out into the wilderness and told that it was time to get our act together. But at least we were given a chance."

It would have been a tragedy if the future of Disney animation had been determined by the failure of *The Black Cauldron*. In actuality, there was no immediate danger of this since Eisner had promised Roy Disney that feature animation would have its opportunity to prove itself. Even before *Cauldron* was released, Disney and Katzenberg had given the green light to another project. In 1982, when *The Black Cauldron* began to show signs of endemic chaos, several artists had asked to be taken off the production and were given the go-ahead to develop a project titled *Basil of Baker Street,* based on the book of the same name by Eve Titus. The principals behind this project were two veterans of the story department (Burny Mattinson and Dave Michener) and two relative newcomers who would play major roles in the animation renaissance (John Musker and Ron Clements). All four would receive director's credit.

Because production of *The Black Cauldron* was so attenuated, members of the *Basil of Baker Street* team had an unusual amount of time to hone their story so that what Katzenberg and Disney were presented with was a very complete and detailed set of storyboards. They liked what they saw and responded with cautious enthusiasm.

"What Jeffrey said," recalls Musker, "was, 'If you can make it in half the time you're used to, for half the money – go ahead.' "

Retitled *The Great Mouse Detective,* the movie was made on budget and in time to be released in July of 1986, just a year after *The Black Cauldron. The Great Mouse Detective* is a far less ambitious movie than its predecessor, but given its modest aims and budgetary restrictions, it is very successful – a thoroughly entertaining film that both pays tribute to earlier Disney masterpieces and points the way to triumphs still to come. Its only serious faults can be blamed largely on the cost cutting that had been demanded. The animation in a few scenes seems sloppy, as if it had been done hurriedly, and there are even instances of backgrounds occupied by static (nonanimated) figures.

Still, *The Great Mouse Detective* is enlivened by some excellent character animation – by the likes of Mark Henn, Glen Keane, Ruben Aquino, and Rob Minkoff – and displays many merits, not the least of which is an emphasis on storytelling that harks back to the glory days.

The story pits a mouse detective called Basil (not without Holmes-like mannerisms) and his sidekick, Dr. Dawson, against the archvillain Ratigan (splendidly realized around the perfectly cast voice of Vincent Price). Aided by Fidget – a peg-legged bat with a sadistic sense of humor – and assorted thugs, Ratigan schemes to kidnap Queen Moustoria and replace her with a clockwork dummy. To build this robot, Ratigan has kidnapped Hiram Flaversham, a master toymaker. It is Flaversham's daughter, Olivia, who begs Basil to take on the case of her father's disappearance. The characters they encounter during their adventures include a sappy hound called Toby (supposedly belonging to Sherlock Holmes himself), an overfed feline executioner named Felicia, and assorted riverfront ne'er-do-wells.

All of these characters, even the minor ones, are well drawn, with Ratigan and Fidget making memorable additions to the ranks of Disney bad guys. Just as importantly, they are woven into a well-thought-out plot that moves forward briskly, never loses sight of where it is going, and is eventually resolved in an entirely satisfactory manner. The movie is full of snappy dialogue and witty sight gags – the latter sometimes more

Made on a low budget, *The Great Mouse Detective,* 1986, proved to be a lively entertainment with strong characters and plenty of humor well integrated into the plot. It demonstrated that Disney feature animation was over its crisis and headed in the right direction. The panoramic layout drawing (center) is by Gil de Cicco

The climactic scene of *The Great Mouse Detective* made use of computer-generated imagery to bring to life the gears and escapements of the mechanism that drives London's Big Ben

reminiscent of vintage Warner Brothers cartoons than of earlier Disney features. It's true to say, in fact, that the new generation of animators had grown up admiring Looney Toons along with the Disney classics, and they were anxious to graft a hipper kind of humor onto the Disney main stem. (Disney had had its share of hip humorists – Ward Kimball, for one – but the wisecrack and the off-the-wall sight gag had found their true home at Warners, where they were nurtured by Chuck Jones, Friz Freleng, Bob McKimson, and others.)

The Great Mouse Detective also featured fine atmospheric backgrounds (some harking back to those painted for *Pinocchio*) and inventive camera work (which is another way of saying that the layout department was making a valuable contribution to the drama and texture of the movie). If the nine old men had come to emphasize character animation at the expense of everything else, the hungry young men and women who succeeded them looked for a new balance in which all departments made a major contribution to telling the story. In this regard, *The Great Mouse Detective* anticipated the major achievements of the Disney feature renaissance.

The film includes one spectacular sequence that depends in part on computer-generated animation. The Studio had had some experience with computer animation in the live-action science-fiction movie *Tron,* which appeared in 1982, but that was outside the feature animation department. The climax of *The Great Mouse Detective* takes place in the clock tower of the Houses of Parliament, with Basil, Olivia, and Ratigan dodging one another along with the cogs, flywheels, gears, and counterweights that drive the clock known to the world as Big Ben. It's a sequence that recalls the splendid 1937 Mickey Mouse short *Clock Cleaners,* but this time the machinery was animated with the aid of a computer, and the result was a mechanical ballet of a complexity and precision that greatly enhances the drama of the moment.

The Great Mouse Detective is a small-scale production, but – like *Dumbo,* another small-scale production – it is consistently entertaining and ultimately satisfying. The public responded to the movie and it turned a respectable profit. The feature animation department having justified its continued existence, new projects were put into development.

Peter Schneider – a young man with a strong theater background – was recruited by Roy Disney to run the department on a day-to-day basis, with the title senior vice president of feature animation. (In 1991 he became president of feature animation.) This was a crucial appointment because, for all the talent it contained, the department had been lacking in hands-on leadership. Schneider provided that leadership and brought a sense of focus. His sound theatrical instincts were soon felt at story meetings and other creative forums, but beyond that he became the person who adjudicated disputes, made difficult decisions, appointed personnel to key positions, soothed sore egos, and generally kept the wheels oiled so that animators and other artists could get on with making movies to the best of their ability.

With Schneider in place, the feature animation department was no longer dissipating its energies. It was he who, with Roy Disney's support, guided the department to the point where it was ready to produce master-pieces like *The Little Mermaid* and *Beauty and the Beast*. And when feature animation became glamorous once more, and immensely profitable, it was Schneider who kept the department on an even keel, shielding it from understandable pressures to increase production at almost any cost and making sure that everyone felt part of its tremendous success.

All this was happening in California, but meanwhile an astonishing Disney project – partly live action but predicated on an acceptance of the universe created by animation – was under way in London.

Film rights to Gary K. Wolf's 1981 book *Who Censored Roger Rabbit?* had been purchased by the Studio's former management. Michael Eisner and Jeffrey Katzenberg looked over the property and were intrigued by the possibilities of a movie in which human actors and cartoon characters consorted together in a never-never land version of Los Angeles. It occurred to them that it was the kind of project that might interest director/producer Steven Spielberg.

Spielberg was fascinated by the idea but said that he would become involved only if he could be guaranteed that the interaction between live-action footage and animation would be seamless and completely naturalistic. Until then, moviemakers who had combined live and ani-mated elements – in *Mary Poppins,* for example – had always shot the live-action elements with a locked-off camera (one anchored to the floor to prevent movement). This greatly simplified the task of combining the diverse elements, but it led to stilted filmmaking. Spielberg insisted that *Who Framed Roger Rabbit* (as the film was eventually called) would have to be made without sacrificing camera flexibility to the needs of animation. He also wanted to see cushions that sagged beneath the imaginary weight of cartoon figures and other instances of interactive naturalism that would make it believable that "toons" could visit our world and that humans could visit Toontown.

Animated characters had been combined with live actors before, but never as effectively as in *Who Framed Roger Rabbit,* 1988

Robert Zemeckis was selected to direct the proposed movie. In London, he discussed the project with the Canadian-born animation director Richard Williams – a legendary figure in the animation world – who was well known to and admired by the Disney animators. Williams had come to the attention of Zemeckis and Spielberg by way of fifteen minutes of animation he had produced, over a period of more than twenty years, for a movie titled *The Thief and the Cobbler*. At first, Williams expressed strong misgivings about *Roger Rabbit* but finally told Zemeckis that he felt the film could be made – if they threw the rule book out.

"We agreed that the key to making the combination work," says Williams, "would be interaction. We thought the cartoon characters should always be affecting their environment or getting tangled up with the live actors."

Williams told Zemeckis that he should just go ahead and shoot the movie the way he would shoot any movie, with fluid camera movements that did not take the animator's problems into account. It would be the animation crew's responsibility to make the cartoons fit into the live-action continuum.

The basic process was somewhat as follows. Scenes that involved both animated and live-action characters were storyboarded, just as for an animated movie. These storyboards were used as a guide for building sets and props and then for directing the live performers (who had to pretend that they were interacting with the cartoon characters). Photostat blowups were made of each frame of live action, and the animators matched their drawings to these photostats, in much the same way that they would normally match them to a layout. The resulting animation drawings could be integrated with the live action with the invaluable help of the optical-effects wizards at George Lucas's Industrial Light and Magic facility.

Not that it was quite that simple. The animation had to mesh precisely with the live action, otherwise it would have been totally unconvincing. It had to be integrated with physical effects and with complicated behavior on the part of the human performers. (Think of the scenes in which

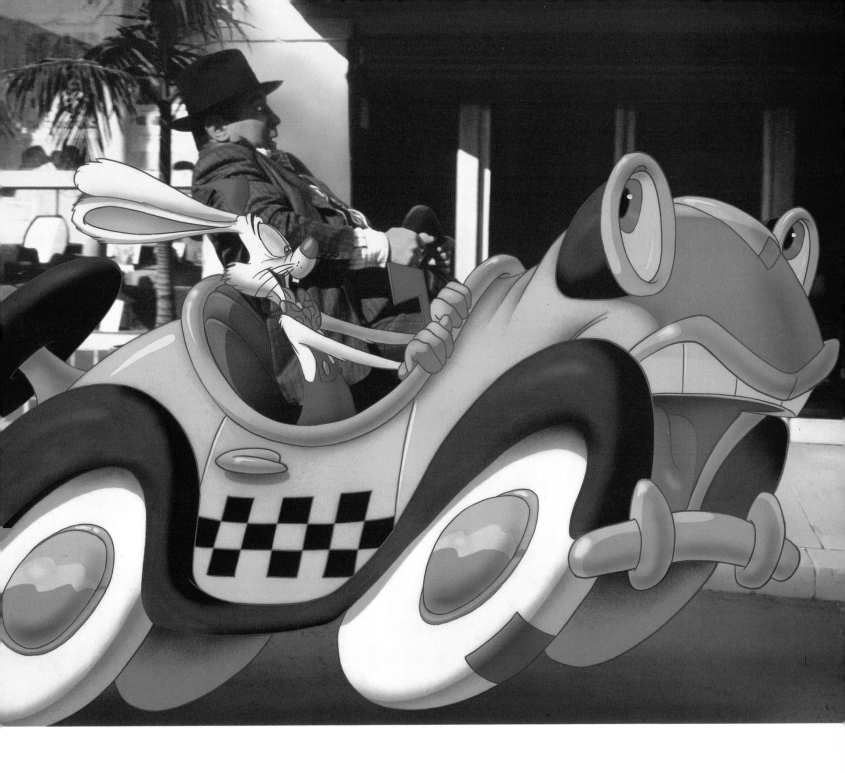

Who Framed Roger Rabbit, 1988, is an astonishing tour de force in which an international team of animators, led by Richard Williams, invented new ways to combine animation with live action so that director Robert Zemeckis could use his actors as flexibly as he would in an all live-action film. In this scene, Roger takes a ride with Eddie Valiant (Bob Hoskins)

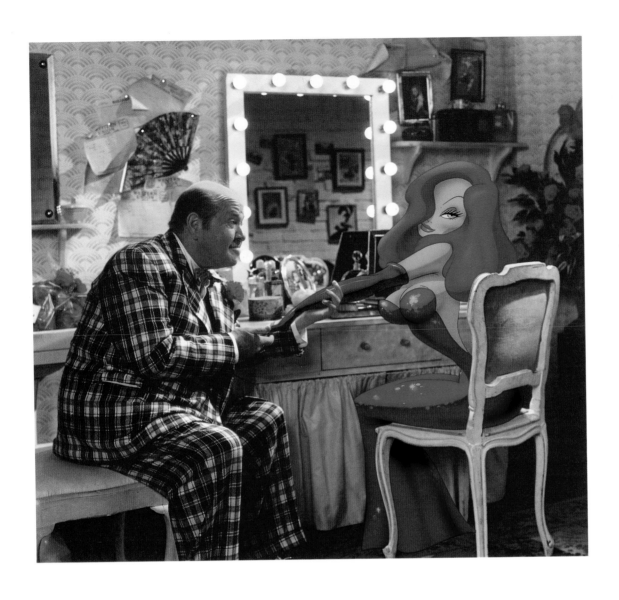

A larger than life presence in *Who Framed Roger Rabbit* is Roger's wife Jessica who proves to be more than a match for the characters played by Stubby Kaye (above) and Bob Hoskins

No more of a cartoon than some Hollywood
actresses of the 1940s and 1950s, Jessica is
pivotal in the artful balancing act that permits
animated and live action characters to interact.
As the Ink & Paint Club's resident chanteuse,
she leaves toons swooning and human customers
thoroughly confused

Overleaf: Traveling in their vintage
Black Maria, Judge Doom's weasel sidekicks
terrorize Toontown

Who Framed Roger Rabbit is full of cartoon gags translated into live-action language, and vice versa

Roger and Eddie Valiant, played by Bob Hoskins, are handcuffed together.) Far from seeking out ways of making things easier for itself, Williams's animation team deliberately created technical problems, always with the idea of emphasizing the interaction between live action and animation. Almost every scene contains some virtuoso touch, and often those touches are used less to move the plot along than to persuade the audience to believe in the reality of this world where toons and humans coexist (if not always peaceably).

The scene for *Who Framed Roger Rabbit* is set by a one-reel cartoon titled *Somethin's Cookin'*, starring Roger and Baby Herman, which has been assigned a fictitious 1947 release date. It is the ultimate parody of the Bugs Bunny/Tweety & Sylvester/Tom & Jerry/Woody Woodpecker/Popeye genre of cartoon short, a brilliant pastiche with more tasteless gags per second than a Friars' Club roast. From the moment it hits the screen, the audience knows that it is in the province of artists who know Mickey Mouse's white gloves – and Wile E. Coyote's paws – as well as they know the backs of their own hands.

The plot of the movie that follows this "Maroon Cartoon" is predicated on the fact that Roger believes that his wife Jessica (one of the sexiest cartoon characters ever) may be having an affair with Marvin Acme (a human played by Stubby Kaye), the gagman and real estate mogul who happens to own Toontown. This initial premise tells how tangled the two worlds are in this movie, and soon we learn that the all-too-human Eddie Valiant, the Chandleresque private eye called in to keep an eye on Jessica, has a grudge against toons because his brother was killed when a toon dropped a piano on his head.

Soon, Valiant and his allies – toons and otherwise – are pitted against Judge Doom (Christopher Lloyd) and his gang of toon thugs. Roger, it turns out, has been set up as the fall guy in Doom's plan to dissolve

Toontown with a toon-obliterating chemical called Dip. The evil judge – a very toonlike human – has already done away with the city's public transportation system (LA's beloved Red Cars), and now he wants to redevelop the site of Toontown as a commercial area that will take advantage of the route of a new freeway.

It's a story, in short, about big business attempting to raze the ghetto in order to generate more big business. This time, though, the ghetto dwellers are toons, and they come with a special set of values and physical abilities that sometimes works in their favor and sometimes works against them. In addition to Roger, Jessica, and Baby Herman, toons developed for the movie include Benny the Cab, Lena Hyena, Bongo the doorman, a spectacular octopus bartender, and the weasely members of Doom's Toon Patrol. All of these characters are splendidly realized and feel as if they belong in our collective memory of the cartoons of the Golden Age. This is just as well since they share the screen with an amazing array of genuine cartoon characters of that period, including – in bit parts and cameo roles – Daffy Duck, Daisy Duck, Donald Duck, Clarabelle Cow, Elmer Fudd, Goofy, Snow White, Speedy Gonzales, Betty Boop, Pinocchio, Foghorn Leghorn, Tinker Bell, Sylvester, Ferdinand the Bull, Bugs Bunny, Dumbo, Clara Cluck, Pluto, the Seven Dwarfs, José Carioca, Woody Woodpecker, Yosemite Sam, Bambi, and many others, not forgetting Mickey and Minnie.

Who Framed Roger Rabbit is an astonishing technical achievement. It is also an amazingly coherent and entertaining film, which enjoyed a great deal of well-deserved box-office success when it was released in 1988. Much of the credit should go to Zemeckis, to the screenplay by Jeffrey Price and Peter Seaman, and to the human performers, especially Bob Hoskins, who displayed an exceptional talent for being able to interact convincingly with cartoons. Still, it would be impossible to overstate the contribution of Richard Williams (who deservedly received an Academy Award for his work on the movie) and his animation crew. It was this team that made *Who Framed Roger Rabbit* the unique cinematic experience that it is.

Even if only a relatively small part of that team came from the Disney animation department – most of the animation was done in London – *Roger Rabbit* is still very much a Disney product. Although fiercely independent, Williams has been a lifelong admirer of the Disney school of animation, maintaining a close relationship over the years with men like Milt Kahl, Frank Thomas, Ollie Johnston, Art Babbitt, and Grim Natwick. This was his opportunity to make his own idiosyncratic contribution to the canon.

Its intrinsic merit apart, *Roger Rabbit* was very important for the future of Disney animation. It was a gigantic success, and it helped reestablish a bond, in the minds of moviegoers, between the Disney name and truly innovative animation. It could not have come along at a better time.

The new management team, meanwhile, was learning about animation and becoming enthusiastic about its future. It was even introducing certain innovations, such as placing an emphasis on the importance of having a screenplay.

In the early days of feature animation, the script had been something that had taken shape largely in Walt Disney's head, with the aid of storyboard artists who worked on the movie scene by scene but had little to say about the overall structure. Later, as Walt began to divide his time between animated features and other projects, the storyboard artists came more fully into their own. After Walt's death, plots evolved on storyboards as a kind of team effort that involved the director (usually Woolie Reitherman), the storyboard artists, and the principal character animators. A single writer – Larry Clemmons – was involved in the process (up to *The Fox and the Hound*), but he had been at the studio since the 1930s and thought like a storyboard artist.

Michael Eisner and Jeffrey Katzenberg came from a live-action background. They were familiar with storyboards as ways of planning, for example, expensive special-effects sequences, but not as a way of generating an entire film. They insisted on screenplays being produced along with the boards (even ahead of the boards), feeling that this would give them the means to come to terms with any given production.

Had they emphasized the screenplay as an *alternative* to storyboards, the results might have been disastrous. The action of an animated movie needs to be developed in primarily visual terms. In fact, the old storyboard methods were left untouched, and the screenplay was used as an adjunct to boards. This proved to be an entirely positive idea since it helped put the emphasis back on carefully thought-out storytelling.

Oliver & Company (1988), the animated feature that followed *The Great Mouse Detective*, was the first to give separate screenplay and story credits. In reality, the story artists and the writers worked together very closely, following a pattern that has little to do with the way live-action movies are scripted. Under the supervision of director George Scribner, more than twenty people contributed story ideas to *Oliver & Company*. At the end of their labors, the story was laid out in two forms – as a set of several dozen boards and as a much more compact screenplay. Each served its own purpose, yet each reinforced the value of the other.

The system was in its early days when *Oliver & Company* went into production, and, in fact, *Oliver* is not as fully realized, from a story point of view, as *The Great Mouse Detective* had been. Loosely based on Charles Dickens's *Oliver Twist*, the screenplay presents Oliver as an orphan kitten and Dodger and the other gang members as canines. Fagin and Sykes (*sic*) are human, though Sykes has animal alter egos in the form of a pair of vicious Dobermans. The setting has been changed from Victorian London to modern-day New York City.

Oliver & Company is notable for the large amount of computer-generated animation – by Michael Cedeno and Tina Price – used to bring to life such elements as cars, construction equipment, and the New York

With its mixture of human and canine protagonists, *Oliver & Company*, 1988, depended on the skills of character animators like Ruben Aquino (top), but the production also made a good deal of use of computer-generated animation, employed to create elements such as automobiles and urban landscapes

subway system. In and of itself, this computer animation is often brilliant, but at times it becomes intrusive and through overuse is allowed to interrupt the narrative flow. Later Disney features would use computer-generated imagery more discreetly and more effectively.

All in all, *Oliver & Company* is a lively movie, if a little awkward and overly cute at times. It contains some fine character animation by the likes of Glen Keane, Ruben Aquino, Mike Gabriel, and Mark Henn, and a mixed bunch of songs enthusiastically performed by a remarkable array of big-name vocalists, including Ruben Blades, Billy Joel, Huey Lewis, Ruth Pointer, and Bette Midler.

One of the *Oliver & Company* songs was written by Howard Ashman, best known at that time for his work on the long-running off-Broadway and Broadway hit *Little Shop of Horrors* (later turned into a movie directed by Frank Oz). Recruited for *Oliver* by Peter Schneider, who had worked for the company that managed *Little Shop of Horrors,* Ashman and his songwriting partner Alan Menken soon attracted the attention of Jeffrey Katzenberg.

"David Geffen was in the middle of producing *Little Shop of Horrors,*" Katzenberg explains, "and when he heard we were using an Ashman song in *Oliver & Company,* he said to me, 'Howard and Alan are geniuses. They love Disney animation and I think you should meet them.'"

Katzenberg did meet them, was greatly impressed, and soon Ashman and Menken were asked to become involved with the Studio's next animated project, *The Little Mermaid,* based on the Hans Christian Andersen story, which was at an advanced stage of preparation with John Musker and Ron Clements slated as codirectors.

"We didn't know much about Howard," says Clements, "except that we liked *Little Shop*. Our first contact with him, I think, was a memo about Sebastian. Sebastian is a crab, and perhaps a little pompous. The way we had developed the story up to that point, Sebastian was probably going to be cast with an English accent. Howard's memo said 'How about making Sebastian a Rastafarian?'"

At first, the idea seemed mildly preposterous – even arbitrary – but in practice it made a great deal of sense because it gave the character a novel personality, and it permitted Ashman and Menken to introduce a couple of lively West Indian numbers into the movie. One of these – "Under the Sea" – went on to win an Academy Award.

Once they had met with Ashman, Musker and Clements were completely won over.

"He knew the Disney films," says Musker, "and he had an encyclopedic knowledge of American musicals. What's more, he showed us how what works for the musical can be made to work for the animated film. Walt understood that, of course – look at *Snow White* – but it was Howard more than anyone who taught it to our generation."

The outcome of all this was that Ashman became the film's co-producer, along with Musker, spending three weeks out of four in Glendale, working on his lyrics but also sitting in on story meetings and sweatbox sessions and contributing to the evolution of the movie in a score of ways.

The Little Mermaid, 1989, was the first Disney animated feature in almost thirty years to tackle a classic fairy tale. It was also the first film produced by the new generation of animation artists to capture fully the imagination of both audience and critics. In this sketch by Bruce Morris, Ariel – the heroine – is shown eluding a pursuing shark

This conceptual painting by Rowland B. Williams was one of many inspirational works produced to help establish the mood of *The Little Mermaid*

Musker and Clements, meanwhile – with the help of art directors Michael A. Peraza, Jr., and Donald A. Towns – imposed a distinctive look on the production that is especially effective in the undersea sequences. Inspiration came from a variety of sources, including pastels by Kay Nielsen, an artist who had contributed to the visual development of the *Night on Bald Mountain* episode of *Fantasia*. In the early forties, Nielsen had storyboarded ideas for two features based on Andersen stories, and these story concept pastels, which had been preserved in the Walt Disney Archives, provided a useful starting point.

Despite this nod to the past, however, Musker, Clements, and Ashman worked hard to make the characters contemporary, even in a period setting. Ariel (who was cast with the voice of Jodi Benson) was not the first spunky Disney heroine, but she was the first one who talked the language of today's teenagers and who expressed herself in ways that post-Beatles adolescents could identify with. Ursula (Pat Carroll), the principal villain of the piece, was portrayed with a self-aware campiness that would have been unthinkable in Disney films even a few years earlier. (The old features are full of campy characters, but – with the possible exception of Cruella De Vil – the campiness is never explicitly acknowledged, as it is with Ursula.)

Although characters like Ariel, Ursula, and Sebastian are treated in a distinctly contemporary manner, the movie plot stays reasonably close to Andersen's tale of the mermaid who falls in love with a human, though the screenplay provides the story with a happy ending that is far from the spirit of the original. Given the conventions of the Disney animated feature (or the conventions of the Broadway musical, for that matter), such a happy ending is acceptable. In this instance, it falls a little flat only because Eric, the human object of Ariel's affections, is boring and two dimensional compared with her. For that matter, the scenes aboard Eric's sailing vessel, and in his Ruritanian kingdom, don't measure up to those that take place beneath the waves.

Ariel rescues Eric

Despite its flaws, the movie never loses the audience, thanks to a wonderful theatricality that must be looked on as Ashman's gift to the evolving Disney animation renaissance (a gift eagerly accepted by Musker and Clements). *The Little Mermaid* unfolds like a great Broadway musical, with Ashman's lyrics and Menken's melodies moving the narrative along with wit and ease. That said, it is important to note that the Disney animation team, under the leadership of Musker and Clements, was able to rise to the occasion. For the most part, the character animation is excellent, and the movie represents an important stage in the resurgence of effects animation. The visual effects department, under the direction of Mark Dindal, was involved in a great majority of the scenes and was given several opportunities to shine, notably in the storm sequences.

Musker and Clements continued the efforts of the new generation of artists to use the whole arsenal of the animation department in the storytelling process. *The Little Mermaid* even involved a handful of multiplane shots.

"We didn't realize quite how expensive and time-consuming they were," says Musker. "And we found that the Studio's old multiplane rig was in poor shape and difficult to use. We ended up farming out most of the multiplane shots to an outside facility."

The effort to use every device available is clearly felt throughout the production, and it supports the fine animation, sound storytelling, and memorable songs in making a movie that deservedly enjoyed great popular and critical success when it was released in November of 1989. For the first time since the 1950s, film professionals and filmgoers alike were talking about a Disney animated feature as something that was more than just another entertaining continuation of the tradition that had begun with *Snow White and the Seven Dwarfs*. Like *Snow White, The Little*

Written by lyricist and producer Howard Ashman (left) and composer Alan Menken, the musical numbers for *The Little Mermaid* (overleaf) helped make the movie an instant animated classic. They would have crucial roles to play in the Disney animation renaissance

The Little Mermaid was marked by art direction reminiscent of Disney animation's first golden age, as exemplified (top) by this background painting by Donald Towns. Also featured were strong supporting characters such as Sebastian (center), and a larger-than-life villainess in the person of Ursula the sea witch

Mermaid has a real sense of magic about it. It reminded people that animation can do things that no other medium can do, and it gave notice that Disney had a new team of artists who understood how to tap into the old wizardry while bringing their own baby-boomer generation sensibility into play.

In one sense, though, *The Little Mermaid* was the last movie of an era – the last feature to be made by the principal Disney animation unit that depended upon hand-painted cels (as modified by the use of xerography that had been standard for almost three decades). The next film to come out of Glendale would employ a totally different system.

In the meantime, however, *DuckTales: The Movie* was in production in various corners of the globe, a movie that was storyboarded, laid out, and art directed in California but animated in France and England, while the cels were painted and photographed in China. (To differentiate it from the classic animated features, it would be released as a Disney Movietoon.)

A spinoff of the *DuckTales* television series, launched in 1987 (see chapter 14), which was inspired by the marvelous Scrooge McDuck comic books created for Disney by Carl Barks, *DuckTales: The Movie* (subtitled *Treasure of the Lost Lamp*) is an animated spoof on the *Raiders of the Lost Ark* type of movie – itself, of course, a spoof of the forties-era Saturday morning serial. The film is hardly a masterpiece, but it is a good deal better than might be gathered from reading the reviews that appeared when the film was released in the summer of 1990. The animation is more than adequate and the action moves along briskly. The production's chief weakness is that the structure of the story is rather sloppy, so that the movie feels like an overextended television episode rather than a true feature.

Far more interesting is *The Rescuers Down Under*, a 1990 sequel to the 1977 adaptation of Margery Sharp's Bianca stories, with Eva Gabor and Bob Newhart once again providing the voices for Miss Bianca and her friend Bernard. *The Rescuers Down Under* can be seen as an attempt to cash in on the popularity of Paul Hogan's *Crocodile Dundee* and things Australian in general. Whether or not this is so, *The Rescuers Down Under* is a modest but generally satisfying movie, though in overall concept it belongs to the middle-period style of Disney feature rather than to the more theatrical style of the era inaugurated by *The Little Mermaid*.

Set largely in the Australian outback, the story centers on a boy named Cody who is friends with the animals, notably Marahute, a giant golden eagle. Meanwhile, a poacher named Percival McLeach is trapping protected wild animals. When Cody stumbles into one of McLeach's traps, the poacher finds an eagle feather in the boy's possession. Thinking that Cody will lead him to the eagle, McLeach kidnaps the boy and makes it appear that Cody has been eaten by crocodiles. A mouse, saved by Cody, reports what has happened, and the news is conveyed to New York by way of the Rescue Aid Society's ham-operator telegraph system.

Two of the architects of Disney's animation revival are Peter Schneider (left), president of feature animation, and Roy E. Disney, Walt's nephew, who many insiders credit as being the savior of the animation department he has headed since 1984

One of the top animators of the younger generation is Andreas Deja, who has helped create some of the Studio's outstanding villains

The Rescuers Down Under, 1990, was conceived as a continuation of the adventures of Miss Bianca and Bernard. This skillfully made movie, which takes the altruistic mice to Australia, has not received the attention it deserves, perhaps because the story harks back to the middle-period kind of Disney feature, and the production as a whole is less rooted in musical theater than the studio's more recent successes.

In one important way *The Rescuers Down Under* looked forward rather than backward. This was the first film in which Disney's CAPS technology was employed. CAPS is a computerized production system that permits handmade animation drawings to be copied and colored electronically (eliminating the need for cels). It also allows different elements of an image to be combined in elaborate ways that formerly would have been almost impossible. CAPS does not generate animation, but it enables hand-drawn animated imagery to be manipulated in new ways, greatly enhancing production values. It can, for example, be used as a very sophisticated multiplane camera, as was the case in the restaurant scene, overleaf

That brings Bianca and Bernard to the rescue. They travel to Australia with the help of an albatross named Wilbur (the brother of Orville from the first *Rescuers* movie). Once there, they join forces with a resourceful kangaroo mouse named Jake, and McLeach's fate is sealed.

Directed by Hendel Butoy and Mike Gabriel and produced by Tom Schumacher, *The Rescuers Down Under* is notable for its strong character animation and imaginative staging of scenes. In the latter regard, the movie was greatly aided by the advent of the Studio's Academy Award–winning CAPS system.

CAPS is a sophisticated computer system dedicated to the task of managing and enhancing animation material. It is not used to generate animation: characters and effects are still drawn by hand, frame by frame. Rather, CAPS takes existing animation drawings and effects and backgrounds and combines them so that they can be seen in video form. It also provides the means to color the images electronically (only the backgrounds are colored with brush and paint). The CAPS system therefore replaces the old ink and paint department, and is operated by former members of that department who were retrained to work at computer workstations, bringing their years of expertise with them.

Enormously expensive, the CAPS system was fought for by Roy Disney and was justified economically because it would speed up production and save money in the postproduction phase. At the same time, it enabled the directors to plan far more complex shots and camera moves. With CAPS there was theoretically no limit to the number of planes or levels of animation that could be included in a single shot. Not only could the CAPS system replace the multiplane camera, it could do its work far more cheaply and with far greater efficiency.

Most significantly, CAPS eliminated cels since it generated finished imagery that could be transferred directly to film, frame by frame.

The use of CAPS in *The Rescuers Down Under* was somewhat tentative since the filmmakers were just beginning to familiarize themselves with the system and could only learn the full extent of its possibilities as they worked with it. Those possibilities are signaled, however, in sequences such as Cody's flight aboard Marahute. CAPS was an important new tool – an amazing electronic paintbrush – and with this system in place, the stage was fully set for the Disney animation renaissance.

11   A Second Flowering

By the end of the decade, there were no longer any doubts about the
new regime's devotion to the future of animation. Michael Eisner and
Frank Wells were clearly aware of the value of the medium to the Studio,
both for its own sake and as a way of generating secondary revenues
(everything from books to games to clothing to new attractions in the
Disney theme parks). Roy Disney was stalwart in his support of the
feature animation department, which Peter Schneider continued to
guide, and Jeffrey Katzenberg had become an enthusiastic hands-on
participant in the process of developing animation projects. It was
in this context that Walt Disney's dream of producing one animated
feature a year was revived.

The efficiency of the CAPS system made the realization of this dream
possible. In order to approach that goal, however, it was necessary to
expand the staff. Talented animators, layout artists, and background
painters were eagerly recruited, and by the time *The Rescuers Down
Under* was released, in November of 1990, feature animation had
spread into several buildings scattered around the same Glendale
industrial park. In addition, there was now a branch of the feature
animation division in Florida where animators and other artists worked
in public view at the Disney-MGM Studios, part of the Walt Disney
World Resort near Orlando (see chapter 17). Far from being just
a sideshow, the Florida unit would play a significant role in many

subsequent feature films, eventually originating its own productions, starting with *Mulan* (1998).

Introduction of the CAPS system was not the only way in which execution had been streamlined. More effective use of manpower also played a major role. Top-flight character animators are rare commodities and in the past they had not always been used in the most efficient way. In the old days, these stars would often labor over drawings until they were almost perfect, so that cleanup artists had only to smooth a line here and erase a slip of the pencil there before the drawing was ready to go to ink and paint.

By the early nineties, all this had changed. It was recognized that the top character animators needed only to produce relatively rough drawings so long as someone else could turn these "ruffs" into CAPS-ready finished art work. The modern cleanup artist does far more than polish existing drawings. He or she takes the character animator's "ruff" as a starting point and actually creates a new, highly finished drawing that retains the feel of the original. Key cleanup artists are also responsible for making sure that characters do not vary in different scenes from the demands of the model sheet. Clearly this requires a different kind of talent – and an important one since it permits the principal character animators to work faster and to farm out more work to less experienced associates. The cleanup keys can be relied upon to iron out differences between the styles of one animator and another.

At its height, the cleanup department, then headed by Vera Lampher, numbered almost one hundred artists. It was their drawings – recorded and colored by CAPS – that actually appeared on screen, and it was in large part due to them that Disney was able to issue animated features with a frequency unmatched since the early forties.

The first movie to take full advantage of CAPS and the streamlining of the feature animation department was a retelling of *Beauty and the Beast* – a film that deserves to be judged by the high standards of the early Disney classics. In fact, *Beauty and the Beast* almost was one of those early classics. Walt Disney had broached the idea of tackling the subject back in the forties – "Probably before *Cinderella*," according to Ollie Johnston's recollections – but had abandoned it when modifying the fairy tale's bleak second half had proved to be uncommonly difficult. The idea was revived forty years later and almost abandoned once more.

There was a desire at the Studio to tackle another movie based on a classic fairy tale. *Beauty and the Beast* seemed like a good candidate, and, after other writers had made a couple of false starts, Linda Woolverton produced a screenplay that succeeded in providing the basis for a viable movie. Don Hahn – fresh from working with Richard Williams on *Who Framed Roger Rabbit* – was assigned to produce, and the original concept called for the British-based American artist Richard Purdum to direct. In the summer of 1989, Hahn took a party of animators and art directors to Europe, where they visited the Loire Valley in France for

Beauty and the Beast, 1991, proved to be a difficult subject to bring to the screen and much preliminary art was produced to help establish plot, mood, and characters. The concept drawing of the Beast carrying Belle through the snow (opposite top) was made by Glen Keane, who would be the principal animator of the Beast. An early version of the story (opposite center) called for a somewhat naturalistic approach and Andreas Deja drew a Gaston who was far more foppish than he later became. The panoramic study (opposite below) was used to help visualize an opening sequence for *Beauty and the Beast* which was eventually abandoned.

Conceptual art by Hans Bacher (right) helped inspire the look and atmosphere of the film. Like other aspects of *Beauty and the Beast*, the character and appearance of Belle (below) evolved a good deal during the conceptual phase. This drawing is by Glen Keane

As the project developed, the Beast underwent radical changes, both physically and psychologically, as can be gathered from early concept drawings such as the examples by Chris Sanders shown here, opposite top

Howard Ashman's story influence led to the Beast's plight becoming pivotal to the story, which is not the case with earlier tellings. It was Ashman too who insisted on characters like Cogsworth, Lumiere, and Mrs. Potts being assigned major roles in order to prevent total gloom from setting in. Lively musical numbers featuring the castle's enchanted objects (overleaf) were introduced into the continuity to provide relief from the somberness of the central theme

In *Beauty and the Beast,* the story builds relentlessly toward its powerful climax. Dramatic as it is, Belle's confrontation with hungry wolves is just one of several sub-climaxes that help to heighten the tension. The Beast's inaccessible castle, below, is a symbol of his isolation

Gaston starts out as something of a comic fool, vain and vapid, but before *Beauty and the Beast* is over he proves to be among the most evil of all Disney villains

The Bimbettes are crazy about Gaston, but in this scene find themselves stuck with his sidekick LeFou

Vera Lanpher (top) is head of the cleanup department. Brenda Chapman (center) has been a key member of the story team for several features, including *Beauty and the Beast* and *The Lion King*. At bottom, directors Gary Trousdale (seated) and Kirk Wise (right), along with producer Don Hahn (rear), headed the team that brought *Beauty and the Beast* to the screen

inspiration and then spent several weeks in London working with Purdum, who, along with his wife Jill, had storyboarded the projected movie.

The Purdums' vision of the tale owed a good deal to classic versions such as that of Madame le Prince de Beaumont, as seen through the eyes of French painters such as Watteau, Fragonard, and Boucher. The boards they had prepared were turned into a story reel which was screened for Jeffrey Katzenberg, who found the approach led to a denouement that was relentlessly grim. This was just as *The Little Mermaid* was being completed, and the very evident qualities of that movie prompted Katzenberg to invite Howard Ashman and Alan Menken to join the *Beauty and the Beast* team.

Ashman met with Katzenberg, Roy Disney, Peter Schneider, Don Hahn, the Purdums, and other key participants and proposed plot changes that led to Linda Woolverton's spending time with him in New York rewriting the script. Ashman's approach emphasized the Beast's story (the unfortunate creature tends to be schematic in most tellings and hardly an object of sympathy). He also worked hard to make Belle more three dimensional, a flesh-and-blood young woman capable of carrying the plot through her passion rather than just a vapid symbol of conventional virtue. Thirdly, Ashman did away with the unmitigated gloom that had plagued the second act by creating prominent roles for members of the castle's staff, who come to effusive life despite having been turned into objects. (This idea was present in the earlier version, but it was Ashman who insisted that characters like Cogsworth, Lumiere, and Mrs. Potts should have fully developed personalities.) Ashman also demanded a larger-than-life villain to be pitted against both Belle and the Beast.

And, naturally, there would be Ashman and Menken songs.

Richard Purdum participated in these revisions but felt the project was turning into something too far from his vision for him to remain with it in good faith. He resigned and was succeeded, as director, by Gary Trousdale and Kirk Wise, known for their strong story skills (though Wise had started his career as an animator). Ashman took the title of executive producer.

The elements of the story began to fall into place, but there were still many other things to settle. The Beast's appearance, for example, would be crucial to the success of the film.

Glen Keane began thinking about that during the preproduction trip to London. Crossing Regent's Park on his daily walk to work, his attention was caught by the wolves loping around their compound at the edge of the London Zoo. Their powerful presence haunted him as he began to visualize the Beast. Inside the zoo, he found Boris, a boisterous mandrill whose facial structure fascinated him. Later, in the Los Angeles Zoo, he sketched Caesar, a 600-pound gorilla who hurled himself against the bars, again and again, in an attempt to frighten the artist.

"I kept reminding myself," says Keane, "that that was how Belle would see the Beast – as this huge, terrifying creature."

Working with animator and sculptor Ruben Procopio, Keane began to combine the characteristics of various animals – gorillas, wolves,

In the Beast's castle, Belle finds her father locked in a cell

mandrills, buffalo, wild boar – until he came up with the creature that eventually reached the screen, a beast whose emotions range from human sensitivity to brutish fury.

The Beast is a formidable creation, but Belle – as animated by a team of artists headed by James Baxter – is a worthy match for him. Her character is effectively spelled out during the opening musical number, at which time we see Belle going about her business in the village where she lives. Dark and faintly exotic-looking (story artist Chris Sanders contributed much to her final appearance), she is addicted to books but, though she enters into the romance of the tales she reads, we understand that she also has a solid, practical streak.

Almost immediately, we encounter Gaston, the villain of the piece, who at first comes across as an arrogant, macho bore (somewhat reminiscent of Brom Bones in *The Legend of Sleepy Hollow*, though with higher social aspirations) – an annoyance rather than a full-blown villain. This deception works well, since the audience is fooled into seeing him as something of a comic character; thus, the full force of his viciousness, revealed only at the movie's climax, comes as a complete surprise. Animated principally by Andreas Deja, Gaston has a unique place in the remarkable canon of Disney villains.

There are several other significant characters in the film, including LeFou (Gaston's clumsy sidekick), Maurice (Belle's inventor father), Mrs. Potts the housekeeper/teapot and her son/teacup Chip, Cogsworth the majordomo/clock, and Lumiere the butler/candelabra, all animated with skill and flair.

The miracle of *Beauty and the Beast* is that these satisfying characters are so effectively woven into the fabric of the story. Each has his or her proper weight within the narrative, and the comedy elements are used to counterbalance the tremendous force of emotion that emerges in the central relationship between Belle and the Beast. Everything seems to contribute to the momentousness of their encounters. Superb work by concept artists like Hans Bacher, by the layout department, the effects animators, the background painters, and especially the art director, Brian McEntee, helped turn the castle and the landscape that surrounds it into elements of the story as crucial as any of the characters. In *Beauty and the Beast,* the entire arsenal of animation techniques is used to drive the narrative.

Computer-generated imagery plays its role, notably in the ballroom scene when Belle and Beast dance through an enchanted environment that could not have been realized without the help of the computer. Meanwhile, the CAPS system permitted the use of camera setups of a complexity that could only have been dreamed of during Walt Disney's lifetime. Some of these setups might, in theory, have been possible before CAPS but they would have been prohibitively expensive to achieve. Others, such as many-layered multiplane shots, would have been physically impossible because of the limitations of conventional camera optics. In addition, CAPS supplied the means to orchestrate the color palette of the movie with a subtlety that had never been approached before.

The voice talent is outstanding, notably Paige O'Hara as Belle, Robby Benson as the Beast, Angela Lansbury as Mrs. Potts, David Ogden Stiers as Cogsworth, Jerry Orbach as Lumiere, and Richard White as Gaston. The songs (which take up almost a third of the running time of the movie) are superb, from the Oscar-winning title song to the memorable "Be Our Guest," as is Menken's score, which won another Academy Award.

All these elements help explain why the public flocked to *Beauty and the Beast,* making it the most commercially successful animated film ever to that point. Beyond the excellence of the components, however, the movie also carries an emotional punch that is astonishing for something that many people still refer to as a cartoon. It was this emotional power that helped pull in an adult audience to supplement the usual family viewers.

Beauty and the Beast appealed as much to dating couples as to kids. In all probability, this had something to do with the fact that the dating couples of the nineties have grown up with daily exposure to animation on television and are in no hurry to outgrow the medium. But that doesn't explain the fact that they came back to see this movie over and over again. The new generation of Disney artists had achieved their goal. They had produced a movie that could be matched against the classics, and they were rewarded with an Academy Award nomination in the category of Best Picture – the first time an animated film had been accorded this honor.

The Studio's next animated feature, *Aladdin,* would prove to be an even greater hit. Except for the element of commercial success, however,

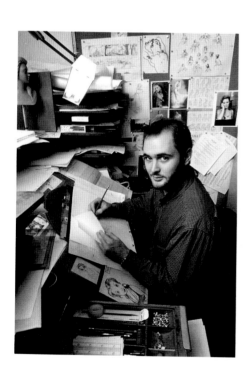

James Baxter headed the crew that animated Belle

One of the greatest challenges of *Aladdin*, 1992, was visualizing the transformations of the Genie, a task that generated thousands of inspirational drawings and storyboard sketches. The upper example is by Eric Goldberg, the lower by Gary Trousdale

Aladdin and *Beauty and the Beast* have very little in common. If *Beauty* depends for its impact upon its ability to plumb emotional highs and lows, *Aladdin* is all witty invention, stylization, and surface flash. That this is so reflects the Studio's determination to avoid the danger of repeating itself and to demonstrate that the new generation of artists is not wholly dependent on the example of its predecessors.

Aladdin evolved as the third directorial outing of John Musker and Ron Clements, who also produced and were the supervising writers. Howard Ashman and Alan Menken were involved once again and wrote six songs for the film (three were used in the final cut) before Ashman, who had been ill for some time, succumbed to AIDS. After his death, Tim Rice – lyricist of *Jesus Christ Superstar* and *Evita* – was brought in to write the remaining songs with Menken.

The basic story of Aladdin and his magic lamp is well known. As with all of their retellings of traditional tales, however, the Disney team looked for ways of making it applicable to a contemporary audience. Aladdin is a Robin Hood–like thief who, in the movie, develops a distinctly twentieth-century conscience. His love interest, the Princess Jasmine, is a spirited young woman with a mind of her own. Finally, it is she who will choose to marry Aladdin, rather than vice versa, and then only when he comes to terms with his problems and admits to his humble beginnings instead of trying to pass himself off as a prince.

In the end, though, conventional narrative is probably less important to *Aladdin* than to any other major Disney animated feature, with the obvious exception of *Fantasia*. Above all, *Aladdin* is a feast for the eyes leavened with wild flights of comedy and imagination.

Much of the look of *Aladdin* – especially in the area of character design – can be attributed to the arrival at the Studio of Eric Goldberg. Like Richard Williams and Richard Purdum, Goldberg had been born in the New World but had achieved success in London, where he headed Pizazz Pictures, a studio that made some of the cleverest animated com-

Few animated films have ever explored the grotesque for its own sake as thoroughly as *Aladdin*. These drawings by Richard Vander Wende are from the film's pre-production phase and give some suggestion of the kind of ideas that were being hatched mercials of the 1980s. Musker and Clements were well aware of Goldberg's talents and were delighted to welcome him to their team.

Goldberg's principal animating assignment was the Genie, but his influence can be felt throughout the movie. Production designer Richard Vander Wende and art director Bill Perkins were working from the supposition that the curvilinear flow of Islamic calligraphy and the graphic poetry of Persian miniatures should be integral to the look of the film. Goldberg took this as a starting point, then turned to one of his heros – the caricaturist Al Hirschfeld – for further inspiration. Hirschfeld's line has the same kind of whiplash expressiveness that can be found in Islamic calligraphy, so that his style of drawing could be incorporated into the texture of the movie without causing any stylistic dislocation.

In the case of the Genie, Goldberg modeled him in part on a Hirschfeld caricature of Maurice Chevalier. (Coincidentally, Chevalier had been one of the inspirations for Lumiere in *Beauty and the Beast*.) Goldberg designed the Genie as a character who is defined by his outline. This may be contrasted with Glen Keane's design of the Beast, which has mass and solidity. For the Beast, that was a necessity since the audience must sense his weight and power. For the Genie, the opposite is needed, as the character is lighter than air and can transform himself into anything from a game show host to a bodybuilder, and it is the infinitely flexible outline that makes this possible. Without Goldberg's mastery of this style it would have been impossible for him to keep up with the verbal and mental acrobatics of Robin Williams, who provided the character's voice.

This emphasis on outline extended to other characters as well. Jasmine, for example, has a basic hourglass figure that registers even if she is seen in silhouette in the far distance.

Goldberg may have been chiefly influenced by Hirschfeld, but he is also a student of Disney animation and an admirer, in particular, of Fred Moore's work on characters like the Seven Dwarfs. This helped ensure that there would be a sense of continuity with Disney tradition, even as the animators moved into fresh territory.

The strongest character in the movie, after the Genie, is Jafar the evil vizier (the voice of Jonathan Freeman), animated principally by Andreas Deja. This was Deja's second villain in a row, following Gaston, but here the challenge was very different. Gaston is rather naturalistic. His jaw and muscles may be exaggerated, but – like the Beast – he is a solid character with weight and mass. Jafar, on the other hand, is strictly two dimensional (from a graphic point of view). With his broad shoulders, his elastic mouth, his haughty eyebrows, and his expressive hieroglyph of beard, Jafar is an invitation to unbridled linear invention, and Deja made the most of it.

Aladdin himself is a slightly annoying character, though the problem has nothing to do with the way he is drawn. With Glen Keane as the directing animator, he is brought to life with enormous skill. The problem has more to do with the conception of the character. The directors perhaps tried *too* hard to make him contemporary, so that he always

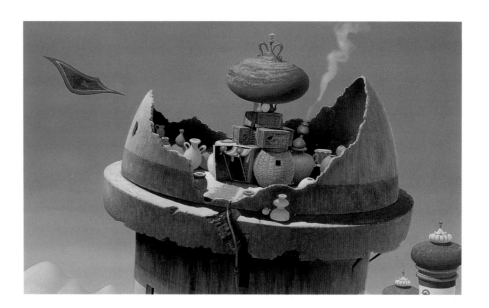

Aladdin was an opportunity for Disney concept artists to exercise their imaginations and their taste for the exotic. Right: a study by Richard Vander Wende. Below: two more by Hans Bacher

Color models for each scene are prepared with the aid of Disney's Academy Award-winning CAPS digital production system. From a model such as this, generated in the computer, each frame in the scene can be electronically colored by a skilled craftsperson. The finished images are scanned directly from the CAPS system onto film stock, thus eliminating the need for cels

Like Ariel and Belle before her, Jasmine is one of Disney's spunky new breed of heroines, a young woman with a mind of her own and a bottomless supply of willpower

Among the notable comic characters in *Aladdin* is the hero's pet monkey, Abu, opposite

Robin Williams provided the voice for the Genie and his wildly improvisational sense of humor. Another inspiration was a drawing of Maurice Chevalier by the caricaturist Al Hirschfeld, whose highly linear, calligraphic style is felt as a strong influence throughout the movie.

Animated by a team led by Andreas Deja,
Jafar is a most demonic villain, a formidable
adversary for Aladdin and Jasmine, and for
the befuddled Sultan

Aladdin was produced and directed by
John Musker (opposite bottom, seated) and
Ron Clements (standing), who made a
brief appearance in the film itself (above),
caricatured as fellaheen on the streets of
Agrabah. Eric Goldberg (opposite top) led
the team that animated the genie and
was to a large extent responsible for styling
Aladdin's cast of characters

seems out of step with the rest of the cast. Aladdin's voice, supplied by Scott Weinger, is also jarringly American in the Middle Eastern context of the movie.

Jasmine is a feisty heroine, and there are many well-realized secondary characters, including Abu, Aladdin's monkey; Rajah, Jasmine's pet tiger; and Iago, Jafar's parrot sidekick, while Randy Cartwright's unit had fun with the flying carpet.

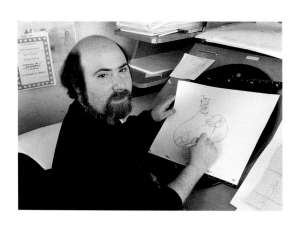

The entire look of the film is fantastic, the Arabian Nights atmosphere having been developed with the aid of more than 1,800 photographs taken by layout supervisor Rasoul Azadani in his hometown, Esfahān, Iran. Along with concept artist Hans Bacher, Azadani was one of the key players in the visualization of *Aladdin,* heading the team that stages the movie and plans the camera moves. Many of the scenes were planned by Azadani himself, taking shape as sketches in workbooks which serve as "bibles" for other artists producing more detailed layouts. Other scenes were developed in sketches by artistic coordinator Dan Hansen.

One of the most remarkable things about *Aladdin* is the way it was choreographed in terms of color. *Beauty and the Beast* had taken this idea quite far. For *Aladdin,* the art director and production designer went even farther, so that no color was used without having some story significance. For example, blue would be used for sky and water, of course, but beyond that it would stand for the good, the positive, the idealistic. Red would stand for evil and the hellish powers of destruction. Not surprisingly, green would represent the earthly paradise while various yellows designated everything from greed (gold) to earthiness (ocher). Richard Vander Wende thought this all through in great detail and even produced a "color script" of the entire movie in which sequences were broken down into schematic representations of their color components, shot by shot.

Like *Beauty and the Beast,* Aladdin contains spectacular backgrounds and astonishing examples of the effects animator's art. The songs are perhaps less important than they were in *Beauty and the Beast* but they do all that is asked of them, and Menken's Academy Award–winning score is first-rate.

Aladdin is full of plums, but in the end what makes the movie unforgettable is the virtuoso collaboration between Robin Williams and Eric Goldberg's animation team in creating the Genie. Williams is famous in his stage performances for his ability to perform stream-of-consciousness ad libs in which his mind turns on a dime then shoots off in any number of directions, each of which provides him with the excuse to invade and inhabit a menagerie of characters – famous, infamous, anonymous, and androgynous. Williams reproduced this routine in the recording studio, improvising around gags devised by story artists and supplying touches of his own. Working to his voice track, the animators succeeded brilliantly in capturing Williams's chameleon persona on film, permitting the Genie to impersonate a dragon, a slot machine, Jack Nicholson, and dozens of other entities.

Aladdin captured the enchanted atmosphere of the Arabian Nights, and it did enchanted business for The Walt Disney Company, like its predecessor breaking all records for an animated film and becoming one of the all-time top money earners among all categories of film.

While *Aladdin* was still in production, another team of artists was preparing *The Lion King* for the moment when the best character animators and other key artists would become available. As with *Beauty and the Beast*, there was a false start in the development stage, but by the end of 1991 things were beginning to take shape.

Tom Schumacher was the original producer, but toward the end of 1991 he was promoted to a newly created position as head of feature animation development and handed over the reins of *The Lion King* to Don Hahn, though Schumacher remained with the project as executive producer. A new directorial duo was created by pairing Roger Allers, story chief for *Beauty and the Beast,* with Rob Minkoff, a gifted animator and story artist who most recently had been working on an aborted Roger Rabbit project. The first thing Allers and Minkoff did, upon being teamed, was to put together a brain trust. For two days, Allers, Minkoff, Hahn, and story head Brenda Chapman shut themselves in a room with *Beauty and the Beast* directors Gary Trousdale and Kirk Wise (co-opted to lend their talent and experience before moving on to a new project of their own). At the end of the two days, many of the plot problems that had been stalling the project were solved.

If *Aladdin* is quite different from *Beauty and the Beast*, *The Lion King* is distinctively different from both of them. The first Disney animated feature ever to be based on a completely original story, *The Lion King* is also the first since *Bambi* to present naturalistic animals in an environment that closely approximates their true habitat. No humans are found in this world, not even the invisible hunters who intrude into Bambi's universe by way of gunshots and carelessly tended campfires.

The Lion King differs from *Bambi* in another key respect. The story of Simba the lion and his adventures in the Pride Lands is a traditional Aesopian fable, so that – for all the surface naturalism – the idea of animals talking to one another and otherwise violating the laws of nature is less disturbing than in the earlier film.

The Lion King presents the rites of passage of Simba, who, at the beginning of the film, is the newborn heir apparent to the kingdom of the Pride Lands, wisely ruled by his father, Mufasa. In early sections of the movie, Simba is shown learning the vital lessons of life from Mufasa. With his best friend Nala, Simba also has an unpleasant encounter, in an elephant graveyard, with a trio of sadistic hyenas. This leads to a final soul-searching session between Simba and Mufasa. Shortly afterward, Mufasa is killed while trying to save Simba during a stampede engineered by Mufasa's evil brother Scar and carried out with the help of his hyena allies.

Finding Simba terrified but unharmed beside his father's body, Scar persuades the cub that he was responsible for Mufasa's death. Guiltily, Simba follows Scar's advice and runs away, certain that he can never go back to the pride. With Simba out of the picture, Scar heads for Pride

ROUGH MODEL SHEET
YOUNG SIMBA
PRODUCTION 0885
"King of the Jungle" 1/13/92

Made for *The Lion King*, 1994, this model sheet for young Simba, drawn by Jean Gillmore, is a good example of the way in which the new generation of Disney artists has learned how to blend humor with naturalism.

Rock, where he tells the assembled lionesses that both Mufasa and Simba are dead. With mock sorrow, Scar assumes reign of the Pride Lands and introduces the horrified lionesses to his army of hyena mercenaries.

Simba, meanwhile, almost perishes in the desert but is saved by an unlikely duo, a meerkat named Timon and a warthog called Pumbaa. Simba joins this pair of outcasts in a jungle paradise which becomes his home as he grows to adulthood. Along the way he absorbs Timon's and Pumbaa's philosophy of life – "Hakuna Matata" – which, they teach him, means no responsibilities, no cares. There comes a time, though, when this point of view no longer satisfies Simba, and he begins to hanker for something more, without knowing quite what. Soon after, Nala appears on the scene, helping to precipitate Simba's return to the Pride Lands and a final showdown with Scar.

The story has a simple arc to it, yet it provides plenty of opportunity for character development and rich detail. The film depends on a strong depiction of the father-son relationship combined with a graphic presentation of the notion that everyone must take responsibility for his or her own life. As usual, all this is backed up by lively comic relief. This may be the first Disney animated film to be written from scratch, but it has

322

The concept studies by Hans Bacher, opposite, show how, at the pre-production stage, *Lion King* artists were already thinking about the way that animals are seen in wildlife documentaries, in which the telephoto lens sometimes causes dramatic optical effects. Throughout *The Lion King*, the African landscape is used to establish both atmosphere and authenticity, as in this image of Rafiki's tree, right

Overleaf: Rafiki holds up Simba's heir for the approval of the denizens of the Pride Lands. A great moment from *The Lion King* – or so it seems. In fact this image does not appear in the movie. It was created for publicity purposes by taking advantage of the CAPS computerized production system to combine elements from different parts of the movie. Simba and Nala have been plucked from a frame at the end of the movie, Rafiki and the cub from a frame near the beginning. Simba, therefore, appears twice – as an adult and as an infant

every bit as much of a mythic feel to it as any of those derived from classic fairy stories.

Like *Beauty and the Beast* and *Aladdin, The Lion King* is a visually exciting movie. The spectacular settings owe much to the concept art prepared by Hans Bacher and the preliminary design work of the layout unit supervised by Dan St. Pierre. The same layout artists did much to give passages of the film the look of a wildlife documentary (typically shot with telephoto or zoom lenses) while maintaining a slightly stylized look that derives in part from African art. Doug Ball's background crew helped give the movie its epic look, also creating a sense of the heat of the savannas. The astonishing wildebeest stampede was achieved by computer animation artists working under Scott Johnston. As for the effects department, headed by Scott Santoro, they had a field day once again, creating notable effects for the opening Circle of Life sequence, the elephant graveyard, the appearance of Mufasa's ghost, and the climactic storm.

It was Allers and Minkoff who determined the overall look of the film, but their ideas were convincingly implemented by art director Andy Gaskill, who was also responsible for the staging of many of the key scenes. (He was promoted to this position because of his highly cinematic storyboarding of the complex opening sequence.) Certain scenes – such as Simba's Busby Berkeleyish musical number, "I Can't Wait to Be King," and the appearance of Mufasa's ghost – were conceived and supervised by production designer Chris Sanders, who also contributed many ideas and visual concepts to the development of the movie as a whole. Another important member of the crew was Randy Fullmer, a former effects supervisor who for this project took on the role of artistic coordinator – a recently created position that has been necessitated by the sheer complexity of animation production today. It is the artistic coordinator's job (along with that of the animation checkers) to ensure that the art coming from the different departments will mesh together seamlessly when they reach the CAPS system. There they are first handled by scene planner Ann Tucker, whose department serves as a bridge between the

The principal villain of *The Lion King* is Scar (opposite bottom), a sardonic egotist skillfully matched to the voice of Jeremy Irons by a team of animators led by Andreas Deja. Scar's allies are the lions' traditional enemies, the hyenas. As a class (above) they are portrayed as goose-stepping fascists. The three principal hyenas (opposite top), however, are anarchistic and manic

hand-drawn animation world and the computer-driven compositing and postproduction zone.

A problem that faced the character animators working on *The Lion King* was a need to work virtually without props (Rafiki's cane is an exception). Props help animators by providing opportunities for "business" and helping define character. (Think of Jiminy Cricket's umbrella or Cruella De Vil's cigarette holder.) It would have been unthinkable, however, to give the king of beasts a crown or have Scar wear dark glasses. The animators were required to aim for convincing naturalism, in keeping with the setting, while still giving the animals some anthropomorphic characteristics. After all, they do speak dialogue and even sing.

As so often in Disney's animated features, the villain comes close to stealing the show. Wittily animated by a team headed by Andreas Deja (his third prime villain in as many films) and greatly benefiting from the sardonic voice inflections provided by Jeremy Irons, Scar is an unforgettable piece of work in more than one sense. The animation of the other characters is up to the same standard, and special note should be made of the work of Mark Henn, Ruben Aquino, Tony Fucile, and James Baxter (who makes a memorable character out of Rafiki). The outstanding comedy figures Timon and Pumbaa were animated by teams led by Mike Surrey and Tony Bancroft, respectively, and brought to life by the voice talents of Nathan Lane and Ernie Sabella.

One of the most spectacular sequences in *The Lion King* is the wildebeest stampede. The animation was computer generated by a team led by Scott Johnston (above), members of which employed their highly specialized skills to capture the spirit of the cataclysmic event that, much earlier, had been suggested in concept paintings such as the one by Hans Bacher, top

Timon the meerkat and Pumbaa the warthog are *The Lion King*'s outstanding comedy characters.

Nathan Lane and Ernie Sabella recording the voices of Timon and Pumbaa

As *The Lion King* approaches its climax,
Simba is shaken from his complacency by an
encounter with his father's spirit which
begins as he contemplates his own reflection
in a pool (above). Returning to Pride Rock,
he finally resolves to confront Scar as the
surrounding landscape burns (opposite top).
Bringing all his cunning into play, Scar almost
manages to win the day, literally pushing
Simba to the edge (opposite bottom), but in
the end justice prevails

The rest of the voice talent is equally strong. Along with Jeremy Irons, it includes Matthew Broderick (as adult Simba), James Earl Jones (Mufasa), Robert Guillaume (Rafiki), and Whoopi Goldberg and Cheech Marin as two of the principal hyenas. There are distinctively flavored musical numbers from the team of Elton John and Tim Rice, and the powerful score, by Hans Zimmer, evokes Africa from the opening moments of the film.

With its immediate predecessors having been received so enthusiastically, expectations for *The Lion King* were positively intimidating. Anticipation began to mount months before the June, 1994 release date when a four-minute promotional clip from the movie was shown in theaters around America. By early that spring, *The Lion King* was being touted as an almost surefire summer blockbuster.

Nothing is surefire, but in this case the film outperformed the most optimistic projections and quickly displaced *Aladdin* as the all-time box-office champion for animated films. By July of 1994, *Daily Variety* – an industry magazine – was predicting that *The Lion King* would be the most profitable movie of all time, animated or live action.

It would also be the last animated feature to be released during Jeffrey Katzenberg's extremely successful tenure as chairman of Walt Disney Studios. Shortly after the film passed the $250 million mark in domestic rentals – and ten years after he joined the Disney team – Katzenberg left the Studio, apparently unhappy at not being appointed president of The Walt Disney Company in the wake of Frank Wells's tragic death in a helicopter accident earlier in 1994.

Katzenberg's departure created a situation in which some of his responsibilities were divided between Joe Roth, a former chief of Fox's movie division, who was appointed chairman of Walt Disney Motion Pictures, and Richard Frank, who was made chairman of the television and telecommunications division (which he had been instrumental in building into an enormously profitable part of the Disney empire). Sanford Litvack, the company's general counsel, was promoted to executive vice president and chief of corporate staff, taking on many of Frank Wells's former responsibilities.

Meanwhile, Roy Disney remained the champion of animation while continuing to exert considerable influence on overall corporate policy from his position as vice chairman of The Walt Disney Company. A strong sense of continuity in feature animation was ensured by Peter Schneider's ongoing role as a very active and effective department head and by the existence of an extraordinarily able creative team of young veterans. In addition, Michael Eisner announced his intention of becoming more directly involved with the day-to-day operations of the department.

Changes of leadership notwithstanding, Disney animation was riding high, driven once again by the kind of inexplicable momentum – a magical conspiracy between artists and audience – that had first been generated more than six decades earlier with the debut of Mickey Mouse.

Rob Minkoff (left) and Roger Allers directed *The Lion King*

12   The Tradition Continues

The magical conspiracy between artist and audience depends upon a number of factors, one of which is surprise. It would be relatively easy for Disney's feature animation team to produce variants on films like *Aladdin* and *The Lion King* well into the twenty-first century. That strategy might even succeed for a while, but before long a certain ennui would set in, on the part of artists and audiences alike.

That the Studio's creative team was determined to avoid this trap is amply demonstrated by *Pocahontas,* a movie very different in mood.

This production is based upon the traditional story of the relationship between Pocahontas, a young Native American woman, and John Smith, a swashbuckling adventurer who was a member of a 1607 British expedition to Virginia. Pocahontas and John Smith were historical characters who did in fact meet in the American wilderness all those years ago. Over the centuries, the tale of their encounter has become woven into the fabric of American folklore and has achieved the status of legend. The Disney retelling of the story draws on the folklore, emphasizing the perspective of the Native American characters, using the Studio's animation expertise as a way of presenting their worldview.

The movie begins in seventeenth-century London where the proud ship *Susan Constant* is readied to set sail for America. Most of those who will embark on this voyage are honest British yeomen looking for a better life, but their leader, John Ratcliffe, is a haughty and rapacious blackguard who sees the New World only in terms of the promise of riches. Among those who have signed on with the expedition is Captain John Smith, who already enjoys a reputation as a formidable Indian fighter.

After a perilous Atlantic crossing, the *Susan Constant* reaches Virginia safely. Pocahontas – daughter of Powhatan, the Indian leader – spies the ship, and soon she spots John Smith, too. Like her, he has an adventurous and inquisitive nature and inevitably their paths cross. While Ratcliffe urges his men to tear up the wilderness in search of gold, Pocahontas and Smith get to know each other and soon Smith begins to understand the Indians' sacred respect for nature.

There are complications ahead, however. Pocahontas is expected to marry Kocoum, a brave but overly serious young warrior who eventually is killed by Smith's friend Thomas. Ratcliffe meanwhile is still hungry for gold. Smith is captured by Powhatan and sentenced to death as Kocoum's murderer. Only Pocahontas can save Smith's life.

Produced by James Pentecost and directed by Mike Gabriel and Eric Goldberg, the Disney version of the tale reinvents the legend once more, providing it with a sense of freshness and a modern perspective on the clash of cultures. The story is told within a visual context of stylized realism that is splendidly effective.

The basic idea for the movie came from Mike Gabriel, who in 1990 had recently finished directing *The Rescuers Down Under* and was looking for a new challenge.

"I was interested in doing something that involved Native Americans," he says. "I began by looking at the most familiar stories and almost

Pocahontas is notable for historically accurate settings, as can be judged from this concept painting of a Native American long-house by Justin Brandstater

Left: Pocahontas observes the departure of the settlers' ship. Storyboard art by Glen Keane. Right: Captain John Smith, seen here in an early concept drawing by John Pomeroy, is significantly different from other handsome Disney heroes, being more fully rounded as a character and decidedly less bland.

immediately the Pocahontas story jumped out at me. It seemed to have all the elements that would make a great Disney film.

With a small team, Gabriel began to develop the idea. When *Aladdin* was completed, Goldberg joined him as co-director, intrigued by the potential of a movie in which a strong heroine or hero would have to carry the story.

"I don't think Disney has ever done anything quite like this before," Goldberg says. "Usually there's a clear-cut villain, and resisting his evil plan is what the film is all about. And usually the comic characters pick up a lot of the slack. We have comic characters, but they're secondary, and our villain, Ratcliffe, is not out-and-out *evil*. He's just a regular, unpleasant, greedy guy who sees the colonies as nothing but an opportunity to make a fast buck. In the end, it's the relationship between Pocahontas and John Smith that has to carry the film. You've got to believe in that relationship or you've got nothing, and that's what makes this picture different. There's never been a Disney animated feature in which the heroine and hero were asked to carry the whole thing."

"This is a film," says producer Pentecost, "in which you see the clash between two cultures, and we've tried to present that in very graphic ways. The landscape itself becomes a key element in the story. When it's seen from the point of view of the Europeans, it's a mysterious new world – both wonderful and scary – a wilderness full of unfamiliar plants and creatures. Seen from the viewpoint of the Indians, it's a completely different place in which the trees and animals are not only familiar but have assigned powers within the mythology by which the tribe lives."

335

Among the artists who helped establish this world was Glen Keane. After his work on *Beauty and the Beast* and *Aladdin*, Keane joined the *Pocahontas* crew at a very early stage and made key contributions not only to the development of the leading characters but also to the evolution of the world in which they act out their destinies.

Keane's primary contribution to the film, however, was probably the inspiration and insight he brought to the character of Pocahontas. While it's true, as Goldberg says, that the relationship between Pocahontas and John Smith must carry the movie, it is Pocahontas who is the key to that relationship. If she were not so captivating and, ultimately, so ready to sacrifice herself, the essential spark would be missing.

Keane designed the character from scratch, thinking about every detail, from the way she moved through the wilderness to the way her hair flowed in the breeze as she ran. Mostly, though, he pondered the way she would think and feel in any given situation, and how this would be reflected in her movements and facial expressions. What were the things, he asked himself, that would define the personality of a seventeenth-century Native American girl? Some of the answers to this came from research. Pocahontas is not a conventional Indian princess, like Tiger Lily in Disney's version of *Peter Pan*. When it came to the appearance of indigenous Virginians, Keane and other Disney artists drew their inspiration from authentic sources, such as the drawings and watercolors of explorer-artists like Jacques Le Moyne de Morgues and John White, who accompanied early expeditions. Correct appearance is only part of the story, and what Keane was equally involved with was the inner life of his character.

The importance of the Pocahontas character can be gauged from the fact that Keane found himself heading a team of no fewer than fifteen character animators devoted to bringing her to the screen – a team that included outstanding talents such as Mark Henn, Pres Romanillos, and Randy Haycock. Whoever did the animating, however, it is very much Keane's vision of Pocahontas that dominates the screen.

Below: This concept painting for *Pocahontas,* by Natalie Franscioni-Karp, evokes the Arcadian world of the American wilderness

Digging for gold, above, Ratcliffe and his men ravish Virginia's forests. Ratcliffe, seen opposite top in a storyboard drawing by Duncan Marjoribanks, is a caricature of the colonizer as blatant exploiter

Overleaf: Pocahontas tracks John Smith as he explores her world

Featuring the voice talent of Mel Gibson and animated by a team headed by John Pomeroy, John Smith is also a strong character. Coming from a European background, he is a less original concept than Pocahontas, but the artists have avoided the pitfalls that might have made him a conventional two-dimensional comic-book hero; thus, he provides the heroine with the kind of foil she needs to be fully effective.

If Disney animated features have had a major weakness, it has been in the portrayal of two-legged heroes, most of whom have approximated the bland Prince Charming stereotype. (Even the Beast becomes one of these royal bores when released from his curse.) John Smith is handsome enough to be a Prince Charming, but he is not bland and he is not stereotypical. He is, perhaps, the most successful leading man Disney animators have so far created, and this bodes well for the future since believable heroes would permit a considerable extension of dramatic possibilities to the animation crews.

Other significant characters are Ratcliffe, the gold-hungry Governor (animated by a team headed by Duncan Marjoribanks), and Powhatan (strikingly realized by a team led by Ruben Aquino).

Stylistically, the film draws somewhat on the American tradition of illustration. The way these influences, and others (especially the look of John White's seventeenth-century watercolors), were integrated into the look of the film was supervised by art director Michael Giaimo and artistic coordinator Dan Hansen. Once again, the layout department –

under the leadership of Rasoul Azadani – and the background artists – headed by Cristy Maltese – made strong contributions to the film.

With songs by Alan Menken and Stephen Schwartz, *Pocahontas* reaches back to the musical approach established for earlier films by Howard Ashman and Menken. If *The Lion King* dipped into a modern pop style – thanks to the contribution of Elton John – the Menken and Schwartz songs, and the Menken score, have much more to do with the Broadway musical tradition.

Perhaps the most notable thing about *Pocahontas* is the fact that it advances the art of feature animation further into the area of movie-making for adults. It is still designed to appeal to a family audience, and there is still comic relief from characters like Meeko, Flit, and Percy, but the relationship between the hero and heroine is portrayed in much the way it might be in a live-action film.

The release of a very different kind of animated feature – *A Goofy Movie* – also occurred in 1995. The second theatrical production from the television animation team, this film is considerably more successful than its predecessor, *Ducktales: the Movie*. Directed by Kevin Lima and produced by Dan Rounds, *A Goofy Movie* blends the brashness and visual inventiveness of the old Disney short cartoons with MTV-generation hipness and – no mean feat – a large dose of tenderness.

In this movie, as in the *Goof Troop* television series (see chapter 14), Goofy is a single dad bringing up – in his own bumbling way – a son called Max. Max is a spunky teenager who finds his mambo-loving father out of touch with rock-era reality. To impress Roxanne, the girl he yearns for, Max disrupts a school assembly with a performance that gets him into deep trouble with the principal, who warns Goofy that Max is hanging out with the wrong crowd and is likely to end up in the electric chair. Visualizing Max as a latent gang member, Goofy decides to take his son on a long fishing trip to straighten him out. Max – who was

A Goofy Movie, 1995, is a feature-length production that successfully captures the spirit of the classic Disney shorts of the thirties and forties

Pre-production art for *The Hunchback of Notre Dame* captured the atmosphere and strong sense of place that are so much a part of Victor Hugo's novel. Lisa Keene's painting of Notre Dame Cathedral (left) was based on a drawing by Darek Gogol. Dave Goetz's study (right) puts gothic architecture to dramatic use

looking forward to his first date with Roxanne – is anything but delighted. The trip is a disaster until Max and Goofy begin to see each other's point of view and join forces to keep an outlandish promise Max has recklessly made to Roxanne.

The high-school scenes are lively and fun – like an animated version of *Grease* – and the ill-fated trip is peppered with good visual gags, some of them apparently adapted from 1930s cartoons such as *Mickey's Trailer*. For the most part the animation is sound and the production values are more than adequate to the task at hand. Best of all, the story line has been well constructed so that *A Goofy Movie* turns out to be a true feature film – much more than just an inflated television special.

Turning back to the feature animation division, the more mature values seen in *Pocahontas* are also to be found in *The Hunchback of Notre Dame*, a retelling of Victor Hugo's famous novel *Notre-Dame de Paris*. First published in 1831, it is best known to Americans through two live-action films based on the Hugo story: one, featuring the great Lon Chaney, made in the silent era; the other, starring the equally magnificent Charles Laughton, released by RKO in 1939. A lesser but not uninteresting French-produced theatrical film version, with Anthony Quinn as Quasimodo, appeared in 1957.

The Disney production team, led by producer Don Hahn and directors Gary Trousdale and Kirk Wise, made an early decision to stay away from these live-action versions – fine as they are – and take Hugo's original as their starting place. This brought with it certain problems (the novel has literally hundreds of individuated characters) but also certain rewards. Chaney and Laughton had both played Quasimodo, the hunchback in the bell tower, as middle-aged. The Disney team was delighted to discover that Hugo's Quasimodo is actually a very young man. By presenting him that way – as a troubled adolescent fascinated by a world he could only experience from a distance – the Disney artists felt they could surprise audiences with a vision of the hunchback that would be fresh to most viewers.

As the directors and the story team (led by Will Finn) struggled to simplify Hugo's sprawling tale into something manageable, other artists began to try to visualize the Paris of the novel and especially the soaring yet confining world of the cathedral church of Notre Dame, with its great stained-glass windows and its grotesque gargoyles.

The story is set at the end of the Middle Ages, when putrid slums with open drains crowded around the cathedral, and around the magnificent homes of the wealthy. Concept artists, and layout artists under Dave Goetz and Ed Ghertner, began to research this world, studying photographs, as well as the works of many artists, including those of Victor Hugo himself, Hugo being a gifted draftsman who created his own gothic visions of medieval Paris. As the research yielded solid results, they began to set down on paper a very concrete image of the city that would appear on screen. The square in front of the cathedral, for example, was established in great detail so that, long before animation began, every shop, every

This elaborate drawing of Quasimodo in his bell tower is by Tom Shannon

Storyboard sketch by Paul and Gäetan Brizzi

The Hunchback of Notre Dame conjures up the teeming streets and underworld of medieval Paris. On this page, a storyboard sketch by Paul and Gäetan Brizzi (right), and pre-production paintings by Don Moore (below) and Rowland Wilson (bottom), the former based on a drawing by Marek Buchwald

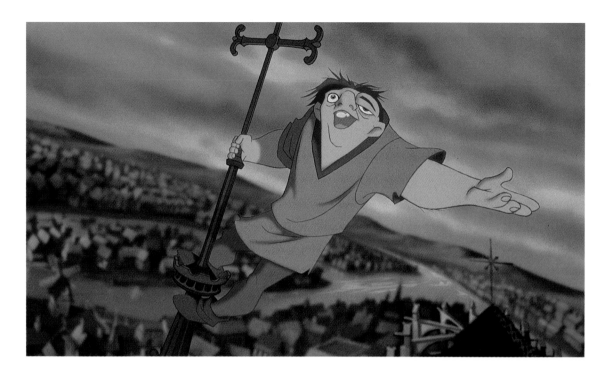

tavern, every home, every warehouse facing onto the square was delineated with as much detail as the facade of the cathedral itself.

The interiors of the cathedral were also explored. In certain scenes, actual interiors would have to be reproduced on screen much as they appear in reality. This would be appropriate to the scenes in which the gypsy girl Esmeralda first seeks asylum in the cathedral. More complex a challenge would be Quasimodo's world within the bell tower. This had to be a magical miniuniverse in which the agile hunchback is completely at home but which anyone else would find bizarre in the extreme. While the bells chime, Quasimodo can swing from beam to beam, dodging the whirring flywheels and escapements as he goes casually about his business in a manner that would spell certain death to anyone else.

Quasimodo is happy among the bells, but he looks down from the tower, at the city from which he has been banished, with infinite sadness. It is his desire to join the crowds that brings him into contact with Esmeralda and embroils him in her complex relationship with Phoebus, the handsome knight home from the wars. It is this desire, too, that brings him into conflict with Frollo, his guardian.

The Hunchback of Notre Dame is a film of immense ambition that sadly is let down by patches of sloppy character animation. During Walt Disney's lifetime, production schedules were – with a few exceptions – determined by the requirements of the animation staff. If the lead character animators felt that more time was needed to fully realize their assignments, then the release date was pushed back. It was the luxury of unhurriedness that permitted the technical perfection of masterpieces such as *Snow White* and *Pinocchio*, as well as of later classics like *Lady and the Tramp*. The only period during which this luxury was taken away was the mid- and late 1940s, when wartime and post-war economics demanded short cuts. Luckily this had little impact on major features, though it's tempting to imagine what might have been done with the

Wind in the Willows section of *The Adventures of Ichabod and Mr. Toad* had the animation staff not been obliged to rush things.

More than forty years later, under the new regime, economics became a factor again, though in a very different way. The tremendous financial success of *Beauty and the Beast, Aladdin* and *The Lion King* had created enormous expectations on the part of audiences, distributors, product licensees, and Disney shareholders alike. Everyone wanted to see at least one new animated feature a year, which placed a tremendous pressure on the animation department. Under the leadership of Roy Disney, Jeffrey Katzenberg, and Peter Schneider, a system had been put in place in which several features could be in different stages of development at any given time, with high production values being guaranteed by modern technology and a large staff of talented artists and craftsmen. Ultimately, however, these movies depend upon the quality of the character animation and the supply of top-class character animators is strictly limited. Occasionally, as was the case with Glen Keane's involvement in the evolution of *Pocahontas*, a key animator would be brought in at an early developmental stage. For the most part, though, top animators did not come into the picture until a movie was completely planned and laid out, and then they would find themselves facing a deadline predetermined by a release date set in response to commercial rather than aesthetic considerations. Scenes featuring the film's hero and drawn by the lead animator might be wonderful, but time pressure would mean that other scenes had to be handled by lesser members of the team, and that could lead to unsatisfactory and even perfunctory results.

There had been hints of this problem in earlier productions, but the sheer narrative momentum of, for example, *The Lion King* had overcome any technical weaknesses. *The Hunchback of Notre Dame* had its basis in a proven great story, but a tricky one for animators to bring to the screen. As animated, the film lacks that relentless momentum and this makes shortcomings in the character animation stand out. Even so, the finished movie has some fine moments and is especially successful in evoking the proletarian energy of the Paris mob. (About ten percent of *The Hunchback of Notre Dame* was actually animated in Paris, where Disney then had a satellite studio.)

If *The Hunchback of Notre Dame* was an ambitious disappointment, *Hercules* (1997) was a flippant failure, sadly so since it was directed by the talented team of John Musker and Ron Clements, previously responsible for *The Little Mermaid* and *Aladdin*, and produced by Alice Dewey. A visitor to the studio when *Hercules* was in pre-production would have seen concept art – including drawings by the British caricaturist Gerald Scarfe – and storyboards that gave promise of a witty, somewhat campy spoof on Greek mythology, cleverly overlaid with deliberate anachronisms, a little like a latter day take on the "Pastoral Symphony" segment of *Fantasia*.

By the time the film reached the screen, however, it had become arch to the point of tiresomeness. The idea of a Greek Chorus in the form of

Although disappointing as a whole, *Hercules* has moments of great visual drama

a Motown girl group probably sounded great when it first came up at a story meeting, but as realized – and despite some decent Alan Menken songs – it's a novelty that soon loses its charm. There's nothing wrong with having fun with the Greek myths, but unless there's a sense of respect underlying the humor (satire would be too strong a word for this production) then the fun falls flat, and that's exactly what seems to have happened here.

As in all the Disney animated features of the nineties, the production values are terrific – the animated flames that dance on Hades' head, for example – and *Hercules* contains some clever visual gags, but it is thin on character and the hero in particular is essentially a sap who, even when he shows signs of achieving his alleged potential, remains silly rather than sympathetic. It's difficult, in fact, to point to a single really sympathetic character – certainly not Meg, the tarty heroine – and a Disney animated movie that lacks the dimension of empathy is doomed to a lowly place in the pantheon. What is missing in this production is the sure touch of Howard Ashman, whose understanding of how campy Broadway wit could be made to mesh with Disney charm might have turned this movie into something special.

A significantly better movie is *Mulan*, which when released in 1998 became the first animated Disney feature to be made entirely outside California, being the product of Disney's now defunct studio in Orlando, Florida. Based on a traditional Chinese folk tale, *Mulan* is the story of a brave young woman who – pretending to be a boy – secretly joins the army in place of her father in order to save his life. After many adventures, she becomes one of China's great heroines.

Mulan was the first feature to be made entirely by Disney's Florida animation unit. The spectacular pre-production painting by Sai Ping Lok (opposite) shows how the movie drew inspiration from traditional Chinese imagery. The film was in fact based on a classic Chinese story and like the original combines contemplative moments (above) and breathtaking action (below)

Clearly this is another example of Disney Animation's determination not to simply repeat its former successes. Like Pocahontas, Mulan is a non-Caucasian heroine, her ethnicity rendered with the graphic simplicity necessary for animation but without any hint of racial caricature. Directed by Tony Bancroft and Barry Cook, and produced by Pam Coats, the movie pays visual tribute to the great heritage of Chinese painting, drawing on both its landscape and genre traditions, and this was matched by the use of Chinese and Chinese American voice talent (Ming-Na and B. D. Wong, for example), though comedy roles were assigned to familiar voices like Harvey Fierstein and Eddie Murphy.

Murphy was given the task of bringing to life Mushu the Demoted One, a small dragon sent by Mulan's ancestors to dissuade her from going to war, though in the end he finds himself helping her to carry out her plans. Mushu is one of the successes of this movie, a film that satisfied the Disney core audience without quite generating the magic that had caused films like *The Little Mermaid, Beauty and the Beast, Aladdin,* and *The Lion King* to be monster hits. In retrospect, *Mulan* is perhaps a little too determined to be politically correct (anachronistic digs at arranged marriages, for example), and a shade too reluctant to go all the way with the traditional Disney virtues of soaring fantasy and character-based humor. Still, it is an entertaining and beautifully crafted movie – a strong story nicely told – that is likely to hold its own against other Disney films when seen in historical perspective.

Another movie with some strong virtues is *Tarzan* (1999), Edgar Rice Burroughs' classic which is said to have been made forty-six times

in live-action versions before the Disney artists set to work on this first
animated production. (*Dracula* is the only story that has been filmed
more often.) From the opening moments of the picture, it becomes evident that animation has some real advantages when dealing with subject
matter of this sort. It's no exaggeration to say that *Tarzan* provides one
of the most gripping openings in the entire Disney repertoire, packed
with drama, tragedy and striking visual invention. A human family is
wrecked on a tropical shore. Simultaneously, a gorilla family loses a
child to a rampaging leopard. Soon after, the same leopard kills the
marooned human parents, leaving the child – the infant Tarzan – to be
discovered and rescued from the big cat by the bereaved mother gorilla,
who adopts the baby, setting up the familiar situation of the man-child
raised by apes in an entirely satisfying way that relies on crisp storytelling devices highlighted by spectacular action sequences.

It is the action sequences – in these opening scenes and throughout
the movie – that make *Tarzan* special. Set pieces such as Tarzan's battle
to the death with the leopard, and his rescue of Jane from a tribe of
baboons bent on separating her bustle from her sun bonnet, are as good
as anything of this sort that the studio has ever attempted. Also spectacular are the scenes of Tarzan moving through the jungle. He does not
merely swing from vines but skims over writhing roots and swollen
stems like a skateboard ace on invisible wheels. This is made all the
more effective by a digitized technique dubbed "Deep Canvas," that
permits the jungle foliage to take on an active semblance of shifting

three-dimensional reality that would have amazed Ub Iwerks and the other pioneers of the multiplane camera.

Apart from the action and the spectacular visual effects, *Tarzan* is convincing in portraying the relationship between the hero and his family of gorillas, and especially good in presenting the growing affection between Tarzan and Jane, who is charmingly brought to life (except for a tendency for her pretty snub nose to crawl around her face in close-ups) with a great deal of help from the voice talent of Minnie Driver. Tarzan himself – largely the work of Glen Keane – is an impressive creation, his physique believably human, his stance adapted to the life of gorillas. Muscular though he is, he is actually smaller than Clayton, the belligerent white hunter villain of the piece. Tarzan's scale relative to both Clayton and the gorillas is key to the sympathy we feel for him.

The weaknesses of the movie include a somewhat mechanical approach to the comedy routines, and especially to the scenes in which pathos is the key element. The Phil Collins songs are disappointing and the "Trashing the Camp" number is a decided letdown to anyone who remembers the musical highlights of *The Jungle Book*. On balance, however, the high points of *Tarzan* far outweigh the lows. For most of its 88 minutes, this is animated filmmaking of a high order.

Long before *Tarzan* was released, some members of the animation department had settled into its new headquarters, across Riverside Drive from the main Burbank lot, a post-modernist fruit sundae of a building designed by Robert A. M. Stern. During the 1990s, when animation production was at its peak, there were active studios in Glendale, Orlando, France, Japan, Australia, and Canada as well as Burbank, but the Stern building, with its Sorcerer's Apprentice hat, was the symbol of animation's new heyday. Appropriately, the hat marked the office of Roy E. Disney, and just as appropriately his chief preoccupation during this period was a sequel to *Fantasia* that in its eventual form would be built around a digitally re-mastered version of the "Sorcerer's Apprentice" segment from the 1940 classic.

This was a heroic undertaking. Like the original, *Fantasia/2000* (as it came to be called) would match state-of-the-art animation with music performed by some of the greatest musicians of the day, including James Levine and the members of the Chicago Symphony Orchestra. And, just like the original, it would be experimental in both form and content, in this instance utilizing both hand-drawn animation and computer-generated imagery. When the first *Fantasia* was released, a handful of theaters were equipped with wide screen and special multi-track sound systems intended to enhance the experience. Where *Fantasia/2000* was concerned, Roy Disney planned to go further, scheduling the initial release for one hundred theaters equipped to project the movie in the eye-popping 70mm IMAX format.

The film opened as planned on January 1, 2000, and the first visual encountered by millennial viewers was a swirling collage of images from the original *Fantasia,* drifting through space. As these faded, the audience

Tarzan (opposite and below) is a movie in which exquisitely realized settings combine with a well thought out narrative to bring fresh life to a familiar story

was confronted with a band of animators and an orchestra of musicians, the artists sharpening their pencils, the instrumentalists tuning up in readiness for their performance. Then, echoing Stokowski's arrival in *Fantasia,* James Levine steps up to the podium, raises his baton and leads the orchestra into Beethoven's Fifth Symphony.

This serves as the accompaniment for a battle between abstract shapes, some hand drawn and triangular, somewhat like butterfly wings, others computer generated and sinister, seeming to seep into the frame like dark shadows that threaten to engulf everything. Immediately the scene is set for a struggle between traditional animation and digitized animation, which in a sense is the theme of the movie as a whole.

In the original, the voice of the writer and critic Deems Taylor was used to introduce the different segments. In *Fantasia/2000,* different celebrities perform this role, and the first to make an appearance is Steve Martin, who provides a brief account of Walt Disney's original vision, then introduces Itzhak Perlman who launches into Ottorino Respighi's "Pines of Rome," called upon here to inspire some spectacular imagery that employs computer-generated animation in conjunction with hand-painted backgrounds and traditional visual effects photography. Here then, handmade imagery and digital imagery are made to work together, the subject matter being exploding stars and whales that learn to fly.

Introduced by Quincy Jones, the next segment is built around George Gershwin's "Rhapsody in Blue." Directed by Eric Goldberg, it follows the interconnected adventures of four characters in Manhattan during the Jazz Age. Goldberg styled the look of this segment to capture the energy of a period when Manhattan was becoming a world capital of popular culture. Wit and jazzy elegance are blended with a lightness of touch that perfectly matches the character of the music.

Next Bette Midler introduces Dimitri Shostakovich's "Piano Concerto No. 2," matched with the Hans Christian Andersen story "The Steadfast Tin Soldier." The animation was based on storyboards that had been prepared at the studio a half-century earlier, and that were now resuscitated under the direction of Hendel Butoy, who also served as supervising

"The Steadfast Tin Soldier," directed by Hendel Butoy and set to music by Shostakovich, combines traditional animation with computer-generated graphics. In the same film, Ottorino Respighi's "The Pines of Rome" provides the musical score for an interlude involving whales that take to the skies (opposite top), while a yo-yo toting flamingo stars in a comic sequence set to Camille Saint-Saëns' "Carnival of the Animals"

director for the entire movie. In this segment, once again, computer-generated imagery and hand-drawn animation are skillfully combined.

Eric Goldberg assists James Earl Jones in introducing Camille Saint-Saëns' "Carnival of the Animals," conceived as an extended comic riff on what would happen if you gave a yo-yo to a flock of flamingos, one of which proved to have a special talent for using the toy in breathtakingly creative ways. A celebration of individuality, this segment relies on traditional animation skills and the use of delicious watercolor stylings.

What follows is a classic of hand-drawn animation, the still marvelous "Sorcerer's Apprentice" – the ultimate in Mickey Mouse spectacles – digitally freshened up but otherwise exactly as committed to film in 1940, with Paul Dukas' program music conducted by Leopold Stokowski. At the conclusion of this segment, Mickey shakes hands with both Stokowski and James Levine, bridging the generations, and Levine introduces the penultimate segment, which utilizes Edward Elgar's stately "Pomp and Circumstance Marches." This features Disney's other early superstar, Donald Duck, in a story based on the Biblical tale of Noah's Ark, during the course of which Donald becomes separated from his beloved Daisy as the flood-waters rise. Needless to say there is a last-minute reunion. Perhaps the most revolutionary segment of the original *Fantasia*, from a musical point of view, was the inclusion of Igor Stravinsky's "The Rite of Spring," which in 1940 was still considered avant-garde and extremely difficult. It was appropriate, then, that Roy Disney decided to include another Stravinsky masterpiece in *Fantasia/2000*. Introduced by Angela Lansbury, this was "The Firebird Suite." Walt Disney had used "The Rite of Spring" as the score to underline an animated history of the evolution of the planet Earth up until the death of the dinosaurs. Now "The Firebird Suite" was called upon to assist in telling a similarly epic tale, the destruction and rebirth of a forest after a volcanic eruption and the fire that it ignites.

Although it is not a part of *Fantasia/2000*, this is perhaps the appropriate place to take note of the completion of *Destino*, an aborted short

In the climactic
sequence of
Fantasia/2000, the
allegorized rebirth
of a forest is set to
Stravinski's "The
Firebird Suite"

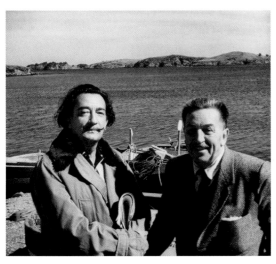

Completed by Roy Disney, *Destino* (top) is the outcome of a collaboration between Walt Disney and Salvador Dalí, seen here together when the man who gave us Mickey Mouse visited the man who gave us melting watches at his home in Spain

film that Walt Disney and Salvador Dalí collaborated on in the forties, for inclusion in one of the anthology movies of the period. While researching *Fantasia/2000*, Roy Disney looked at the art that had been prepared for *Destino,* by Dali and Disney artist John Hench, and decided that the project should be finished. Luckily, although Dali was dead, his wife had kept notes on her husband's ideas for the movie, and John Hench was very much alive and well, so that it appeared possible to pick up the threads with a solid hope of fulfilling Dali's intentions. This proved more difficult than expected, but eventually the movie was completed and has enjoyed considerable success including an Oscar nomination.

Like *Hercules, The Emperor's New Groove* (2000) takes a mythological world – this time suggestive of the empire of the ancient Incas – and uses it as a platform for anachronistic jokes and slapstick humor. In this case, the device works rather better, perhaps because the film is utterly unpretentious.

Kuzco (the voice of David Spade) is the cocky young emperor of this zany world. When his advisor Yzma (Eartha Kitt) tries to have him poisoned, he is accidentally turned into a talking llama. With the aid of Pacha (John Goodman), Kuzco attempts to regain his throne, and his

The Emperor's New Groove (top) unfolds in a colorful Pre-Columbian setting. *Atlantis: The Lost Empire* (above) attempts to bring new life to an old myth

Treasure Planet is a science-fiction update of Robert Louis Stevenson's *Treasure Island*

human form. That is the bulk of the plot, though it is of course peppered with many dastardly deeds and comic setbacks. The gags come fast and frequently, and in general this movie (directed by Mark Dindal) lives up to its modest ambitions as a light-hearted romp.

One of the most disappointing Disney animated releases of any period was *Atlantis: The Lost Empire* (2001). The concept of the movie – a search for the lost continent of Atlantis, set in the Edwardian era – seemed promising enough. What reached the screen, however, was decidedly a let down.

Atlantis provides some well-staged set pieces, especially in the battle scenes, and is generously larded with the special effects and production values expected by audiences in the CAPS era. The character animation is distinctive, based as it is on the drawings of comic-book artist Mike Mignola whose stylized approach must have been somewhat challenging to translate into cinematic terms. *Atlantis* was doomed to failure, however, by the story team's inability to make any sense of disparate and unrelated plot elements. Nobody expects this kind of animated adventure to adhere strictly to the Aristotelian dramatic unities, but it does require its own kind of internal logic and in this instance the fantasy is undermined by blatant narrative nonsequiturs. The movie falls apart for lack of thematic structure.

Another disappointment was *Treasure Planet* (2002), a retelling of Robert Louis Stevenson's *Treasure Island* in the form of a very fanciful space opera complete with pirate galleons and caravelles cruising the universe powered by "solar sails." Long John Silver has been transformed into a kind of bionic renegade, his sidekicks such as Ben Gunn have

357

become robots or cyborgs, even his parrot is a morphing alien. Stevenson's classic tale is sturdy enough to stand changes of this kind, but somehow the film fails to capture any of the magic of the original novel, or the romance of the 1950 Disney live-action *Treasure Island* with its scenery-chewing performance by Robert Newton.

Also released in 2002, *Lilo & Stitch* – animated at the Florida studio – turned out to be the most commercially successful picture to emerge from the Disney animation department since *The Lion King*, and deservedly so since it was one of the most adventurous and satisfying movies the Studio had produced in years. Not especially innovative from a technical point of view – its glorious use of watercolor is actually a throwback to the days of *Snow White* and the great shorts of the early Technicolor era – its strength comes essentially from the way it exploits Disney's most basic value, believable character animation. The film is adventurous in that it takes that fundamental virtue and adapts it to human types who are utterly unclichéd, then mixes those down-to-earth characters with creatures from post–*Star Wars* era science fiction to create a comedy of misunderstandings that has at its center a difficult family situation that always threatens to spin out of control.

The story begins in deep space where a mad scientist, Dr. Jumba Jukiba, has unleashed a genetically engineered monster on the universe. Genetic Experiment 626 has the intelligence of a super computer allied to the brattiness of a disturbed three-year-old. To complicate things, he is indestructible. When the United Galactic Federation attempts to rid itself of 626, he escapes to Planet Earth – Hawaii, to be exact – where he poses as an especially ugly and improbable stray dog. In this guise, he is adopted by a little girl called Lilo, as full of rage and destructive impulses as 626, having lost both her parents. Naturally Lilo and 626 – renamed Stitch – hit it off, but that is just the beginning of their troubles since their combined fury tends to create problems for everyone around them.

Set in Hawaii, *Lilo & Stitch* features believeable humans (left) and spectacularly zany space creatures, most notably Stitch (right), an indestructible bundle of unbridled intergalactic energy. These pre-production drawings are by Chris Sanders

Featuring some of the Disney Studio's best
recent character animation, *Lilo & Stitch*
proceeds from one crisis to the next with
imagination and humor

The relationship between disaster-prone
Stitch and easily riled Lilo (top) is at the heart
of the movie. Stitch's occasional attempts to
endear himself (above) are seldom greeted
with success

Despite the inner rage that boils over at the least provocation, Lilo is devoted to Nani, her older sister

Central to this story is the relationship between Lilo (beautifully animated by a team led by Andreas Deja) and her older sister Nani (supervising animator Stéphane Sainte Foi) who has become her guardian. Drawn in a style that is far removed from any Disney conventions of prettiness, these characters are amongst the most fully realized by the current generation of Disney animators. Lilo is chunky and sometimes surly, but always full of vital energy. Nani is attractive, even sexy, without being a stereotype. Their relationship, compounded of love and exasperation, is completely believable.

The visitors from the United Galactic Foundation are in every sense from a different world, sometimes resembling characters from some surrealistic 1940s Warner Brothers cartoon short, but they work well enough within context. Stitch (supervising animator Alex Kupershmidt) is altogether more complex than the others, being asked to evolve from an amoral monster into a loving being with human emotions, which he achieves quite convincingly.

Written and directed by Chris Sanders (who also provides the voice for Stitch) and Dean DeBlois, and produced by Clark Spencer, the movie is marked by high production values throughout. Some of the swimming and surfing scenes are especially enjoyable to watch, with smooth transitions between conventional and underwater viewpoints, and the fact that Lilo is an Elvis Presley fan makes for a solid sound track.

Also produced by Disney's Florida animation unit, *Brother Bear* (2003) is another very good film, directed by Aaron Blaise and Bob Walker, and produced by Chuck Williams. It's tempting to say that it's *two* very good films because its structure is that of a movie within a movie, and the two stories unfold in very different narrative and visual idioms: one a traditional Disney-style, Aesopian fable with cartoony, talking animals and large dollops of comic relief – not far removed from *The Lion King* or even *The Jungle Book* – and the other human-centered, naturalistic and filled with spiritual longing. Each part contains enough high drama for half-a-dozen action films.

Set in the age of the wooly mammoths, in a spectacular version of the American Northwest, *Brother Bear* is a cinematic re-imagining of a

Brother Bear weaves together two interrelated narratives, one a tale of animals in an ancient Western wilderness, the other the story of a band of Native Americans in that same wilderness, which they see as being filled with the spirits of their ancestors. Pre-production art (bottom) by Paul Felix

Right: The Great Spirits descend upon Kenai
Below: Research into everything from costumes to customs brought an air of authenticity to *Brother Bear*. This concept drawing is by Harald Siepermann

Native American myth that succeeds brilliantly in drawing in a twenty first–century audience. The first section of the movie tells the story of three brothers, Sitka (the voice of D. B. Sweeney), Denahi (Jason Raize), and Kenai (Joaquin Phoenix). Kenai, the youngest, desperately wants to prove himself a man and is bitterly disappointed when the community's shaman presents him with his totem – the talisman by which he must live – a bear that represents love. He must suffer the teasing of Denahi, who believes "love" is for girls, and then discovers that, thanks to his carelessness, a bear has been able to steal a basket full of fish. Furious, he impulsively sets out in pursuit of the bear. Knowing that Kenai has the kind of temperament that is likely to get him into trouble, his brothers try to catch up with him. Their journey takes them to high icy wastes where there is a dramatic confrontation with the bear. To save his brothers' lives, Sitka, the eldest, sacrifices his own. The bear survives and now Kenai is more than ever determined to have his revenge. Another battle with the bear ensues and almost by accident Kenai manages to kill the creature. At that moment, the Great Spirits, appearing in the form of the *aurora borealis*, descend and, enveloping Kenai, transform him into a bear.

Now Kenai's sole contact with his former existence is through Tanana (Joan Copeland), the Shaman, who tells him that it is the spirit of his brother Sitka that is behind this transformation, and that he can find Sitka "on the mountain where the lights touch the Earth." determined to return to human form, Kenai sets out to find this magical place, accompanied only by a bear cub named Koda (Jeremy Suarez) that has been separated from its mother. The search brings them into contact with many and varied inhabitants of the tundra, including a couple of intellectually challenged moose brothers (Rick Moranis and Dave Thomas, sounding very much like SCTV's Bob and Doug McKenzie). High drama is generated by the fact that Kenai is being pursued by Denahi, who believes that Kenai, in his bear form, is responsible for the death of both his brothers.

The film makes the most of its setting, with striking visuals that range from pastoral springtime scenes, presented in a cheerful, California

Left: In this storyboard sequence
by Richard Chavez, Kenai is
transformed into a bear
Opposite: *Brother Bear* is filled with
a rich cast of characters, both animal
and human

Impressionist palette, to sweeping panoramas as the camera's point of view soars over mountain peaks, glaciers, white water rivers, and icy fiords. As in *Lilo & Stitch*, the character animation is excellent overall, with strong contributions from Brian Howard, James Young Jackson, Tom Gately, Anthony Wayne Michaels, Alex Kupershmidt, and the ever-reliable Ruben Aquino, as well as from the cleanup team supervised by Philip Scott Boyd and Christine Lawrence Finney. The movie's comic relief scenes do not get in the way of the action, and Phil Collins' songs – much stronger than those he contributed to *Tarzan* – help move things along efficiently. If there is a major criticism to be made of this picture, it is that the two parts of the story are so different in idiom that there are moments where they do not mesh convincingly. This problem, however, is easily outweighed by the movie's many virtues, and there are stretches in the first twenty minutes or so – as the three human brothers pit themselves against nature in pursuit of the bear – that are as powerful dramatically as anything in the Disney oeuvre.

One thing that *Brother Bear* illustrates very clearly, as was also the case with *Lilo & Stitch*, is that when it comes to humans (and even to a lesser extent with mammals), Disney's traditional brand of hand-drawn character animation is still streets ahead of anything that has been achieved with computer-generated animation. Pixar's CG films (see chapter 13) can do wonders with toys and beetles and monsters and fish, and they create marvelously convincing three-dimensional worlds, but they are not yet able to compete when it comes to putting characters like Nani and Denahi on screen. Sadly, *Brother Bear* would be the last film to emerge from the Orlando studio, closed in 2003 as part of a restructuring program that saw all animated feature production consolidated in Southern California.

Disney's 2004 hand-animated entry, *Home on the Range,* includes human characters but is essentially a talking-animal film in the tradition of *Lady and the Tramp*. More specifically, *Home on the Range* is a classic Hollywood western, except this story is told from the point of view of the cows rather than the cowboys. Three members of a dairy herd – Mrs. Caloway, Maggie, and Grace (Judi Dench, Roseanne Barr, and Jennifer Tilly) – become bounty hunters in order to save their farm from foreclosure. Their aim is the capture of the most feared cattle rustler in the West, Alameda Slim (Randy Quaid). Vying with the bovine trio for this rich prize is a glory-seeking horse named Buck (Cuba Gooding Jr.). The consequence of all this is comic mayhem punctuated with musical interludes from the team of Alan Menken and Glen Slater. The farm is the property of one of the human characters, Pearl (the voice of Carol Cook) who is about to default on her mortgage and has nowhere to turn. The bevy of buxom bovines searches for a way out of this mess.

Directed by Will Finn and John Sanford, and produced by Alice Dewey, *Home on the Range* is a comic romp made in a retro style that faintly recalls the Disney anthology movies of the 1940s, and even more so the "modernist" short cartoons – like *Gerald McBoing-Boing* and the Mr. Magoo films – made in the 1950s by the UPA Studio.

Home on the Range features an egotistical bounty hunting horse named Buck (top), and a trio of feisty cows (bottom)

The style of animation featured in *Home on the Range* is reminiscent of old Disney movies such as *Fun and Fancy Free* and *Melody Time*

To compare this production to classic Disney feature animation, or even to recent successes like *Lilo & Stitch* and *Brother Bear*, is beside the point. *Home on the Range* provides another example of Disney animators going out on a limb, and one hopes that such experiments will continue to be encouraged, by studio and audiences alike.

Home on the Range was the last production to employ the CAPS system, in use at the Studio for twenty years. Despite many improvements that had been made over that period, CAPS was showing signs of age and by the time *Home on the Range* was in the can, an entirely new digital platform was in place, this one capable of replacing CAPS for 2-D animation and also of sustaining state-of-the-art computer-generated animation.

Appointed head of feature animation in January 2003, David Stainton emphasizes the importance of staying abreast of the technology:

"There was a time, a few years ago, when our production methods became top-heavy – obese if you like – partly because of the way we were trying to get the most out of the CAPS system. A film like *The Lion King* was actually made with a relatively modest crew. Later we tried to step up production by setting a lot of manpower loose on every project. Things got out of hand, and what we're finding now is that we're able to put a quality movie together with a much more streamlined crew.

Glen Keane in his animation studio

"A good animated film still sells a lot of tickets, but that doesn't mean a thing if it costs too much to make in the first place. What we're concentrating on is efficiency without loss of quality and our new computer platform helps us achieve that. *Lilo & Stitch* and *Brother Bear* demonstrate that there's still a market for 2D animation, but we have to face up to the fact that the public is very intrigued by the novelty of computer-generated animation. The Pixar movies prove that. I believe that our future will find room for both kinds.

"Good CG work demands the same quality of character animation you need for a 2D movie. Here at the studio, we've found that it pays to retrain traditional animators – people who can draw – to work with the computer, and we're beginning to retrain computer-competent people in basic animation skills. The two disciplines come together, and combining them becomes easier since the students who graduate from programs like Cal Arts and the Ringling School in Florida emerge with both drawing and computer skills.

"We're working on cracking problems such as the perception that CG animation cannot deal adequately with human characters (see chapter 13). For an upcoming film, *Rapunzel Unbraided*, we challenged Glen Keane to demonstrate that computer-generated animation *can* develop convincing human characters. He in turn has challenged a whole team of animators and the results so far are extremely promising. I'm reminded of what happened when Walt Disney asked his artists to produce convincing human characters for *Snow White and the Seven Dwarfs*.

"I believe our Disney department is healthier than it has been for some time, and audiences will be pleasantly surprised by what we have to offer in the next couple of years."

13 Digital Dreams

The dream of digitally-generated animation has been around since
computers were born, or at least since they ceased to be a monopoly
of the Pentagon and the aerospace industry. Crude digital animation,
good enough for daytime TV, has been possible for some time, but if you
asked Disney animators of the first golden age – the generation of the
Nine Old Men – whether computer animation would ever achieve the
standards that would make it suitable for feature film production, they
would respond with a weary sigh: "Never," was the generic answer. "It's
not even good enough for feature-quality in-betweening. It's simply too
mechanical. Computer-generated drawings lack any sense of weight."

In the long run, however, the great majority of veteran animators have
been won over by the undeniable achievements of Pixar Animation
Studios. Retrospectively, it can be seen that the veteran animators were
making the mistake of assuming that, in order to meet their standards,
computer-generated animation would have to ape *their kind of animation,*
and this assumption was shared by many of the top character animators
of the *Little Mermaid* and *Lion King* generation. From at least the time
of *Oliver & Company* (1988), however, the younger animators did accept
the use of computer-assisted production techniques in creating mechanical forms such as automobiles and in plotting shifting perspectives for
layouts. With the arrival of CAPS, production values came to rely more
and more on digital technology, but even so, in movies like *Pocahontas*

and *Tarzan*, all the spectacular effects and crowd scenes and thrilling simulated camera movements remained subsidiary to traditional character animation, which in turn relied upon skill with a pencil.

Elsewhere, however, animators were beginning to think along very different lines. Prominent amongst them was John Lasseter, a young Disney veteran – and a product of the Disney-inspired training program at Cal Arts – who in 1985, during the period of *The Black Cauldron* fiasco, moved from Burbank to the San Francisco Bay Area where he joined the computer division of Lucasfilm, George Lucas's production and post production facility. The following year, the division was purchased by Steve Jobs, a co-founder of Apple Computer, and renamed Pixar. Under Jobs' direction, which demanded creativity and innovation, Lasseter and CGI innovator Ed Catmull worked on developing software that would create the illusion of three-dimensional animated characters that could appear naturalistic right down to the textures of hair, skin, and fabrics. Together they formed the core of the Pixar team, Catmull's prowess having contributed much to the success and evolution of the company's technical artistry and future releases. Their early experimentation led to RenderMan, a program that permits computer-generated footage of, for example, dinosaurs to be slotted digitally into live-action film, a technique that has enhanced many features. It also led to the development of animated commercials and shorts, made in collaboration with directors Andrew Stanton and Pete Docter. An early short, *Luxo Jr.* – a story of desk lamps that come to life – was nominated in 1986 for an Academy Award. In 1988, Pixar produced another short, the Oscar-winning *Tin Toy*, in which a small child causes havoc with his playthings. By that point, Jobs, Lasseter, Catmull and their team were increasingly thinking in terms of feature animation, and their ambitions were beginning to seem believable.

One reason for their confidence was that they had seen through the basic error of the Disney veterans' condemnation of computer animation. Their digitally-produced imagery did not in any way resemble classic Disney animation. It had its own very different look, so that no obvious stylistic or technical comparisons could be made. Pixar animation was about volume as much as about line, about naturalistic texture as much as about color, about realistic depth as much as about surface pattern. It was original, and it succeeded brilliantly on its own terms.

Still there was a link between Pixar animation and classic Disney animation, a strong one, that came as a consequence of the fact that so many Pixar employees were steeped in Disney tradition, either from having worked at Disney, or having trained with Disney veterans at Cal Arts, or both. At Pixar, they were evolving a whole new approach to animation, exploring radical new possibilities and taking chances, but they did so having absorbed the key lessons that Walt Disney had taught – the importance of story and character.

Not surprisingly, the Disney front office took a considerable interest in what was beginning to evolve in Northern California. As it became clear that Pixar was on the verge of being able to produce full-length

For *Toy Story*, Disney teamed up with Pixar Animation Studios to produce the first feature made entirely with computer-generated 3-D animation. Leading the cast of resourceful toys were the cowboy Woody (below and opposite) and the astronaut Buzz Lightyear (opposite)

animated films, Disney struck a deal with Steve Jobs' studio. The first feature, *Toy Story*, was financed 100 percent by Disney, but after that film the deal was renegotiated to give Disney a fifty percent share in the ownership of Pixar's feature releases in return for a fifty percent investment in those productions. In addition, Disney would distribute the pictures for which they would receive an additional fee.

The first feature to go into production was *Toy Story*, which would prove a sensational success when it hit screens across America during the 1995 Christmas season. With its theme of a child's playthings coming to life, it belonged to a genre that can be traced back through *Tin Toy* to some of Walt Disney's early cartoon shorts such as *Midnight in the Toyshop* (1930). Where it differed was in the scope of its ambition and in its presentation of a fully developed, slyly hip yet emotionally satisfying story. Developed by John Lasseter and a team of storyboard artists and screenwriters that included *Buffy the Vampire Slayer* creator Joss Whedon, the narrative tells of the rivalry between Woody, a much loved but now shopworn cowboy doll (the voice of Tom Hanks) and the new arrival in the playroom, a pumped-up toy astronaut named Buzz Lightyear (Tim Allen) whose sense of mission far exceeds his sense of humor. These antagonists battle for the affections of both Andy, their owner, and the rest of the toys in Andy's room, including an attractive shepherdess doll (Annie Potts), a Mr. Potato Head (Don Rickles), a Slinky Dog, and a platoon of toy infantry men. Their adventures take them out of the playroom and into a scary world of gaudily lit strip mall attractions and suburban streets populated by Soccer Moms speeding to their next drop-off. Eventually, Buzz and Woody are forced to team up to defeat the common enemy – Sid, a sadistic neighborhood kid whose greatest pleasure in life is destroying toys.

The story provided situations that children could identify with, while allowing plenty of room for savvy, pop culture gags and glosses to amuse their parents – the perfect combination for a film that can genuinely appeal to the entire family. On top of that, the imagery that appeared on screen was sensational.

When animators like Winsor McCay first brought drawings to life, it seemed to an unprepared public like some kind of voodoo. *Toy Story* achieved something almost as astonishing, introducing a new kind of magic that shocked and delighted even sophisticated late twentieth-century audiences made up of people who thought they had seen just about everything. Pixar's artists seemed to have the power to actually bring "real" toys – not just graphic representations of toys – convincingly to life and set them loose in a world that appeared very close to the real world. In this breakthrough film, three-dimensional forms, no matter how complex, are naturalistically shaded, even when set in motion and lit from multiple sources. In this respect, characters produced by Pixar's digital animation techniques resemble those created using Claymation or filmed three-dimensional stop-action models – such as King Kong – rather than those that are the result of conventional animation drawings. Pixar's world, however, is far more fluid and true to life than that of the stop-action animator, and *Toy Story* simply bowled over viewers with its ability to mimic reality. At the same time, its artists borrowed freely from whichever techniques of conventional animation remained applicable, understanding for example that the key to a character's personality is to be found in his or her eyes. Woody, for instance, has eyes that are as soulful as those of Geppetto in *Pinocchio*, or Belle in *Beauty and the Beast*.

If there is a weakness to *Toy Story,* it is in the animation of the human characters. The Pixar artists were, in fact, confronted with the same problem faced by artists like Grim Natwick and Art Babbitt at the time of *Snow White and the Seven Dwarfs*. It's one thing to bring toys to life, but creating a convincing human presence on screen is far more difficult because the viewer instinctively knows how humans look and move, down to the tiniest flick of an eyelash. In the case of *Toy Story,* the weakest characters are Andy and Sid, the two children involved. Fortunately, the story was conceived in such a way as to require the minimum of screen time for the humans, so that the weakness was minimized and did little to interfere with the overall triumph of the movie.

In Pixar's next film, that problem was avoided because the focus was placed on the insect world. *A Bug's Life* (1998) is as full of vitality as a forest glade in springtime. It positively swarms with vim and vigor, and the vegetation that provides the setting is itself almost as animated as the arthropods, myriapods and acridians that dwell under leaves and stones and amongst the vines and creepers.

In creating the world of *A Bug's Life,* the Pixar artists made brilliant imaginative use of the computer's ability to replicate natural forms such as leaves and dandelion seeds

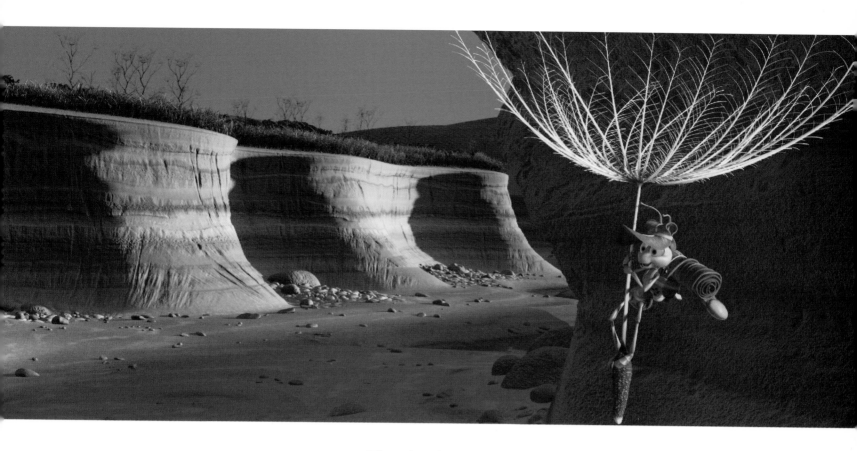

The tribe of ants on which the story centers turns out to be made up of lively personalities rather than the single-minded and almost robotic creatures that we tend to see when they invade our living rooms. The plot involves a threat against the ants by mobster-like grasshoppers led by a character named Hopper (the voice of Kevin Spacey). In order to protect themselves from this aggression, the ants, led by Flik (Dave Foley), seek help from the members of a flea circus and other bugs with specialized skills.

Already, a Pixar-type plot was beginning to emerge, a swiftly flowing kind of narrative in which non-human characters with humanoid characteristics are called upon to right wrongs in storylines that leave plenty of room for hip humor seamlessly integrated into the texture of the movie. It is an effective formula, especially when combined with the kind of special effects that can be achieved with the help of computer-generated animation. Like its predecessor, *A Bug's Life* was a critical and box-office triumph.

Inevitably, the runaway success of *Toy Story* demanded a sequel and soon Woody, Buzz Lightyear, and their pals were back on the Pixar storyboards in preparation for *Toy Story 2*, which would appear in 1999. Loaded with dazzling set pieces, this film has the advantage of working with already familiar characters, so that little exposition is required. Instead of conventional scene setting, the picture opens with a brilliantly staged tease from a Buzz Lightyear videogame that takes our hero into outer space where he confronts myriad dangers. This is sheer, vertiginous action that propels the viewer into the main body of the movie, where we find that all is well in the playroom, with Buzz and Woody now the best of friends. An "injury" to Woody's right shoulder, however, leads to him missing his annual trip to Andy's cowboy camp, and then, while trying to save a fellow toy from a fate dreaded by all toys – being placed in a garage sale – Woody winds up trapped there himself. He is spotted by Al McWhiggin (Wayne Knight), a slimy antique toy dealer who recognizes Woody as a rare collectible spawned by a 1950s TV puppet show titled *Woody's Roundup*. As cheap as he is nasty, McWhiggin tries to bargain for Woody, who has been marked down to a mere 25 cents. To the relief of Buzz and the other toys, watching from the playroom window, Andy's mother removes Woody from the sale, but the dastardly McWhiggin kidnaps him, thus precipitating the rescue efforts on which the rest of the movie is predicated.

Along the way, Woody meets up with spunky cowgirl Jessie (Joan Cusack) – another character doll spun off from *Woody's Roundup* – who proves to be a major addition to the company. Everything propels the movie toward a dazzling climax, which finds Woody and Jessie having to escape from the cargo hold of a jetliner at the moment of takeoff. Directed by John Lasseter (who also executive produced along with Steve Jobs) and co-director Lee Unkrich, the movie featured production values that were better than ever, and snappy songs by Randy Newman.

Toy Story 2 (1999) took the steadfast band of heroes introduced in *Toy Story* and sent them on a new adventure

Right: Drawn by Ricky Nierva, this is the first sketch ever made of Mike Wazowski. While the look of James P. Sullivan – known to his pals as "Sulley" – evolved through 30 different 3-D "sculpts," Mike's basic appearance remained the same. Below is more concept art by Ricky Nierva

Overleaf: *Monsters, Inc.* creates a convincing world in which monsters generate energy to power their city by scaring children. This takes courage since they are themselves terrified of kids

2001 saw the release of *Monsters, Inc.,* a tour de force of computer-generated animation, which brought to life another original story (by Pete Docter, Jill Culton, Jeff Pidgeon, and Ralph Eggleston) combining action, hilarity, and pathos in the now familiar Pixar idiom. The action of the movie is set in Monstropolis, an industrial city with residential areas that resemble the older parts of Brooklyn. Except for the fact that they are monsters, the inhabitants of these brownstone-lined streets are regular blue-collar guys who almost without exception work for Monsters, Inc., the local power company, which generates energy in an unusual way. Inside a gargantuan and highly automated factory, "Scarer" monsters on the "scare floor" are confronted by doors, through which they are required to plunge into another dimension – the one inhabited by human beings. Specifically, they burst from children's closets, in the middle of the night, waking the little darlings and capturing the resulting terrified adrenaline rush – a form of pure energy – to be stored in giant canisters. What makes this task heroic is the fact that the monsters are as scared of the kids as the kids are of them. As Monsters, Inc.'s crabby boss, Waternoose (James Coburn) explains, "there is nothing more terrifying than a human child."

The top "Scarer" at Monsters, Inc. is James P. Sullivan (John Goodman), better known as Sulley – 800 pounds of pastel-colored, furry, polka-dotted sweetness who has the ability to transform himself, for a few seconds at a time, into an ogre so terrifying he can trigger a 10,000 volt panic attack in any child whose room he finds himself in. Aided by his lime green, monocular pal Mike Wazowski (Billy Crystal), Sulley finds himself in competition with Randall Boggs (Steve Buscemi), a lizardlike monster so loathsome he disgusts even the other monsters. Randall covets Sulley's MVP status and will do anything he can think of to sabotage the big guy's career. He gets a helping hand when Sulley unwittingly brings a small child, Boo (Mary Gibbs), to Monstropolis, where her presence sets off alarms and spreads consternation like meltdown in a nuclear plant.

Complicating matters, Boo is not in the least frightened of monsters and thinks that Sulley is cute. She even has a soft spot for the paranoid Mike whose understandable instinct is to send her back where she belongs before she makes life impossible. This situation leads to a rich variety of cleverly developed situations, culminating in a chase scene that makes the airport climax of *Toy Story 2* seem almost tame by comparison. Nor is this the end of the movie. The makers of *Monsters, Inc.* pile climax upon climax, each one topping the last until the audience is left breathless. Directed by Pete Docter, co-directed by Lee Unkrich, and produced by Darla K. Anderson, this is a movie that leaves the viewer both satisfied and exhausted.

Directed by Andrew Stanton and co-directed by Lee Unkrich, Pixar's 2003 entry, *Finding Nemo*, became animation's biggest box office success ever, surpassing even *The Lion King*. Based on an original story by Stanton, this film tells the tale of Marlin, a clown fish, in search of his lost son, Nemo. By comparison with its predecessor, which displayed all the edgy hipness that has accrued to the Pixar name, *Finding Nemo* has a plot that is close to old-fashioned, feel-good Disney story-telling. It's possible to imagine a version of this story being produced, using conventional hand-drawn animation, by the Disney feature animation department at almost any time in its history. There is even a scene, inside a whale, that inevitably calls up memories of *Pinocchio*.

That said, *Finding Nemo* exploits the possibilities of digital animation to the fullest – to orchestrate large schools of fish, for instance,

Below: Storyboard drawings of Dory and Marlin by Ronnie del Carmen

Bottom: This pastel of the underwater world in a fish tank is by Dominique Louis. Layout by Nelson Bohol

The vivid array of settings in *Finding Nemo*
is full of exotic creatures and unexpected
encounters. At top is Nemo's undersea
school, and below, Nemo is face-to-face
with his first human

Marlin and Nemo, reunited
in Sydney Harbor

and especially to generate marvelous undersea effects that convincingly
recreate the world we have come to know through the lenses of the
underwater cameras of Jacques Cousteau and his many successors.
At times, these effects almost overwhelm the story, and it is easy to see
how the Pixar artists became infatuated with the possibilities inherent in,
for example, the tidal movement of seaweed, or the passage of a finned
character through the deceptively beautiful tendrils of a sea anemone,
much as they fell in love with the motion of grassy fronds and falling
leaves in *A Bug's Life*.

Fish proved to have potential as characters for computer-generated
animation. They are so various in appearance that it becomes easy to
delineate personality by means of color and form, and their oddly
mechanical movements, their sudden bursts of speed, lend themselves
well to digital replication. In this instance, creation of character was
further enhanced by some inspired choices of voice talent, notably Albert
Brooks as Marlin, and Ellen DeGeneres as Dory, his scatter-brained
companion.

The Incredibles (2004) represents a return to the hipper kind of Pixar
picture in which sentiment is balanced by a kind of wised-up humor.
Written and directed by Brad Bird – known for his work on *The Simpsons*
and for his acclaimed animated film *The Iron Giant* – this movie takes
as its premise the idea that the golden age of the superhero (or Supers as
they're known here) is over. There have simply been too many lawsuits
caused by civilians who are angered by Supers whose heroics have ended
in unfortunate mishaps. The consequence is that many Supers have had
to take advantage of a government-sponsored relocation program.

One such redundant Super is Mr. Incredible, now known as Bob
Parr, who with his family – all of them, except the baby, incredible in
one way or another – has been living for some years a more or less
normal existence in a suburban community. One day, though, the lure
of a secret mission awakens his Super spirit. He struggles to squeeze his

Opposite top: The fish tank crew
manages to find a way out of
captivity, only to be faced with
yet another obstacle – plastic bags.
Center: Marlin meets Bruce, the
Great White, for the first time.
Bottom: Terrified, Marlin
tries to stop Dory from touching
the deadly jellyfish

Mr. Incredible – also known as Bob Parr – squeezes into his Super suit

no-longer-svelte-form into his old Mr. Incredible suit, and the battle with evil is rejoined, despite every impediment the modern world can throw in his path. His wife, Helen Parr (better known as Elastigirl in her Super years), has not lost the ability to stretch herself out of shape in order to badger a bad guy. As for their teenage daughter, Violet, she is so shy she would like to become invisible, and has the Super ability to do just that. She can also create force fields, while her younger brother Dash has the power of speed.

It would be difficult to think of a better concept for a Pixar picture, a dramatic situation that plays directly to the strengths of the Pixar team – wild invention, knowing humor, and strong character development.

One question remains: How would Walt Disney have felt about computer-generated animation? The answer seems obvious. Walt Disney never shied away from innovation. I believe he would have been Pixar's greatest admirer.

The Incredibles is the story of a family of superannuated Supers who, having been put out to pasture, find themselves called upon to save the world one more time

III Live-Action Films and the Stage

14 Muskets and Mouseketeers

Walt Disney's greatest contribution to the motion-picture industry was the genius he brought to the art of animation. After World War II, however, his studio became well known for its live-action movies and also for its television shows. The live-action movies ranged from low-budget nature films to lavish productions like *20,000 Leagues Under the Sea*. The one thing they all had in common, during Disney's lifetime, was that they were carefully tailored for family audiences in the most traditional sense of the term.

Although the Alice Comedies had included live-action material, *The Reluctant Dragon*, released in 1941, was a major departure for Disney. At one level, it is a documentary about Disney animation – complete with cartoon inserts – but it is much more than that because of a linking live-action narrative which sees the comic writer and actor Robert Benchley set loose on the Burbank lot, with predictably amusing consequences. Unpretentious and charming, *The Reluctant Dragon* presents an interesting, if somewhat fictionalized, picture of the Disney Studio during its Golden Age.

A little later, in the mid-forties, segments of live-action footage found their way into package films such as *The Three Caballeros* and *Fun and Fancy Free*, but the real breakthrough had come with *Song of the South* (1946), in which a full complement of professional actors was used to tell an entirely fictional story. The three cartoon segments helped sell the movie – as did scenes that combined live action and animation – but the success of the movie depended chiefly on strong performances (notably by James Baskett as Uncle Remus), crisp direction, and the cinematography of Gregg Toland, best known for his work on *Citizen Kane*.

A little more than two years later, Disney released *So Dear to My Heart,* which, like *Song of the South,* was a costume drama starring Bobby Driscoll and Luana Patten and set in rural America. A minimal amount of animation was employed, but to all intents and purposes this was an entirely live action film.

The next phase in the development of Disney live-action production came about largely as the result of a historical accident. Because of postwar monetary restrictions, a sizable amount of Disney capital was frozen in the United Kingdom. This money could not be taken out of the British Isles, but it could be used there, and, on the advice of his brother Roy, Walt Disney decided to utilize these funds to make live-action films in Britain. The fruits of this venture – *Treasure Island, The Story of Robin Hood and His Merrie Men, The Sword and the Rose,* and *Rob Roy, the Highland Rogue* – were released between 1950 and 1954.

These are well-told, satisfying adventure stories full of muskets and longbows and appropriate period detail. *Treasure Island* is a minor masterpiece of the genre, a faithful rendition of Robert Louis Stevenson's classic novel, highlighted by Robert Newton's mesmerizing performance as Long John Silver. With his wooden leg and almost mechanical manner-isms, Long John resembles one of Disney's great animated villains, both menacing and funny. As played by Newton, he is also very human.

The other British costume dramas featured fine performers such as Richard Todd, Jack Hawkins, James Robertson Justice, and Glynis Johns, introducing Disney to the reservoir of acting talent available in London, one he would draw upon often for future projects. Beyond that, the movies made imaginative use of the natural beauties of the British landscape. Disney himself was very much in charge of these productions, spending extended periods each year in the United Kingdom.

Modest as these movies were, they did a good deal to restore the Studio's fortunes and must have made Disney increasingly aware of the part that live action would have to play in his future plans. By the early 1950s, he was fully committed. Animation would continue, but the Studio's facilities would be modified and expanded to accommodate other kinds of production.

The Disney Studio had one great advantage over its competitors. Because of its background in animation, it was equipped to deal with unconventional ideas. Of necessity, Walt Disney had become unusually resourceful as a filmmaker, unbound by convention when it came to imagining what might make a commercial movie. Ideas that would have been thrown out at other studios were actively sought by Disney.

At some point soon after the war, he began to think about making a film about America's last frontier – Alaska. Instead of hiring a writer to script an epic, he got in touch with Al and Elma Milotte, who ran a

In *The Reluctant Dragon,* 1941, Robert Benchley finds himself on the loose on Disney's Burbank lot. In the bottom picture, Benchley is seen with Clarence Nash and Florence Gill, the voices of Donald Duck and Clara Cluck

Although it includes fine segments of animation, *Song of the South*, 1946, is primarily a live-action film highlighted by James Baskett's outstanding portrayal of Uncle Remus

Starring Robert Newton and Bobby Driscoll,
Treasure Island, 1950, was the first of a series
of costume dramas filmed in the British Isles

camera store in Alaska. The Milottes were nature buffs and had some experience with 16mm cinematography. Disney asked them to film glimpses of Alaskan life that might suggest possible lines of development. After sending back footage on a variety of topics, from salmon fishing to gold mining, Al Milotte wrote to ask if Disney would be interested in material about the tens of thousands of fur seals who inhabited the Pribilof Islands – bleak rocks in the Bering Sea. Disney wired his approval, and soon reels of seal footage began to arrive at the studio. According to James Algar, one of those entrusted with shaping the material, it was difficult at first to make sense of the footage they were screening. But Disney saw something that held his interest. The seals were acting out a primitive rite that had been repeated for thousands of years. The problem was to present this rite in dramatic terms that would be readily under-stood by a theater audience. The Disney staff began to research the subject and to put together the story of the seals' life cycle. The film sent by the Milottes was tailored to fit this story, and the result was a twenty-seven-minute picture titled *Seal Island*, released in 1949.

At first, *Seal Island* attracted little attention, but after it won an Academy Award for best short subject of that year, it received wide dis-tribution. Its success led to Disney launching a whole series of nature documentaries which he called True-Life Adventures. Most ran between twenty and thirty minutes, but six feature-length movies were also produced – *The Living Desert, The Vanishing Prairie, The African Lion, Secrets of Life, White Wilderness,* and *Jungle Cat.*

The Milottes were involved in several of these productions, but many other cameramen also contributed to the True-Life Adventures – most of them trained naturalists. The same basic formula was used for all these films. Location or laboratory footage was shot and then sent to Hollywood to be edited into usable form by a team headed by James Algar, Winston Hibler, and Ben Sharpsteen. Trained in the animation side of the business, they tended to look – sometimes too assiduously – for the humor in any given subject and were not above tinkering with their raw material, in the cutting room, to bring out its gag potential. Anthropomorphism was also emphasized – probably a necessary technique for selling the idea of nature documentaries to the public at a time when they were a complete novelty and considered decidedly uncommercial.

Some of the later True-Life Adventures, such as *The African Lion,* were more objective, less influenced by "animation thinking." And even the corniest of these movies was full of wonderful cinematography. Disney gave naturalists the time and equipment they needed, and they repaid him with footage of a quality that had never been seen before. For all their defects, the True-Life Adventures pioneered a genre which was to become a staple of television programming in the form of shows like the *National Geographic* specials.

Spin-offs from the True-Life Adventures included the People and Places documentary series and, more significantly, the many Disney films – such as *Nikki, Wild Dog of the North* and *The Legend of Lobo* – that blended documentary animal footage with staged footage (sometimes involving

Seal Island (top) was the first of Disney's True-Life Adventures, a pioneering series of wildlife films that also included *The African Lion* (center) and *The Living Desert*

Al and Elma Milotte shot the footage used to produce *Seal Island* and *The African Lion*

human actors) in order to create a dramatic story. Other studios had used this technique for series such as *Lassie* and *Rin-Tin-Tin* that featured canine stars, but Disney producers often employed nondomestic animals including bears, coyotes, and even wolves and wolverines, in this way.

Movies of that genre demand great patience on the part of both animal handlers and cameramen, and producers like Algar, Hibler, Harry Tytle, Ken Peterson, and Roy E. Disney developed remarkable expertise in this field.

As far back as the 1930s, Walt Disney had been aware of the potential importance of television – Mickey Mouse cartoons were used in early tests of transmitting equipment – and Disney was careful to retain television rights to all of his films. In the late 1940s, when other studios were trying to make quick money by selling the home-screen rights to their film libraries, Disney resisted the temptation.

Given this foresight, one might have expected Disney to be eager to involve the Studio in television production, but that was not the case. As the television boom gathered momentum, he turned down series opportunities (but did produce Christmas specials in 1950 and 1951). Finally, in 1954, he agreed to develop a series for the American Broadcasting Company. This had little to do with enthusiasm for television but a great deal to do with the fact that ABC was prepared to make a sizable investment in Disney's proposed theme park in return for Disney lending his prestige to the network. Appropriately, the new series was titled *Disneyland*.

Now it became apparent that Disney had been very smart to hold on to the television rights to his library of back products. Major features like *Bambi* could be reissued theatrically while lesser productions, including shorts, could be recycled as part of the television series. Still, a good deal of new material would be needed, and one of the first ideas slated for

Buddy Ebsen (left) and Fess Parker starred in *Davy Crockett*, Disney's first television hit

production was *Davy Crockett,* scheduled as a three-parter starring Fess Parker and Buddy Ebsen. According to Bill Walsh, the series producer, the subject was picked by sheer dumb luck: "At that time [Davy Crockett] was considered just one more frontiersman."

When the three episodes were edited, they ran a little short, and Disney suggested that they fill in the needed time with a montage of evocative drawings. The drawings were just fine but a little dull, so Disney suggested a song to go with them. Tom Blackburn, who had written the script, and George Bruns, who composed the score, went off for about twenty minutes and came back with a song that began "Born on a mountaintop in Tennessee. . . ." Walsh thought it sounded pretty awful, but there was no time for anything else.

The song was, of course, "The Ballad of Davy Crockett," and it became a smash hit on both sides of the Atlantic. The three *Davy Crockett* shows were equally successful, creating a craze for coonskin hats and providing ABC television with an enormous boost. (Later, *Davy Crockett* was recut and released as a feature film.)

The *Disneyland* series itself went from strength to strength. Later its name was changed several times (to *Walt Disney Presents,* then *Walt Disney's Wonderful World of Color,* then *The Wonderful World of Disney,* then *Disney's Wonderful World,* and finally *Walt Disney*); its time slot moved from Wednesday to Friday to Sunday, and the show even changed networks, in 1961, from ABC to NBC, and in 1981 from NBC to CBS; but these changes had no effect on the fact that the sixty-minute weekly format Disney developed in 1954 remained successful for twenty-nine seasons.

Another hugely popular Disney show, *The Mickey Mouse Club,* was launched on ABC in 1955, running each weekday afternoon until 1959.

Again, Bill Walsh was entrusted with getting the series off the ground, and his first task was to find the right kind of young performers.

"I remember Walt saying, 'Don't get me those kids with the tightly curled hairdos – tap dancers – get me children who look like they're having fun. Then later we can teach them to tap dance or sing or whatever.' He suggested that if we went to ordinary schools and watched the kids at recess, pretty soon we'd find there'd be one we would watch – whether he was doing anything or not. . . . And that would be the kid we wanted for the show. So we used this technique and we found Annette and Darlene and Cubby and the bunch."

The show developed a pleasant, informal format with which children could identify. The talents of the Mouseketeers were combined with old Disney cartoons and many other kinds of material. Dramatic serials, such as "Spin and Marty," became a popular feature of the program.

All of the Mouseketeers became popular, but from the beginning it was Annette Funicello who attracted the most fan mail. Walsh and the other producers tried to maintain an ensemble feel, but gradually Annette's inescapable popularity caused more and more of the show to be keyed to her. The show was still receiving excellent ratings when it ended, but it had become very expensive to produce and Walt Disney was feuding with ABC over the number of commercials the network wanted to insert into the program. Annette was also beginning to outgrow her role. For these combined reasons, it was decided to take the show off the air. (*The Mickey Mouse Club* format was revived in 1977 and 1989.)

Annette moved on to film stardom outside the Disney Studio orbit, but she was still under the guidance of Walt Disney, who continued to own her contract.

In 1954, the year in which the *Disneyland* series was launched, the Studio released 20,000 *Leagues Under the Sea*, easily its most ambitious live-action picture to that point – a big-budget movie using major Hollywood stars (Kirk Douglas, James Mason, Paul Lukas, and Peter Lorre) and state-of-the-art special effects.

The film 20,000 *Leagues* came into being as a by-product of the True-Life Adventures. Bill Walsh and Card Walker had raised the possibility of making an undersea film for the nature series, and this triggered the idea of bringing Jules Verne's classic to the screen. Disney was not enthusiastic at first but eventually bought the rights to the property from MGM and called in Earl Feldman and Richard Fleischer – known for their imaginative B movies – to write and direct the film.

The project demanded elaborate sets and a great deal of trick photography. Much of the action was shot in a large water tank on one of the Disney soundstages; other scenes were filmed in an outdoor tank at the Fox lot, and location work was done in Jamaica and off San Diego. One high spot of the action is a violent fight between the crew of the submarine *Nautilus* and a giant squid – a sequence that called for all the ingenuity the Studio could muster. The first version, shot at tremendous expense, did not satisfy Disney. The squid did not look real enough and the action

The Mickey Mouse Club featured the Mouseketeers, a group of children with no previous show-business experience. Although no one performer was designated as the show's star, Annette Funicello emerged as a great audience favorite and went on to a career in movies

20,000 Leagues Under the Sea, 1954, was a big-budget adventure film with an all-star cast that included James Mason (top), Kirk Douglas, Peter Lorre, and Paul Lukas

Hayley Mills, second from left, starred in several Disney films, including *Pollyanna*, 1960

was filmed against a pink sky, which provided quite the wrong atmosphere. A new squid was prepared and the sequence reshot, this time during a simulated storm.

James Mason is splendid as the heroically demented Captain Nemo, and Kirk Douglas has fine moments as the stalwart whaler Ned Land. The contrast between these two characters is a little overstated, but *20,000 Leagues Under the Sea* grips our imagination because it is convincing as a battle of ideas and emotions.

Released in 1960, *Swiss Family Robinson* is another big-budget movie taken from a classic adventure story. With John Mills in the lead role, we see how a shipwrecked family learns to cope with life on a tropical island, how they bring European ingenuity to bear on their unfamiliar environment, and how they deal with a band of pirates that invades the island. The production offers some excellent scenic photography, but in the end, the movie lacks the dramatic tension of the best Disney adventure films.

The Shaggy Dog, released in 1959, was the first of the Studio's zany comedies. It starred Fred MacMurray, who had been seen in many of the screwball comedies of the thirties and early forties. *The Shaggy Dog* was to some extent an update of that kind of film, though aimed chiefly at the juvenile market. It was a box-office success and was followed by other similar vehicles tailored to MacMurray's talents, notably *The Absent-Minded Professor*, 1961, and *Son of Flubber*, 1963. The young British actress Hayley Mills also starred in several Disney films during this period, including costume pieces such as *Pollyanna* and contemporary comedies like *The Parent Trap*.

In 1964, Disney released *Mary Poppins*, a film which became one of the greatest hits in the history of the motion-picture industry to that date.

Adapted from P. L. Travers's children's stories, the movie provided Julie Andrews with a spectacular screen debut and smashed box-office records at home and abroad.

Walt Disney had been aware of Travers's remarkable nanny for many years and had made several attempts to obtain the rights to the Poppins stories, probably intending to adapt them for an animated feature. The author resisted his overtures until he visited her in London and persuaded her that the time was ripe to bring her world to the screen. (By then, several other studios were bidding for the rights, and Rodgers and Hammerstein were interested in turning the stories into a musical.)

Back in Burbank, Bill Walsh – who would coproduce the movie – and Don DaGradi began to work on a script that would weave fragments from the original stories into a continuous narrative. The brothers Richard M. and Robert B. Sherman were called in to write music and lyrics.

Next came the crucial matter of casting an actress to play Mary Poppins herself. Mary Martin and Bette Davis were considered front-runners, but Disney had seen Julie Andrews on stage in *Camelot* and was taken with her. He especially liked the way she whistled. The part of Mary's friend Bert went to Dick Van Dyke, whose television show was at the peak of its popularity and who was the only American principal in the cast. The children who become Mary's charges were played by Matthew Garber and Karen Dotrice, both of whom had earlier Disney experience. Glynis Johns, another Disney veteran, was cast as their mother and David Tomlinson as their father. Yet another Briton, Robert Stevenson, was assigned to direct.

Mary Poppins lacks the ethereal charm of Travers's stories, but it has its own virtues. In providing the movie with a coherent structure, Walsh and DaGradi transformed those stories into something more robust than the original. But then again, Julie Andrews is a far more glamorous and youthful version of Mary Poppins than the one we meet on the printed page. She brings a charm and spark of her own, and her singing voice and

Released in 1964, *Mary Poppins* combined live action with interludes of animation and became the biggest commercial success that the Studio would enjoy during Walt Disney's lifetime

An airborne tea party that ends in hysterical laughter is one of many special effects sequences that contribute to the magic of *Mary Poppins*

dancing ability – matched to memorable songs – are great assets. In the end, though, the key to her performance is her ability to seem prim and proper yet be perpetually on the verge of some kind of marvelous insanity.

Dick Van Dyke's attempt at a cockney accent leaves much to be desired, but the rest of the cast is excellent, and Edwardian London is evoked with a good deal of feeling for atmosphere, clever use being made both of remarkable special effects and of simple sets that would not seem out of place on the stage of a Broadway theater. Throughout the film, the real and the imaginary are combined in inventive and believable ways, though the scenes that combine live action with animation now seem stiff and dated in the wake of *Who Framed Roger Rabbit*.

In the production of *Mary Poppins*, all of the Studio's resources were pooled to produce a motion picture that probably could not have been made anywhere else.

The greatest of those resources, Walt Disney himself, would soon be gone, but the kind of live-action family films he had espoused continued to be produced at the Studio. *The Love Bug,* 1969 – developed, written, and produced by Bill Walsh – inaugurated a series of movies about Herbie, a Volkswagen with a mind of its own. *Bedknobs and Broomsticks,* 1971, was a lively fantasy adventure featuring Angela Lansbury, and *Freaky Friday,* 1976, was the best of a number of Disney films that starred future Academy Award–winner Jodie Foster.

Walt Disney picked Julie Andrews to
play Mary Poppins in part because he was
impressed by her whistling ability

David Warner was one of the stars of *Tron*, 1982, which made use of electronic effects to place human protagonists inside a video game

The Love Bug, 1965, was the first of several successful comedies conceived by producer Bill Walsh and built around Herbie, a Volkswagen with a mind of its own

In 1979, there was an attempt to cash in on the science-fiction movie craze by producing a space-opera version of *20,000 Leagues Under the Sea* titled *The Black Hole*. It was strong on special effects but weak on story and fared miserably at the box office. Another disappointment was the video-game fantasy *Tron*, which made spectacular use of computer-generated imagery but failed to generate any empathy between protagonists and audience.

Tron was made during the brief tenure of Tom Wilhite – former head of the Disney publicity department – as vice president of creative development. Along with *Tron*, Wilhite was largely responsible for some interesting movies, such as *The Last Flight of Noah's Ark* and *The Devil and Max Devlin* (both starring Elliott Gould) and the powerful rite of passage drama *Tex* (starring Matt Dillon).

The problem was that the family film market was proving demographically less profitable than the young adult audience, and, despite strong efforts like *Tex*, the Studio had a problem expanding its live-action production in a direction that would appeal to those young adults. As noted in chapter 10, testing showed that the Disney name was actually off-putting to young adults since they associated it with the world of childhood from which they were trying to graduate.

With this in mind, Ron Miller, then head of production, decided in the early eighties to begin issuing a new and more adult-oriented line of films for which a different brand name – Touchstone – was eventually

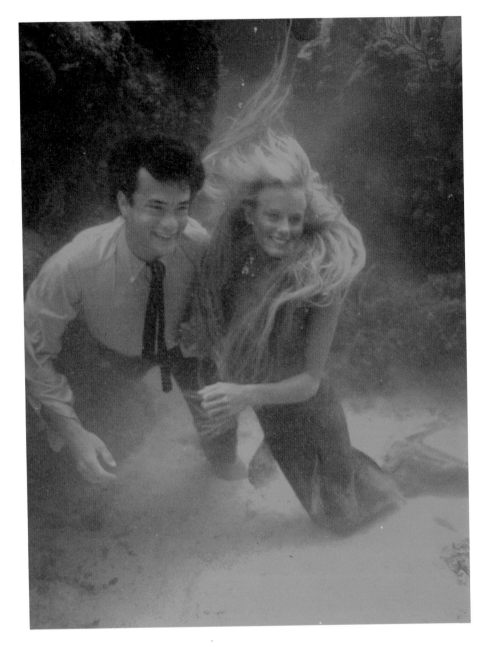

Splash!, 1984, was the first Disney feature to be aimed at a sophisticated adult audience

adopted. With Wilhite in charge of this program, the first Touchstone movie was *Splash!*, starring Tom Hanks and Daryl Hannah and directed by Ron Howard. It was released in 1984 with much fanfare and enjoyed considerable critical and commercial success.

Clearly, Touchstone was a good idea, but it came too late to help save the Studio from being plunged into a state of turmoil later that year. Touchstone would come fully into its own only after the team led by Michael Eisner, Frank Wells, and Roy Disney took control of the Studio and began to restructure the entire production program.

15 Expanded Horizons

One of the first films to go into production after Michael Eisner and Frank Wells took control of the Studio was *Down and Out in Beverly Hills* (1986), Paul Mazursky's very adult (and very funny) comedy starring Bette Midler, Richard Dreyfuss, and Nick Nolte. It was a signal that the production team, spearheaded by Jeffrey Katzenberg, was ready to expand into markets where Disney had seldom, if ever, ventured before.

Still, while Eisner's mandate to Katzenberg emphasized broadening the Studio's scope (so that Disney could have a full range of pictures that would enable it to compete with companies like Columbia and Paramount), it also included a directive to make "real Disney" movies once again – the kind of family-oriented productions for which the Studio had made its reputation. To produce the more adult-oriented films, two new entities were set up: Touchstone Pictures and Hollywood Pictures. These went on to release such hits as *The Color of Money* (1986), *Good Morning, Vietnam* (1987), *Dead Poets Society* (1989), *Beaches* (1989), *Pretty Woman* (1990), *Father of the Bride* (1991), *The Joy Luck Club* (1993), and *Sweet Home Alabama* (2002). Meanwhile, live-action family fare – like animation – was released under the Walt Disney name, and it is primarily those movies that this chapter is concerned with.

Team Disney (as the new executive group was dubbed) soon had a success with a youth-oriented picture that Walt Disney would surely

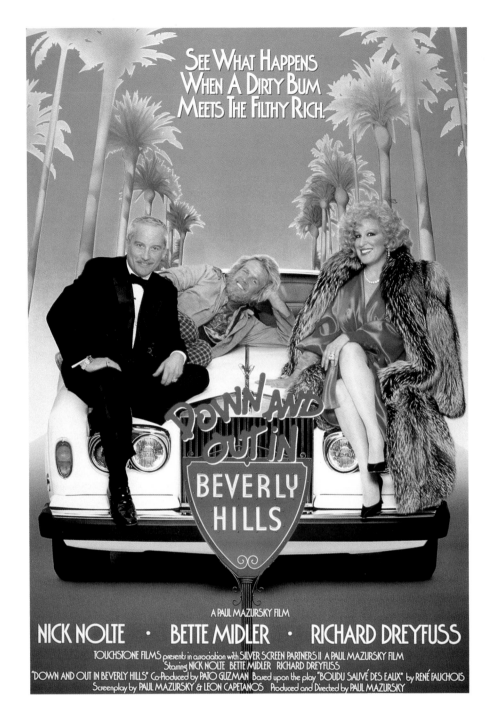

Directed by Paul Mazursky, *Down and Out in Beverly Hills*, 1986, signaled a move toward more adult-oriented films instigated by new Disney chairman Michael Eisner and his studio head Jeffrey Katzenberg

have approved of. This was *Flight of the Navigator* (1986), a science fiction fantasy directed by Randal Kleiser, who is perhaps best known for *Grease* (produced at Paramount under Katzenberg's auspices). The following year the Studio inaugurated a series of decidedly juvenile comedies starring Jim Varney as Ernest P. Worrell. Also in 1987, *Benji the Hunted* revived a favorite Disney genre of the fifties and sixties, the fiction film that blends staged and documentary footage into a rousing entertainment with ethics that have more to do with man's view of the world than with the laws of nature.

1988's *Who Framed Roger Rabbit* (see chapter 10) proved that Katzenberg and Eisner were serious about making the kind of movies that would recapture the old magic. In 1989, they had a solid family-oriented hit with *Honey, I Shrunk the Kids*, very much a throwback to

A variation on the Pygmalion theme in which the heroine is a Hollywood hooker rather than a cockney flower girl, *Pretty Woman* was one of the major hits of 1990. Here the camera sets up to shoot the movie's star, Julia Roberts

Honey, I Shrunk the Kids, 1989, was a successful return to the kind of special-effects comedy the Studio had exploited effectively in the sixties and seventies

Honey, I Blew Up the Kid was a sequel set in Las Vegas. A third film in the series was titled rather lamely *Honey, We Shrunk Ourselves*

the kind of Disney special effects movies that Bill Walsh used to produce, full of trick shots and oversize props. Directed by Joe Johnston and starring Rick Moranis, the film's success inevitably led to a sequel, *Honey, I Blew Up the Kid* (1992), this time directed by Randal Kleiser. A television series followed.

In 1990, Touchstone released *Dick Tracy*, Warren Beatty's entry into the big budget comic-strip hero genre, which co-starred Dustin Hoffman, Al Pacino, and Madonna. Also drawing on a 1930s pop culture background was 1991's *The Rocketeer* – set largely in pre–World War II Hollywood – the story of a young aviator (Bill Campbell) who accidentally comes into possession of a rocket pack that enables him to fly Buck Rogers–style. Directed by Joe Johnston, this film is a little long-winded but has some nice inside jokes for movie buffs, and features everything from Nazi spies to a flamboyant matinee idol.

Hollywood Pictures' *Encino Man* (1992) tickled the funny bones of teenagers with the story of a cryogenically preserved caveman who becomes the most popular dude in the San Fernando Valley. Another Disney hit that year was *The Mighty Ducks*, the story of the triumph against the odds of a peanut league hockey team (which eventually led indirectly to the establishment of a National Hockey League franchise of the same name). Its success gave rise to sequels, and also to a skein of similarly themed sports movies that includes *Cool Runnings* (1993) and *Angels in the Outfield* (1994).

The year 1993 saw the release of Tim Burton's *The Nightmare Before Christmas*, a stop-motion animated musical feature produced by Burton, who before his success with movies such as *Beetlejuice* and *Batman* had been an artist in the Disney animation department. *Homeward Bound: The Incredible Journey* (1993) was a remake of Disney's 1963 film about a trio of pets that find their way across country under trying circumstances. This time, we get to hear them speak, with

Scenes from *The Mighty Ducks* (top, left) starring Emilio Estevez as an ice hockey coach, and *Angels in the Outfield* (top, right) with Danny Glover as the team manager. Released in 1990, *Dick Tracy* (above) was an imaginative exploration of pop culture directed by Warren Beatty, who also starred

Opposite: Tim Burton's *The Nightmare Before Christmas*, 1993, added stop-motion animation to the Disney repertoire

Tim Burton with some of the characters created for *The Nightmare Before Christmas*

the borrowed voices of Michael J. Fox, Sally Field and Don Ameche, a gimmick that does nothing to enhance the story, but which proved successful enough commercially to lead to a 1996 sequel in which the trio wanders the streets of San Francisco.

By then, Jeffrey Katzenberg had departed the Studio and Joe Roth – whose Caravan Pictures had already come under the Disney umbrella – had replaced him as head of production. Earlier, in 1993, Disney had purchased Miramax, which continued to operate as an independent company, making films primarily for the art houses and winning a sack full of Academy Awards along the way.

In 1994, the Studio had a Christmas hit with *The Santa Clause*, directed by John Pasquin and starring Tim Allen. That same season saw the release of *Rudyard Kipling's The Jungle Book*, a disappointing live-action exploration of the material that had inspired the animated classic. A still more disappointing sequel followed in 2003. Yet another less than sparkling gloss on familiar material was 1995's *A Kid in King Arthur's Court*.

Frank and Ollie (1995) is a handsome and deserved documentary tribute to Frank Thomas and Ollie Johnston, the last survivors amongst Walt Disney's Nine Old Men, directed by Theodore Thomas, Frank's son. The following year saw an outstanding release in the form of *James and the Giant Peach*, an imaginative adaptation of Roald Dahl's story about a boy who flees the unpleasant realities of his life by hitching a ride in the world's largest piece of fruit, which turns out to be populated by a varied and lively group of characters. Directed by Henry Selick, the film starts in live action then switches to a very sophisticated version of stop-action animation that permits the magic of Dahl's imaginary world to be caught on film.

There were two remakes of Disney classics: *101 Dalmatians* in 1995 and in 1997 *That Darn Cat*. *101 Dalmatians* is a live-action re-enactment

The Santa Clause, starring Tim Allen, was a substantial box office hit

James and the Giant Peach made use of stop-action animation and special effects to recreate Roald Dahl's world of fantasy

101 Dalmatians was a live-action remake of *One Hundred and One Dalmatians*, the new version starring Glenn Close as Cruella De Vil

A smart and savvy remake of the 1961 original, *The Parent Trap* starred (left to right) Natasha Richardson, Lindsay Lohan, Dennis Quaid and, yes, Lindsay Lohan

of the 1961 animated favorite *One Hundred and One Dalmatians*. Directed by Stephen Herek, and with Glenn Close as an effective Cruella De Vil, the film starts out well enough, but eventually descends into overdone and rather ham-fisted slapstick that is not likely to make anyone forget the tightly staged climactic scenes of the original. This did not prevent the making of *102 Dalmatians*, released in 2000. *That Darn Cat* is an update of the 1965 Dean Jones vehicle, which manages to demonstrate that cats were funnier in the sixties.

Air Bud (1997) is a pleasant kid flick about a stray dog with a talent for shooting basketball hoops. *RocketMan* (1997) is a science fiction comedy that must be among the unfunniest movies Disney has ever released. With *Flubber* (1997) we are back in the world of Disney remakes. It would be tempting to say that this is a world that should have been left uninhabited, but 1998's *The Parent Trap*, directed by Nancy Meyers, bucked the trend, being an entirely satisfying update of the 1961 film with Lindsay Lohan in the dual Hayley Mills roles.

Directed by David Kellogg, 1999's *Inspector Gadget* – based on a television cartoon series – starred Matthew Broderick as a kind of comic cuts bionic man who plays for laughs while in pursuit of the bad guys. *The Straight Story*, also released that year and directed by David Lynch, is a far more interesting film, based on the true tale of a seventy-three-year-old man who drove his lawn mower 300 miles in an attempt to make up with his estranged and ill brother whom he hadn't spoken to in a decade.

Dinosaur (2000) is a Disney-produced partially computer-generated film in which digitized giant reptiles are combined with live-action backgrounds. It tells the story of a young dinosaur, separated from his parents while still an egg, then brought up by a family of lemurs, with whom he is forced to flee a bombardment of meteors, such as has been surmised

Dinosaur employed digital effects to recreate a realistic prehistoric world

to have precipitated the dinosaur extinction. The dynamics of the plot are predictable, and there is nothing here to match the super smart humor of the Pixar movies, but some of the visuals are striking and the opening sequence is a spectacular mini melodrama that sets the tone for the whole movie.

The Country Bears, the first of a trio of films to be based on attractions in Disney theme parks, was released in 2002. Other than marking the beginning of this trend, it caused very little stir. Far more successful, and an enormous box office hit, was the Jerry Bruckheimer produced *Pirates of the Caribbean: The Curse of the Black Pearl* (2003), a swashbuckling extravaganza featuring Johnny Depp as a dashing, delinquent sea dandy, Captain Jack Sparrow, a role that would once have gone to Errol Flynn. Under the direction of Gore Verbinski, Sparrow is led on a merry chase as he attempts to recapture his ship, *The Black Pearl,* from the villainous Captain Barbossa (Geoffrey Rush) who, along with his crew, has joined the ranks of the living dead, thanks to a curse. Compounding his crimes, Barbossa has kidnapped the beautiful Elizabeth (Keira Knightley). In order to pursue Barbossa, Sparrow and an old friend of Elizabeth's, Will Turner (Orlando Bloom), "borrow" the Royal Navy's fastest ship, H.M.S. *Interceptor*. This annoys His Majesty's servants in the region so that Sparrow and Turner are themselves pursued by H.M.S. *Dauntless*, which not entirely by chance happens to be under the

Inspired by the popular Disneyland attraction, Jerry Bruckheimer's *Pirates of the Caribbean: The Curse of the Black Pearl* was an enormous hit starring Keira Knightley (opposite top), Johnny Depp (opposite top and bottom) and Orlando Bloom (opposite bottom). Some scenes from the movie (above) recall elements in the theme park attraction

command of Elizabeth's fiancé, Commodore Norrington (Jack Davenport). Needless to say, a desert island and a treasure are also involved. In fact, all the elements of classic pirate melodrama are present and they are exploited to the fullest.

To the casual observer, the film version of *Pirates of the Caribbean* might seem to have little to do with the venerable Disneyland attraction. Disneyland aficionados, however, will find that the movie is peppered with insider references – including such tiny details as a crab in the sand next to the skeleton of a man who has been stabbed in the back – that bring an extra layer of meaning. In fact, the art directors used Marc Davis' original story sketches for the ride as research material.

Davis' influence is apparent again in *The Haunted Mansion* (2003), a film based on another theme park attraction to which the veteran animator contributed many ideas. In the movie version – directed by *Lion King* director Rob Minkoff, and featuring spectacular special effects makeup by Rick Baker – a real estate salesman played by Eddie Murphy becomes trapped, with his family, in a spook-filled *antebellum* Southern mansion. The gags come as fast and furious as in an old Mickey Mouse cartoon.

Also appearing in 2003 was *Freaky Friday,* a remake of the 1976 film starring Jodie Foster and Barbara Harris, based on a novel by Mary Rodgers that tells the story of a mother and daughter who gain respect for one another after swapping places for a day. This was an instance of a remake being a very good idea. The original movie was terrific and the new version, starring Lindsay Lohan and Jamie Lee Curtis, was if anything even better, with Lohan delightful and Curtis putting in one of her funniest performances since *A Fish Called Wanda*. Directed by Mark Waters from a smart script by Heather Hash, this movie is a splendid example of how the old type of Disney family film can be brought up to date.

Since the original *Disneyland* show, Disney has always had an important presence in broadcasting. In 1983, the Disney Channel became an early entry into the cable television field, and on July 31, 1995, The Walt Disney Company shocked the entertainment industry by announcing

Another successful remake was the 2003 update of *Freaky Friday* in which a mother and daughter – Jamie Lee Curtis (left) and Lindsay Lohan – find themselves in one another's shoes, not to mention inside one another's skins plans to acquire Capital Cities/ABC Inc., in a $19 billion deal that would create the largest media group in the world, as of that time. When the merger was finalized, it meant that Disney had assumed ownership of the ABC television network along with its eight local affiliate stations – all in choice markets – a network of twenty-one radio stations, newspapers, magazines and other publishing interests, and also had acquired an 80 percent interest in several more cable channels, most notably ESPN.

It is fair to say, then, that Disney is an enormous presence in the broadcasting industry, both on the entertainment front and in the arena of gathering and dispensing news. Most of this falls outside the scope of this book, but brief note must be taken of some of the company's activities in this area, especially in the field of animation for television (and of movies for direct release to video, mostly handled by the television animation division).

Long before the merger with Capital Cities/ABC, Disney had been providing entertainment fare for network TV, often as co-producer with companies such as Witt-Thomas-Harris. Arrangements of this sort led to a number of hit situation comedies such as *The Golden Girls, Blossom* and *Home Improvement*. Disney-sponsored live-action production for television has continued since that time, especially for the Disney Channel and for the ABC Family cable channel. This has resulted in scores of shows that have carried on the traditions of quality television established while Walt Disney was still alive, and a number of popular series such as *Lizzie McGuire*.

During Walt's lifetime, the Studio had stayed away from television animation, except to the extent that it recycled its theatrical releases for the smaller screen. In the early eighties, however, the possibility of creating animation specifically for television began to seem financially attractive, and it found a champion in the form of Gary Krisel who had spent several years reviving the fortunes of Disney's music and merchandising divisions. The advent of the Disney Channel meant that Disney back material would now be used there. It was Krisel's theory that Disney should be developing new material for the networks, and Ron Miller, then Studio head, gave him the go-ahead to explore the possibility. When, shortly after, the Eisner-Wells team took charge, Krisel's plans were given a cautious boost. The huge success of *The Gummi Bears*, one of the new division's first shows, provided great impetus to move on to fresh projects, including both programs based on all new characters and others based on existing Disney characters. In the latter category, both *The New Adventures of Winnie the Pooh* and *Ducktales* (based on the Scrooge McDuck comic books of Carl Barks) were major hits. *TaleSpin* was an interesting novelty, set in the town of Cape Suzette and featuring characters out of *The Jungle Book*, but casting them against character – Shere Khan became a sort of Daddy Warbucks type – in a retro setting reminiscent of old Warner Brothers movies. Other series based on in-house properties included one derived from *The Little Mermaid* and *Goof Troop*, starring Goofy as an incompetent but loving single parent.

New characters were the stars of *Darkwing Duck*, which featured a

Disney's animated television hits have included *TaleSpin* (top), *Darkwing Duck* (center) and *Goof Troop*

Ducktales was one of the success stories of
Disney's television animation division

feathered hero who was a remote cousin of old comic-book private eyes like Will Eisner's *The Spirit*. That was essentially a humorous show, but quite different in tone – dramatic and even sinister – was *Gargoyles*, about stone figures from Scotland that attain the ability to come to life when they are incorporated into a Manhattan skyscraper.

All this was before the merger with ABC, and many of these series continued to thrive after it had taken place. Later they were joined by others such as *Mickey MouseWorks*, *Hercules*, *The Mighty Ducks*, and *Kim Possible*.

Meanwhile, the television animation division had taken on the responsibility of producing occasional theatrical films, such as *A Goofy Movie* (see chapter 13) and many feature length titles intended for sale and rental in video stores. The first of these was *The Return of Jafar*, a sequel to *Aladdin*, and other entries have included both sequels to older Disney classics *(Lady and the Tramp II)* and many titles that have capitalized upon the characters appearing in recent Disney theatrical features.

Like much of the material produced for TV, most of the animation for these video releases is farmed out to studios abroad, especially in Japan and Australia. These productions do not in any way aspire to the standards seen in the work that comes out of feature animation, but the best examples are entertaining and competently-animated stories, made with the kind of expertise that you would expect given that they bear the Disney name.

In this popular television series, Kim Possible is a typical teenager except that she also happens to be a savvy martial arts expert who is frequently called up to rid the world of its dastardly criminals and supervillains

16 Broadway

Disney's contributions to the tradition of the American musical began as early as *Snow White and the Seven Dwarfs,* in which songs were integrated into the narrative in a fluid way that anticipated the revolutionary leap taken by Rodgers and Hammerstein at the time of *Oklahoma!* (see chapter 4). Until 1994, however, that contribution had been made entirely by way of the movies. On April 18, 1994, however, all that changed as Broadway critics and first nighters crowded the lobby of the Palace Theater to greet the premiere of the stage production of *Beauty and the Beast.*

The story begins several years earlier when Michael Eisner began to think about the possibilities of Disney becoming involved with Broadway. His interest had been piqued by director Robert Jess Roth who had come to him with a stage treatment based on the film version of the story. The idea seemed to make sense. After all, *Beauty and the Beast* was a proven vehicle. While developing the animated version, Howard Ashman had solved many of the plot's inherent dramatic problems. In addition, it had terrific songs by Ashman and Alan Menken, and it had been a box office success. On top of that, the story presented fine opportunities for the kind of elaborate special effects stage magic demanded by modern Broadway audiences – opportunities that in time would be seized upon by illusion specialists John Gaughan and Jim Steinmeyer.

Linda Woolverton, who had worked closely with Ashman while scripting the film, was called upon to provide the book. Songs were added, some with lyrics by Tim Rice, and Roth was engaged to direct. With choreography by Matt West, sets by Stan Meyer, costumes by Ann Hould-Ward, and lighting by Natasha Katz, this was a full-blown Broadway production designed to compete with blockbusters like *Cats* and *The Phantom of the Opera*.

In the original cast, Susan Egan starred as Belle and Terrence Mann as the Beast. The show delighted audiences, and at the time of this writing, it is still running on Broadway a decade later. It enjoyed comparable success in other theater capitals like London, Sydney, and Tokyo, while road companies took the show all over America and beyond.

Beauty and the Beast only hinted at the scope of Eisner's Broadway ambitions and commitment. A transplanted New Yorker, he was very much aware of the attempts that were being made in the 1990s to refurbish the Times Square area, after decades of decay and civic indifference, and was eager to become involved in the process. Disney representatives began to look at various theaters in the Broadway theater district with the idea of purchasing and renovating one. Peter Schneider and Thomas Schumacher were asked to supplement their animation department duties by looking into the feasibility of stage adaptations of existing Disney material.

The stage adaptation of *Beauty and the Beast* borrowed directly from the animated film version in terms of characterization and costume design. Seen here (left to right) are Heath Lamberts, Stacey Logan, Gary Beach, and Beth Fowler as servants who have been transformed into, respectively, a clock, a feather duster, a candlestick, and a teapot. Photograph by Joan Marcus

Dianne Pilkington as Belle and Alex Bourne as the Beast in the 2002 British touring company of *Beauty and the Beast*. Photograph by Catherine Ashmore

Another smash at the movie box office, *The Lion King* was a challenging yet intriguing candidate for translation to the stage. Like *Beauty and the Beast*, it offered a strong plot and memorable songs. In the case of *Beauty* however, it had been relatively easy to translate the look of the film to a live production. By contrast, bringing *The Lion King* to the stage would pose a challenge for even the most imaginative theater director. An entirely different approach would be called for. The element of familiarity would be lost, but the loss would provide the opportunity for a radically fresh treatment of the material, one that could take audiences by surprise and give the story a new life.

While a team was being assembled to explore this possibility, the search for a theater was narrowed down and eventually came to focus entirely on the New Amsterdam, built in 1903 and once the home of the Ziegfeld Follies. The theater was converted to a movie house midcentury, and in 1980, the building was listed by the National Register of Historic Places because of its importance in the evolution of Broadway, its sumptuous interiors – part Baroque, part Art Nouveau – and its pioneering use of cantilever construction. This innovative technology did away with pillars, thus permitting unobstructed views of the stage from all parts of the auditorium. Listing saved the theater from the wreckers'

TAYMOR

Opposite top: Director and creative visionary Julie Taymor is shown sculpting the head of Scar from clay. In the foreground are prototypes of the Simba and Mufasa masks that will be used on stage. Photograph by Kenneth van Sickle. Opposite bottom: Julie Taymor's costume studies of animated plants for the "Can You Feel the Love Tonight" scene in *The Lion King* (left), and her study of a dancer manipulating body puppets representing gazelles (right). Photographs by Kenneth van Sickle. Above: The imaginative theatrical effects employed in *The Lion King* include a dancer-operated cheetah and giraffe puppets built around actors on stilts. Photograph by Joan Marcus

ball, but it could not guarantee that it would remain occupied and later in the same decade it was abandoned. When the Disney team first saw it, it was in a sadly dilapidated state, but its grandeur could not be entirely disguised. In 1995, The Walt Disney Company set up the New Amsterdam Development Corporation for the specific purpose of returning the building to its original glory.

Meanwhile, development of *The Lion King* for stage presentation had been continuing, based on the movie's plot and utilizing the Elton John and Tim Rice songs, but employing an entirely different visual approach, one that was in fact quite close to one of the original concepts for the movie (see chapter 12), which had explored the possibilities of a highly stylized look, drawing upon the shapes and forms of African art.

A key moment in the evolution of the production came when Julie Taymor, largely at the behest of Thomas Schumacher, was hired to direct the show. In addition, she designed the costumes, worked with Michael Curry on masks and puppets, added scenes and musical numbers, and even contributed lyrics to new songs. Best known for her experimental use of masks and puppets, some skeptics thought Taymor a risky choice. In fact she proved the ideal person to handle a complex and difficult task that demanded original thinking and a high level of risk-taking.

Seen here in silhouette is a model of the Gazelle Wheel, which plays a key role in *The Lion King*'s Circle of Life theme. The full-size version of the wheel is pushed across the stage, and as it moves forward the gazelles are propelled into balletic leaps. Photograph by Kenneth van Sickle

Taymor is fond of saying that the magic of theater resides not in spelling everything out but in permitting members of the audience to fill in the blanks and complete the picture. Under her auspices, *The Lion King* became the kind of show in which a waterfall could be represented by a bolt of silk rippling in the breeze from a fan, the savannahs themselves by dancers in headdresses made of grass. Antelopes and gazelles would be conjured up with the help of contraptions that seemed part puppet, part bicycle. Men on stilts would be transformed into giraffes. Some performers would wear giant masks, representing the kind of animals they were portraying, or else operate stylized shoulder-mounted puppets that almost doubled their height – ideas that were clearly and effectively derived from the costumes worn by some African tribal dancers. Allowing for the sophistication of the stage devices, one could say that Taymor's concept for *The Lion King* was not far removed from what might have been expected had a tribe from East Africa been asked to stage its own version of the story.

The show that began to evolve was one in which the imagination of the director and the other creative talents would challenge members of the audience to exercise their own imagination. Before it reached Broadway, however, it had to undergo much testing, transformation, and fine-tuning. The first try-outs in front of a ticket-buying audience took place at the Orpheum Theater in Minneapolis during the summer of 1997. The reception was generally good, but the show was running long, certain props did not work as designed, and some of the performers seemed to be taking longer than others to adjust to the novelty of a production in which puppets are often allowed to upstage human performers. One thing that everybody agreed about was that the opening "Circle of Life" number – with its scores of animal puppets crowding on stage, and its full sized elephant (a man in each leg) – was as spectacular as it had been in the movie, so much so that one local critic said he would pay to see the show again if only for the first five minutes.

Taymor and her team worked hard to implement the lessons they had learned in Minneapolis, and by November 13, 1997, when the show opened at the lavishly renovated New Amsterdam, everything was working smoothly. There was still some apprehension as to how this kind of stylized production would be received on Broadway – where the naturalism of *Les Miserables*' barricade scene, and *Miss Saigon*'s helicopter, was the order of the day. The reaction of the audience during the "Circle of Life" opening soon allayed any fears. As media reaction poured in, it became clear that *The Lion King* was destined to be a giant hit. At the time of this writing, it is in its seventh year on Broadway, and continues to play to sold out houses around the world.

If the first Disney stage musical was a fairly safe choice, and the second an adventurous one, the third came totally out of left field – at least so far as audiences were concerned. Behind the scenes, *Aida* had briefly been thought of as a project for the animation department, but instead had been developed as a live theater piece. Songs would be provided by Elton John and Tim Rice – following up on their collaboration in *The Lion King* – and the book was entrusted to *Beauty and the Beast's* Linda Woolverton.

Woolverton's work was to be based upon the libretto for Giuseppe Verdi's opera *Aida,* commissioned by the Khedive of Egypt for the opera house he was building to celebrate the 1869 completion of the Suez Canal. The libretto was a tale of Ancient Egypt inspired by a story written by a famous French archeologist of the day, Auguste Mariette, who was later appointed by the Khedive to supervise the sets and costumes of the original production, which premiered in Cairo in 1871. Mariette's story told of a tragic love triangle involving a warrior named Radames and the two

The lyrical simplicity with which *Aida* is staged can be illustrated by this effectively minimal set. Aida's exile in Egypt is suggested by a gangplank and the reflections of silhouetted palm trees evoke the river Nile. Photograph by Whitney Cox

Left: Elton John with *Aida* musical director Paul Bogaev. Photograph by Joan Marcus. Right: A concept drawing of the Mantle of Authority, which, in the stage performance, is presented to Aida by Nubian slaves. Photograph by Marc Bryan-Brown

women who love him, Amneris, an Egyptian princess, and Aida, an enslaved Nubian princess.

To some opera purists, the idea of making a pop version of *Aida* was scandalous. In fact, the Disney version has little to do with Verdi but rather is simply the retelling, in a modern musical idiom, of a story he once used. In this sense it might be compared with Verdi's *Falstaff* which is a retelling in his musical terms of Shakespeare's *Merry Wives of Windsor.*

The most noticeable structural changes from the opera libretto occur at the beginning and the end of the show. Where Verdi's work ends tragically, the ending of the Disney musical offers a glimmer of hope. The Disney opening also differs from the original, but in a manner the composer might have found intriguing. The characters who are to become Radames and Aida are modern-day visitors to the Egyptian galleries of a museum. They examine the artifacts as Amneris comes to life from behind a showcase as she sings the song "Every Story is a Love Story." From then on, the narrative unfolds in the ancient world, but with a strong contemporary emphasis on the interracial love between Radames and the title character.

Reportedly, the project got off to a great start with Elton John and Tim Rice tossing off a score of songs in less than a month. Many problems lay ahead, however, not the least of which was the fact that no one seemed to have a firm grip on how to sell this story to a modern audience. At one point the title of the piece was changed to the klunky *Elaborate Lives: The Legend of Aida* – which probably would have kept the target audience at arm's length. In 1998, the show went into tryouts in Atlanta, where it was beset by a variety of problems.

Disney did not abandon the project, however. The title reverted to *Aida,* cast changes were made, Tony-award winner Robert Falls was hired to direct, and Bob Crowley was brought in to redo the sets and costumes. The result was a lean, streamlined production that relied more on imaginative lighting (Natasha Katz) and slickly staged choreography (Wayne Cilento) than expensive set pieces. This faster moving, more polished version was presented in Chicago in 1999 where during previews there was another major setback when part of a set collapsed, injuring two of the principles. The show carried on, however, opening on Broadway, at the Palace, on March 23 of the following year.

Although it did not receive the rapturous welcome accorded *The Lion King*, *Aida* quickly proved to be popular with audiences who connected strongly to the production's rich emotional core, and it became one of Broadway's top grossing shows.

To date, the story of Disney on Broadway is the tale of three enormous hits. The theater world is very different from the movie world, however, in that success is measured in terms of long runs in a single theater (or a small number of theaters) rather than in terms of the money brought in during a relatively short run in a very large number of theaters. The latter requires a company to release many movies every year, hoping that some will be successful. Success in theater can require years of time and work in order to ensure the longevity and ultimate success of a production.

Certainly there is no reason to believe that Disney's Broadway adventure is over, though Broadway is not the only destination involved. A stage version of *Mary Poppins* is scheduled to have opened in London's West End by the time this book is published. With Thomas Schumacher in charge (Peter Schneider having left the company in 2001), the theatrical division has at least two other productions in the pipeline – adaptations of *Tarzan* and *The Little Mermaid*. Apparently, the adventure is just beginning.

IV   The Magic Kingdoms

17   Beyond Film

Walt Disney was a man with a knack for doing the right thing at the right time – a person with an almost uncanny instinct for gauging what the public wanted and the courage to act on his intuitions. It is essential to realize, though, that his intuitions were backed up by hard work and thorough preparation. Never was this more evident than in the most important of his postwar endeavors.

Disneyland Park grew from a seed that had been germinating in Disney's mind for fifteen or twenty years, since the time he had taken his young daughters to local amusement parks and wondered why there could not be a place that was as entertaining for adults as it was for children. There is some evidence to suggest that he was thinking about specific rides as early as the late thirties, but economic realities made it impossible for him to pursue such ideas at the time.

Shortly after World War II, Disney's doctor suggested that he find a hobby to counter the stress of running the Studio. Disney – who had been a news butcher on the Santa Fe Railroad (see chapter 1) – had always loved trains and was aware that two of his top animators, Ollie Johnston and Ward Kimball, were serious railroad buffs. He admired Johnston's backyard railroad and decided to build one for himself in his own garden. Next he began thinking about running a full-size narrow-gauge railway around the Studio, using engines that had been built for the 1915 Pan American Exposition in San Francisco. He soon decided

DISNEYLAND

SCHEMATIC AERIAL VIEW
APPROX. 45 ACRES
WITHIN RAILROAD TRACKS
DESIGNED BY WED ENTERPRISES

Opposite left: Walt Disney's passionate interest in railroads had an important influence on his plans for Disneyland

Opposite right: Disney stands beside the trolley tracks on Disneyland's Main Street

Before he committed himself to the Disneyland that has become so familiar, Walt Disney briefly considered the possibility of building an amusement park directly across the street from the Burbank home of the Studio. This plan gives some idea of what that park might have looked like

This imaginary aerial view of the proposed park, drawn by Herb Ryman, was used as a sales tool when Walt Disney was presenting the idea of Disneyland to potential investors. A 1958 map of Disneyland, overleaf, shows how the final plan evolved

that there wasn't enough room to install a railroad at the Studio, but he began to think about that innovative kind of amusement park again: a railroad circling the perimeter would make a wonderful feature of such a park.

In 1952, Disney set up an organization called WED (his initials) to begin planning the park in earnest. At first WED consisted of a few designers – men like Claude Coats and John Hench, mostly co-opted from the animation department – who understood how Disney worked and who were well equipped to interpret his ideas. (They would be called Imagineers, and later the company was renamed WDI, for Walt Disney Imagineering.)

Plans and models were made for an as yet unchosen site. There were thoughts of building in Burbank, directly across the street from the Studio, but that idea was abandoned and the Stanford Research Institute was called in to recommend a suitable location for the Park within the greater Los Angeles area. Soon Disney owned 160 acres of orange groves in Anaheim, to the south of Los Angeles. The land was relatively inexpensive, yet it was adjacent to the planned route of the Santa Ana Freeway, which soon would link Orange County with metropolitan Los Angeles. The mild climate would permit year-round operation of the Park.

With conventional Coney Island–type parks failing in many parts of the country, an amusement park hardly seemed like a sound investment. Disney sought out the advice of experts, all of whom told him he had invented a new way of losing money. Some officers of Disney's own company – his brother Roy included – were also skeptical about the venture, but Walt went ahead with his plans, financing development from his own pocket and with funds from companies that agreed to pay advances on Disneyland concessions.

Major progress came in 1954 when the American Broadcasting Company-Paramount Theaters group agreed to purchase slightly more than one-third of the shares of a company called Disneyland, Inc., in return for Disney's providing ABC with a prime-time television series, *Disneyland* (see chapter 13). The remaining shares were divided between Walt Disney Productions, Walt Disney himself, and Western Printing and Lithographing, which had a longtime association with the Studio. Before long, Walt Disney Productions was able to buy out the holdings of both Western and ABC–Paramount.

The improved financial situation of Disneyland, Inc., offered banks more than adequate security, and funds were advanced, setting the stage for construction to begin. Meanwhile, Disney planned the television series in such a way as to afford Disneyland maximum publicity.

His overall concept for the Park had its own kind of logic, which has proved enormously effective over the years. The plan called for a vintage railroad defining the perimeter of the Park, with its main station right at the entrance. Once past the station, the visitor would have to pass down Main Street – an idealized reproduction of a small Midwestern town of the sort Disney himself had known as a boy. Main Street was calculated to correspond with one of the archetypes of the American imagination, establishing an ambience that would put visitors in an appropriate frame of mind. Its scale would be slightly less than life-size, enhancing the sense of friendliness and intimacy. Transportation would be available – vintage trams and horse-drawn trolleys – but people on foot would be drawn down Main Street by the imposing edifice at its far end – Sleeping Beauty Castle – the likes of which had never been seen in any Mississippi Valley community. In fact, all of Disneyland was conceived in terms of visual magnets that would draw people through the Park and keep the crowds moving. Sleeping Beauty Castle was the greatest of these magnets, and all paths would converge on the traffic circle immediately in front of it.

A visitor who followed a clockwise route from this central feature would find himself, first of all, in Adventureland, next in Frontierland, then in Fantasyland, and finally in Tomorrowland. Each of these areas would have a specific atmosphere, appropriate to its name. Disney characters and references to Disney movies and television shows would be found throughout, but in a sense the Park was conceived in such a way as to seem like a tribute to the Hollywood movie tradition as a whole. Many of the familiar genres were there, from Westerns to science fiction and from costume dramas to exotic safari sagas. If there was an emphasis on material derived from animation, that was understandable. The bottom line was that visiting Disneyland would be like spending a day *inside*

Walt Disney welcomes visitors to the park

a cluster of Hollywood films, each one spilling magically into the next. Entering the Park would permit people to visit places where only the camera had taken them before.

Some of the individual features of Disneyland had been foreshadowed at Coney Island, and especially at fairs like St. Louis's Louisiana Purchase Exposition and Chicago's Century of Progress Exposition. What made Disneyland very different was the fact that it was organized in a way, and built on a scale, that was user-friendly decades before that term was coined.

Disney's plan was sound. It had a sense of structure and continuity that was new to this kind of enterprise, it exploited genres of popular culture that had already demonstrated their staying power, and it capitalized fully on the established Disney image. Every element had been thoughtfully considered and imaginatively developed.

Disneyland was opened on July 17, 1955. Television crews were on hand to record the opening ceremonies while thirty thousand guests thronged Main Street and explored the farthest reaches of the complex. Millions more witnessed the event on their home screens. No entertainment facility had ever received this kind of publicity, and Disneyland became a national phenomenon overnight.

Walt Disney had built the Versailles of the twentieth century – but it was a Versailles designed for the pleasure of the people rather than the amusement of the nobility.

At the time of its inauguration, it was not, of course, quite the dense complex we find today. As yet, no monorail had been installed, no New Orleans Square linked Adventureland to Frontierland. A grove of trees stood where the Matterhorn would one day rise. Disney had created an unusual and agreeable environment suitable for further expansion but already providing novel entertainments for both children and adults. The Park could be enjoyed by those who were anxious to participate as well as by those who chose to stroll and observe. It was a place for families, a place to visit – and revisit – for the whole day, an environment that seemed inexhaustible. Hours could be spent just browsing in the stores along Main Street (this at a time, it should be remembered, when the galleria-type shopping mall did not yet exist).

Apart from the originality of its plan, what made Disneyland radically different from other earlier amusement parks was the fact that it resembled the back lot of a movie studio. The skills that go into building movie sets are the same skills that have gone into Main Street and Frontierland. The differences are that Disneyland's "sets" are built to withstand extended use and that, while a movie street may consist of facades that open onto storage areas or empty spaces, Disneyland's thoroughfares are punctuated by doors that give access to shops and restaurants along with rides and entertainments.

Filmmakers are trained to think sequentially: One situation must lead to another to create a narrative flow. These same narrative skills were employed in planning the layout of the Park. As the visitor is drawn from one place to another, calculated scenic changes give the impression of a

This aerial view of The Magic Kingdom at Walt Disney World in Florida shows a Main Street parade in progress. Overleaf: Cinderella Castle at Walt Disney World (left) and Sleeping Beauty Castle in Disneyland, with Anaheim's version of the Matterhorn in the background (right)

Modes of transportation, from horse-drawn trolleys to rockets, play an important role in establishing the atmosphere of the theme parks. Above: the Walt Disney World edition of Tomorrowland with Space Mountain silhouetted against the sky; left: the *Mark Twain* cruises sedately through Frontierland at Disneyland; opposite top left: the Disneyland railroad; opposite top right: transportation in Town Square at Disneyland; opposite bottom: the Walt Disney World monorail glides through Epcot

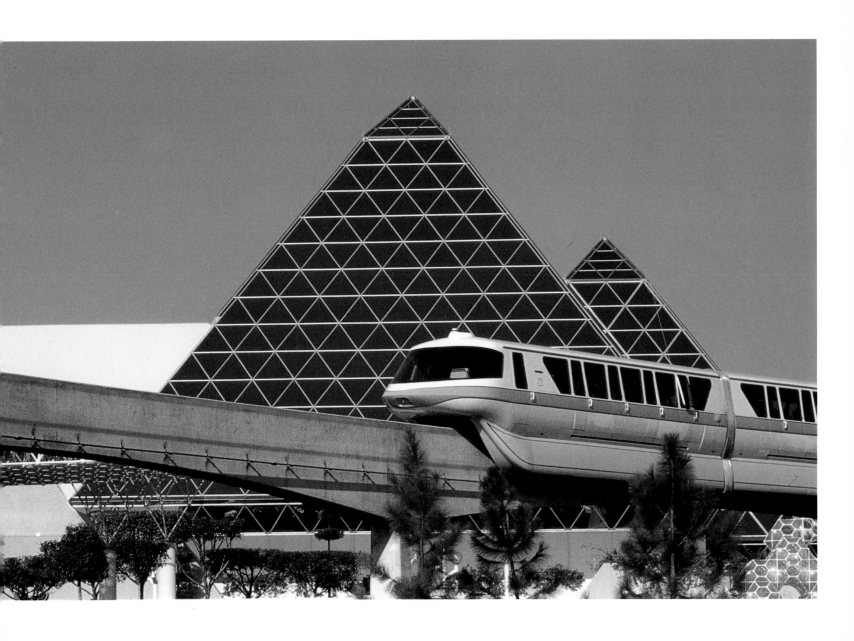

definite and satisfying sequence of events. The difference is that a movie narrative moves in a straight line, from beginning to end, whereas a visitor to the Park is free to choose among many options, as in an interactive video game. He can, in effect, write his own story, although its basic elements have been carefully preplanned by the designers.

A plaque in Disneyland's Town Square reads as follows:

TO ALL WHO COME TO THIS HAPPY PLACE:
WELCOME.
DISNEYLAND IS YOUR LAND. HERE AGE
RELIVES FOND MEMORIES OF THE PAST . . .
AND HERE YOUTH MAY SAVOR THE CHALLENGE
AND PROMISE OF THE FUTURE.
DISNEYLAND IS DEDICATED
TO THE IDEALS, THE DREAMS, AND THE HARD
FACTS THAT HAVE CREATED AMERICA . . .
WITH THE HOPE THAT IT WILL BE A SOURCE OF
JOY AND INSPIRATION TO ALL THE WORLD
JULY 17, 1955

When those words were written, even Walt Disney cannot have imagined quite how thoroughly his park would capture the imagination of the world. For a while, at least, Disneyland must have seemed like an end in itself. Before very long, however, Disney was beginning to think about how ideas implicit in his first theme park could be expanded elsewhere. The 1964 New York World's Fair provided opportunities to experiment, and then he turned his attention to Florida.

Walt Disney and Card Walker visit the site of Walt Disney World

In part, Disney's intention was to build a theme park that would be a magnet for the East Coast as Disneyland had become a magnet for the West Coast. Beyond that, he wanted to avoid some of the problems that had plagued the first theme park. When it opened, Disneyland had been an island of fantasy set in an ocean of orange trees. That soon changed as urban sprawl arrived to surround the park with motels, gas stations, and fast-food joints. Walt Disney watched these haphazard developments with displeasure and vowed that in Florida he would build a Magic Kingdom that was completely insulated from the outside world.

To this end, he set out to acquire a large tract of land that could accommodate not just a Disneyland-type theme park but also other attractions – including EPCOT (then thought of as an experimental community) – served by Disney-operated hotels and other visitor services. Every effort would be made to preserve as much as possible of the existing topography, to control pollution, and to maintain an ecological balance.

The success of Disneyland made financing for Walt Disney World Resort (as the project was named) relatively easy. Locating the right property was the next order of business. A Disney publication tells the story in the following words:

"Sheathed in necessary obscurity, Disney representatives set out early in 1964 to obtain control of a large area straddling the line separating Orange and Osceola counties in central Florida. Located between the cities of Orlando and Kissimmee, the site is at the crossing point of several heavily travelled highways.

"By October, 1965, they had put together 27,443 acres – almost 43 square miles – at a cost of just over $5,000,000. This size would permit for plenty of future expansion and would assure control of its perimeter. For comparison: Walt Disney World covers about the same land area as the city of San Francisco; it is about twice the size of the island of Manhattan."

On November 15, 1965, accompanied by Florida Governor Haydon Burns, Walt and Roy Disney spoke to the press and officially launched the Walt Disney World project.

Surveying his property from the air, Walt Disney decided that the shore of Bay Lake – the largest natural body of water – was the spot to begin Phase One of the development. Just months after the first earth-moving equipment arrived at the site, however, Disney was in the hospital and dying. During this final illness, he could think of nothing but the Florida project and spent his remaining reserves of energy describing every detail of his vision to his family.

John Hench, a senior vice president of WDI and dean of the Imagineering team, describes Roy Disney's report of one of his last visits to his brother. "Walt was hallucinating, but it was as if he could see this map of the property on the ceiling, and he was pointing to it with one hand and describing it, explaining why we'd have to build an east-west road running through, and so on. It was as if the whole thing was there in full detail. He was obsessed."

"And Walt was right," Hench adds. "We did have to build that east-west road to make the whole thing work."

"The problem was," says Marty Sklar, president of WDI, "that, when Walt died, many people thought that we couldn't carry the thing through without him, especially since Florida was looked on as an extension of the New York market, where Disney had never performed as well as in the rest of the country. People within WED, like Dick Irvine and John Hench, had to persuade management that some version of Walt's vision was still possible."

Normally a fiscal conservative, Roy Disney was the easiest member of the management team to convince.

"He had seen how important it was to Walt," says Sklar, "and as a result he really dedicated the rest of his life to beginning Walt's dream. It wasn't EPCOT, which is what Walt had really cared about most, but it *was* Walt Disney World, and that provided the foundation for everything else that has been done down there since. EPCOT was always the underlying aim – the building codes were written with that in mind – but the key thing was to get something going and building the Magic Kingdom first was the wise thing to do, I believe. It gave people something they could identify with the Disney name. It didn't frighten anybody. Roy got wholeheartedly behind that.

" 'Personally I had my doubts,' Roy told Hench, 'but I knew I had to do it for Walt – because if I hadn't he would have given me hell when I died.' "

As scheduled, Walt Disney World was opened by Roy Disney in October of 1971. A few weeks later, just five days before Christmas, Roy Disney – who had been looking forward to retirement – was dead, his life shortened, some speculated, by his exertions in realizing his brother's last dream.

18 Magic Kingdoms

Expansion in Florida, and later into Japan and Europe, has enabled Disney's Imagineers to explore many aspects of the theme park concept, from the creative marriages of entertainment and science found at Epcot to the cultural variations on basic Disney themes introduced at Tokyo Disneyland and Disneyland Paris (originally known as Euro Disney). Those themes still find their archetypal expression in the two original Magic Kingdoms, in Anaheim and near Orlando. From the beginning, they contained the seeds of much that would come later (Tomorrowland, for example, anticipated EPCOT Center). Over the almost three decades since Walt Disney's death, many additions and alterations have been made to the Magic Kingdoms, providing visitors with new experiences, from Space Mountain to Mickey's Toontown to the the multimedia Alien Encounter, yet these primary parks are still essential expressions of the original vision.

For more than forty years, John Hench has been a key creative figure in the organization first known as WED, then WDI. Along with Claude Coats, Marc Davis, Herb Ryman, and a handful of other animation veterans, he was handpicked to work on Disneyland. While Davis periodically returned to the animation department, Hench stayed on and remains at WDI today – the individual who, next to Walt Disney himself, has probably had the greatest input into design decisions relating to the theme parks.

Hench has given extensive thought to the reasons for Walt Disney's success, both with regard to the parks and to his career in general:

"Part of it, I suppose, was Walt's exploitation of very old survival patterns. He had an instinct for this. I think that if anyone really wanted to take the time to examine it, he would see that these survival patterns are the basis of our aesthetics, our sense of pleasure. We've carried these things around for twenty million years, in our DNA chains or whatever it is. We are the successful survivors, so we must still carry those mechanisms with us. The things that please us are obviously the ones that boost our survival potential – and the ones that we don't like are those that threaten us."

Hench illustrates Disney's instinct for exploiting survival patterns by referring back to the early cartoons:

"Mickey was so-called Lollipop Art – because he was made from circles. I'm oversimplifying it, but circles have never hurt anybody – they are women's breasts and clouds and other soft forms. Felix the Cat, on the other hand, was full of angles and sharp points, and I really think this was the difference between the two. It explains the success of Mickey, who just won't quit. Walt was a highly intuitive person and he sensed these things, and, as a result of this, the Studio has probably developed more awareness than any other design group in this field.

"A lot of designers allow contradictions into their work because they're careless or because they don't really understand what they're doing. These contradictions will cancel out what they're trying to say. If someone wants to make an automobile that will look slick and powerful and he designs something that triggers a very old image of a dead whale on the beach, the customers won't buy it. Look at the Hudson. It was a perfectly good car, but nobody would believe it. I haven't really analyzed the Edsel, but again it gives you an example of [something designed by] a company which was perfectly skilled at engineering, and did a wonderful job of preselling the car – but nobody would touch it."

Hench, whose animation experience included stints as a background painter, a layout artist, an effects animator, and an art director, emphasizes the ways in which Walt Disney's unique cinematic background influenced the design concepts that give the Magic Kingdoms their special character:

"Walt had a high sensitivity, I think, for timing and the way things relate to each other – and this, of course, came from the film work. This is what film is all about, connecting ideas so they relate to one another. A motion picture is an act of communication. It consists of ideas – sometimes very complex ones – that you want other people to understand, and you want them to understand them the way you intended them to, without wandering off on their own. So you want to keep the structure clean and simple. Live-action filming has to count on a lot of accidents, but in a cartoon we could gradually eliminate the things that contradicted what we were trying to say. With the background we had, this was a very easy thing to apply to the third dimension."

As has been seen in earlier chapters, animation is the most controlled form of filmmaking imaginable, with everything preplanned and nothing

Previous pages: Mickey Mouse plays host in Mickey's Toontown left to the temperament of stars or the vagaries of light and weather. The Magic Kingdoms are controlled environments engineered to conform to the principles Disney had evolved while making his animated films. All the elements of an animated movie must be planned so as to complement each other, and this same criterion was adapted to the design of the theme parks.

"It's a concept of relating things in a noncompetitive way," Hench explains. "One of the worst things about, for instance, a World's Fair is that every facility is trying to outshout the others. People are subject to pressure from the Russian pavilion as opposed to the French, as against the Italian – and it does make for a curious kind of mental fatigue. Also, you have to pick up ideas and then drop them completely as you go on to another exhibit – it's like overrecording on a tape, I guess. Eventually you get very confused. Most people have this experience when they go to a World's Fair. They walk out absolutely exhausted and then can't remember very much of what they've seen – most of the attractions have cancelled each other out, as they were probably designed to do.

"Disneyland is a much more pleasant experience – and Walt Disney World, too – because at least there's an attempt to relate one idea to the next. You don't have to drop one before you pick up another – they carry through. This again comes from the motion-picture background. The division into related themes gives a sense of continuity."

The motion-picture influence is most obvious within the context of the individual attractions. Each version of the Haunted Mansion, for example, presents the visitor with a ride that unfolds in time in exactly the same way a movie does. A movie transports an audience from point A to point Z by means of a carefully structured sequence of visual devices – the camera following the action and the audience traveling with the camera. In other words, the camera is a moving vehicle which carries the audience through the narrative, following its assigned route. In the Haunted Mansion, as in other attractions of that type, a car that runs on rails is substituted for the camera. In the Disneyland edition of the ride, the visitor is first ushered into a gothic lobby where he finds himself in a crowd of people in a circumscribed space overhung by cobwebs and surrounded by sinister portraits. A disembodied voice issues a few words of warning, then the lights are extinguished and the show begins with a teaser – a device designed to establish the atmosphere and to draw the visitor into the unfolding scenario. The floor begins to drop and a body suddenly appears, hanging by the neck from the ceiling high above. The sinking floor immediately establishes a feeling of insecurity, but it has the added practical purpose of bringing visitors down to a basement level where they board the "doom buggies" that take them through the rest of the show. These vehicles carry the visitors through a series of spooky environments, each of which exposes them to a new kind of "supernatural" phenomenon. The "buggies" are wired for stereo sound and are built in such a way that the rider can see only what is directly in front of him. Each vehicle is on a swivel so that it can be turned, by electronic signals,

The Haunted Mansion at Walt Disney World
looms in the night. Like other attractions in
the theme parks, the interiors of the various
versions of the Haunted Mansion are developed
from continuity drawings like those, opposite,
which are used in much the same way that
storyboard drawings are used in the planning
of an animated film

to face just what the designers want it to face at any given moment.

In such traditional Magic Kingdom rides, the rider is not given the choice of where to look. That decision has already been made by the designers, who determined what will be seen just as a movie director determines what a movie patron will see. For one recent attraction, however – Roger Rabbit's Car Toon Spin in Mickey's Toontown at Disneyland Park– a variation on this approach has been successfully used.

Mickey's Toontown is a new section of Disneyland which derives in part from the film *Who Framed Roger Rabbit* but also provides a home for venerable Disney cartoon characters like Mickey, Minnie, Goofy, and Donald. Planned under the supervision of senior show manager Dave Burkhart and senior concept designer Joe Lanzisero, Toontown is a three-dimensional, walk-through cartoon world featuring, among its other attractions, many interactive gags. (A mailbox talks back to anyone who attempts to deposit a letter. A manhole cover protests when stepped on.)

The designers decided to make the Roger Rabbit ride itself as interactive as possible. For this attraction, visitors are seated in Lenny the Cab (a lookalike cousin of Benny, the cartoon taxi featured in the movie). Lenny then takes the rider through a toonscape peppered with suitably toonish adventures. What makes this ride different, however, is the fact that the occupants of the cab have some control over its movements. They can manipulate the steering wheel and alter the direction in which they are facing and therefore have some choice as to how each set piece of the ride is viewed.

"You can take this ride any number of times," says Lanzisero, "and never repeat exactly the same experience."

That limited control enhances this particular ride – providing novel perceptual pleasures while adding to the sense of careening through cartoon space. The route of the vehicle through the set pieces is as fixed as it is with any more traditional ride. It is only the viewpoint that can be manipulated, and, oddly enough, the degree of control the vehicle's occupant is provided with actually creates the illusion of being *out* of control, as though in a skidding car. In the end, the interactive element built into this highly enjoyable ride is really another form of illusion.

This cinematic sensibility is evident throughout the Magic Kingdoms, though – as noted in the previous chapter – it is necessarily deployed in a less deterministic way. The parks are planned to give visitors a pleasant experience (free of those World's Fair pressures described by Hench) no matter which route they happen to select.

To get a full sense of the cinematic character of the Magic Kingdoms, one need only sample their various transportation systems. Like the parks as a whole, these systems deal in everything from unadulterated nostalgia to space-age technology. Main Street is served by trolley cars and horse-drawn vehicles, yet a short walk will take the visitor to a streamlined Monorail. The engines and rolling stock of the railroad circling the Park conjure up the golden age of steam, but the PeopleMover that runs through Tomorrowland is a silent, electrically powered system that addresses the late-twentieth-century need for nonpolluting vehicles

An aerial view of Big Thunder Mountain at Walt Disney World (top) and a building on Big Thunder Mountain which shows how the Disney Imagineers have transformed what is essentially a simple roller coaster by adding a level of scenic detail found in the movies

Roger Rabbit's Car Toon Spin offers visitors
to Disneyland an opportunity for interactive
fun (right). Goofy's Gas Station (below) offers
a good idea of the cartoonlike architecture
and props that give Mickey's Toontown its
special character

(which Walt Disney was already thinking about in the fifties). Other forms of transport abound, meshed into a complex network made up of components that are designed to afford the visitor pleasure by taking him on a cinematic ride through or around the Park. Their routes are planned not as the shortest way between A and B, but rather so as to afford the rider the greatest possible degree of visual satisfaction. The Florida monorail offers its passengers impressive panoramas of the lakes and the surrounding countryside blended with glimpses of fairy-tale worlds that are conjured up as, for example, it glides out of the futuristic Contemporary Hotel, affording distant views of the turrets and spires of Cinderella Castle.

The theme parks exploit all kinds of technical novelties, the most celebrated of which (though they are no longer unique to Disney) are the *AUDIO-ANIMATRONICS*® figures that provide "animation in the round" for so many of the Magic Kingdom attractions.

    Long before he began to build Disneyland, Walt Disney had been a collector of clockwork toys. In the mid-forties he began to experiment with mechanical puppets, filming a Buddy Ebsen dance routine, which was then reproduced in the form of a miniature figure built by Studio engineers. The Ebsen puppet worked, but the machinery involved was too clumsy and bulky to suggest any immediate application.

    The building of Disneyland prompted a new round of experiments with mechanical figures. At first Imagineers worked with models that had simple cam and lever joints, but before long they began to try out more flexible systems employing pneumatic and hydraulic power transmission controlled by electrical inputs. This was efficient enough to supply the kind of crude movements needed for such things as the animals dotted around the jungle ride. Then someone came up with the idea of using sound,

Soon after World War II, Walt Disney tries out a dance routine with Buddy Ebsen. Ebsen's routine was filmed and served as the basis for Disney's first mechanical figure, the ancestor of all the *AUDIO-ANIMATRONICS* figures in the parks

Brought back to life by *AUDIO-ANIMATRONICS*, President Lincoln confronts his audience recorded on magnetic tape, to activate the pneumatic and hydraulic valves. At that point, the potential of *AUDIO-ANIMATRONICS* began to be realized. Sound impulses triggered mechanisms, buried within lifelike plastic figures, that could control movements down to the flicker of an eyelid. The tape system also permitted these movements to be synchronized with prerecorded dialogue or music, as well as with lighting effects and whatever else might contribute to the atmosphere of the ride.

The first *AUDIO-ANIMATRONICS* figures were some exotic birds, which eventually formed the basis of the Disneyland Enchanted Tiki Room. It was at the 1964 New York World's Fair, however, that *AUDIO-ANIMATRONICS* had its first major outing. Disney contributed a number of the fair's major attractions, including the Ford Motor Company's "Magic Skyway," General Electric's "Carousel of Progress," and Pepsi-Cola's "It's a Small World" (all of which were later adapted for the theme parks). The most dramatic exhibit was "Great Moments with Mr. Lincoln," which Disney prepared for the Illinois pavilion.

Visitors were confronted with a startlingly lifelike facsimile of the nation's sixteenth president. Lincoln not only spoke but also emphasized his thoughts with naturalistic gestures. His eyes raked the audience as though challenging opponents to debate. He shifted his weight from one foot to the other and his expression changed with the sense of his words. The impact was extraordinary.

This success was not easily won. Indeed, only a few months before the opening of the pavilion it seemed that Lincoln might never be ready in time. The sheer energy locked up in the pneumatic and hydraulic systems of any AUDIO-ANIMATRONICS figure is considerable, and unless this energy can be precisely regulated the figure is apt to become violent. Before he was finally tamed, Mr. Lincoln smashed his chair and threw mechanical fits that threatened the safety of the men working on him.

Just in time for the fair, the power was harnessed, and soon equally sophisticated AUDIO-ANIMATRONICS figures were being featured at Disneyland and Walt Disney World, populating attractions such as Pirates of the Caribbean, the Mickey Mouse Revue, the Country Bear Jamboree, and the Hall of Presidents (which once again featured the words of Abraham Lincoln, who this time appeared surrounded by his peers).

Later, computer chips and other electronic innovations helped make the mechanical figures still more sophisticated, but always their effectiveness has been predicated on the Disney artists' years of experience with animation. They understand, for example, the importance of animating the eyes because, as in film animation, the attention of the audience is instinctively drawn to the eyes. If they are not convincingly naturalistic, the entire illusion will break down. The Imagineers also understand, from two-dimensional animation, that a sense of reality may often be best expressed by suppressing or limiting movement. A character may express surprise more effectively by raising an eyebrow than by throwing up his hands in shock. It is this kind of knowledge that has made AUDIO-ANIMATRONICS so valuable an asset to the parks. Without it, the engineering skill that goes into these figures would be wasted.

For all the technological innovations to be found in the Magic Kingdoms, the Disney organization's primary area of expertise is show business. The theme parks are a kind of total theater which exceeds the wildest dreams of dramatists and which provides entertainment for millions of visitors each year.

19 Themes and Variations

In its early days, Walt Disney World consisted of the Magic Kingdom, three hotels, various satellite resort areas (including campgrounds), a small model community (Lake Buena Vista), three golf courses, and a magnificent 7,500-acre wildlife preserve designed to save the last vestige of the Central Florida wilderness. (The sections of the property that have been developed were not part of this wilderness and do not impinge upon it since it was carefully isolated from the resort areas before building began.)

Already, in this skeletal form, Walt Disney World was a test bed for enlightened technology, innovative urban planning, and responsible environmental management. The advanced building code encouraged the use of state-of-the-art construction techniques so that, for example, some buildings on the property pioneered a new method of modular construction using lightweight steel frames. The Magic Kingdom itself was built on a giant platform which permitted a network of corridors, storage areas, and service systems beneath the surface of Main Street and the other principal areas of the Park. This infrastructure provided all kinds of advantages. Supplies and costumed employees could be delivered to any point in the Park without ever appearing on the streets. Garbage could be disposed of without benefit of conspicuous trucks.

Elsewhere in the Park, an advanced wastewater treatment plant was constructed, and experiments were conducted in treating wastewater by natural means that could generate methane gas as a by-product. Water

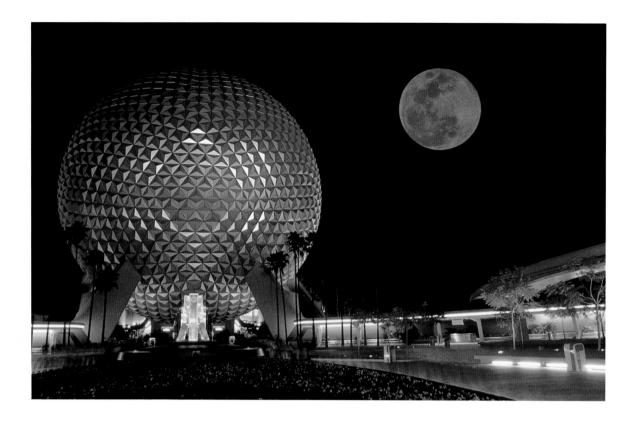

management in general was handled with great care, so as to maintain the ecological balance of the area, while the use of solar energy was also explored in one of the complex's office buildings.

In many ways, getting Walt Disney World up and running was rather like building a medium-size city from scratch:

"There was nothing there," says John Hench. "We had to install everything from a power plant to a laundry. You couldn't get phone calls in and out until equipment was put in. Even a simple thing like paint – there was nowhere to get it locally so you had to bring it in from somewhere else. And, of course, there was no trained work force available. When it came to staffing the Park and the hotels, we had to hire people wherever we could find them and train them ourselves."

All this effort and experimentation pointed toward EPCOT Center, the Experimental Prototype Community of Tomorrow that had been Walt Disney's main reason for wanting to develop the Florida property.

Disney envisioned EPCOT as an actual community; when he announced the project, in 1966, he described his aims in the following terms.

"I don't believe there's a challenge anywhere in the world that's more important to people everywhere than finding solutions to the problems of our cities. But where do we begin . . . how do we start to answer the great challenge?

"Well, we're convinced we must start with the public need. And that need is not just for curing the ills of the old cities. . . . EPCOT is . . . an experimental prototype community that will always be in a state of becoming. It will never cease to be a living blueprint of the future. . . .

"We don't presume to know all the answers. In fact we're counting

The focal point of EPCOT Center, comparable to the castles in the Magic Kingdoms, is Spaceship Earth (top), a geodesic sphere housing a theme show devoted to the history of communications.

When EPCOT Center was being planned, a flexible master model (above) enabled Disney's Imagineers to experiment with many arrangements of the various elements on the cooperation of American industry to provide their best thinking during the planning of our . . . community. And most important of all, when EPCOT has become a reality, and we find the need for technologies that don't even exist today, it's our hope that EPCOT will stimulate American industry to develop new solutions that will meet the needs of people expressed right here in this experimental community."

The participation of industry was to be a big part of the scheme.

"It seems clear in retrospect," says Marty Sklar, "that Walt used the 1964 New York World's Fair as a stepping-stone toward EPCOT. Certainly we didn't need the extra work at the time, but it gave Walt access to the chief executives of GE and other companies he would want to deal with in the future."

The first designs for EPCOT show a domed city that has its roots both in the work of visionary planners like R. Buckminster Fuller and in pop culture versions of the future that might be found in a Buck Rogers comic strip.

"Had Walt Disney lived," Michael Eisner speculates, "I'm sure that EPCOT would have evolved, just like everything else he worked on. It would have changed. What he left behind . . . is just the first expression of an idea that he didn't have time to follow through on."

This is probably true. Still, there is something about the vision of an experimental community that is a perfect expression of the belief in progress that was so characteristic of Americans of Walt Disney's generation.

For Disney the distance from Main Street to EPCOT Center was not so very far.

On opening day, in the fall of 1971, people responded to the inauguration of Florida's Magic Kingdom by staying away in droves, and for several weeks Walt Disney World was half empty. Disney's critics had a field day, gloating that such a theme park could never succeed on the "more sophisticated" East Coast. By Christmas, however, customers began to pour into the park, and the critics were having to eat their words. Apparently, families had stayed away at first only because they had anticipated that the crowds would be overwhelming. Very quickly, business built up to the anticipated level, then easily surpassed it. Projections for the first year had called for WDW to greet six million customers, about the annual attendance level of Disneyland in those days. In fact, ten million people streamed through the gates of the Magic Kingdom during its first twelve months of existence.

"Once again," says Marty Sklar, "we had to put EPCOT on the back burner for a while because the Park became so successful so quickly that for the next four years we were running just to keep up with demand in the Magic Kingdom. For example, Walt Disney World had no thrill rides when we opened. We had no Space Mountain, a very sparse Tomorrowland, no Pirates of the Caribbean. Shows we had thought of for Disneyland had to be adapted for Florida. It was a full-time job just getting more capacity into the Park. It would have been difficult to think seriously about

EPCOT, in those early days, let alone to get any work done on it."

By the mid-seventies, EPCOT was under serious consideration again, with Walt Disney's protégé Card Walker, now president of Walt Disney Productions, as its champion. Walker realized that the original experimental community idea would be difficult to sell to the financial community. (To mention just one problem, how could such a community guarantee the democratic rights of its residents while functioning under the corporate control that would be necessary to justify its existence?) There is some evidence that Disney himself had recognized these difficulties before he died. In any case, Walker decided that the only way to realize a viable version of Disney's dream was to reconceptualize EPCOT as a theme park that would be "a showcase for prototype concepts," which would provide "an ongoing forum of the future" and would serve as "a communicator to the world . . . a permanent international people-to-people exchange."

In a sense, this new version of EPCOT would be something like a permanent World's Fair, with one group of pavilions presenting man's technological challenge (Future World) and another presenting the cultures of various nations (World Showcase). It would differ from a World's Fair, however, in that the pavilions would complement one another rather than compete for attention. To this end, it would be pleasingly organized around circular ponds and a large circular central lagoon that would help create a soothing environment for the visitor.

The multinational aspect of the concept was not new. One of the earliest ideas for Disneyland had been an international street (it was to branch off from Town Square), and EPCOT would present an opportunity to implement that concept on a much grander scale. Similarly, Future World had its roots in Tomorrowland. At the crossroads between Future World and World Showcase would be an exhibit called the American Adventure inspired by Herman Melville's observation that "America has been settled by the people of all nations. . . . We are not a nation so much as a world."

"Around 1975," says Sklar, "after we'd finally gotten Space Mountain open, and some other key rides, we were able to focus on what we were going to do with this EPCOT idea. Our first move was to hold a series of meetings in Florida. We had conferences about energy and about health and about communications. It was pretty extraordinary because we were able to bring in all these dozens of experts and there were very few of them who didn't believe that Disney had an important role to play as an agent of change, and as a communicator who could bring people together. That was how we defined our role. We knew how to communicate ideas, but we didn't claim to know what it was that should be communicated. We left that to the experts.

"I remember one meeting we had when we were doing the Living Seas pavilion. Bob Ballard – the guy who found the *Titanic* – told us, and his fellow experts, that everybody had been wrong about what was at the bottom of the ocean. 'We've found that there's life down there.' It changed everybody's thinking. We already had a story for the film we were doing in connection with the pavilion, but the advisory board told us, 'You can't do that.' So we had to start over again. And this was typical. We weren't looking to present propaganda. We wanted to have the best people in any given field tell us what we should be doing."

WED's best talents – young men like Randy Bright and Tony Baxter, along with veterans John Hench, Marc Davis, and Herb Ryman – were turned loose on EPCOT, which finally opened in October of 1982, eleven years after the opening of Walt Disney World. Visitors could eat shepherd's pie in an English pub or *foie de veau* in a French bistro, then move on to the AT&T pavilion, where Walter Cronkite narrated a show based on the concept of spaceship earth.

As had been the case with the Magic Kingdom, early attendance figures were disappointing, and some visitors found certain of the exhibits overly didactic, but ticket sales built steadily. Over a period of time, EPCOT Center, as it became known, developed into a formidable foil for the Magic Kingdom – a totally novel kind of theme park in which the magic had more to do with scientific and cultural curiosity than with fairy tales and nostalgia.

Over the years, it has expanded – with spectacular new shows, such as the Living Seas, featuring "sea cabs" and an underwater restaurant – and, most importantly, the Imagineers back in California, along with their panels of experts, have kept close tabs on developments in the various fields of endeavor represented at EPCOT Center with the intention of updating films and exhibits. By 1994, almost everything in EPCOT Center was scheduled for renewal.

"The Energy Pavilion is a case in point," says Sklar. "There have been major developments in the energy field since that was built, and we are now in the process of rethinking it completely to reflect new discoveries and possibilities."

EPCOT Center was a new kind of theme park, but it was by no means the final development at Walt Disney World. Early in 1985, Michael Eisner raised the idea of an arts pavilion for EPCOT Center. This quickly evolved into a concept for a motion-picture arts pavilion, which fit together nicely with the notion of a movie ride that had been suggested by parks chief Dick Nunis.

Eisner and Frank Wells (whose earliest responsibilities at Disney included making the already profitable parks still more profitable) began to think that this concept had too much potential to be contained by a single pavilion shoehorned into EPCOT Center. Why not develop a whole new theme park that was also a working motion-picture studio, where visitors could enjoy movie- and television-related rides and exhibits? They could also have the opportunity of watching a film being made on an actual sound stage and see animators at work on a forthcoming Disney feature.

To maximize the appeal of such a facility, it was considered desirable to supplement automatic access to the Disney backlog of films by acquiring rights to another library of film classics. The library that proved to be

The World Showcase section of Epcot utilizes
expertise derived from filmmaking to evoke
different countries and cities, such as Japan
(above), Venice (opposite top), and Paris. In the
case of Paris, the Eiffel Tower is built as a
large miniature projecting above the mansard
roofs, just as it might be for a movie set. The
illusion is quite striking, especially at dusk
when the surrogate tower becomes a silhouette
against the Florida sky

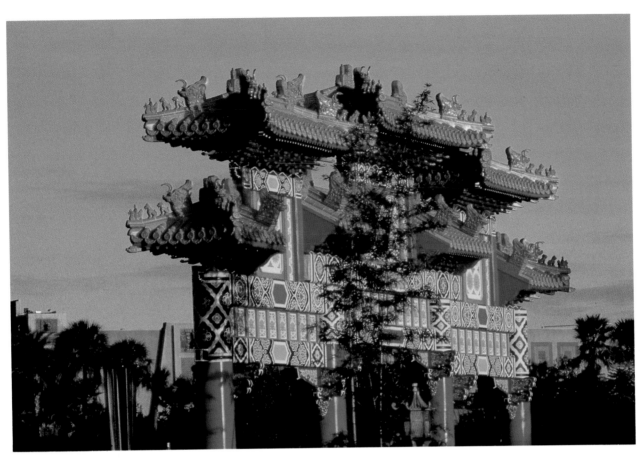

The World Showcase pavilions at Epcot are notable for their wealth of decorative detail. Above: a traditional gateway welcomes visitors to China. Below: the statue of St. George and the Dragon in Germany is a copy of a famous original in Munich's Marienplaz

Scenes from Epcot: A diver feeds a dolphin in The Living Seas pavilion, and a robot valet performs his duty in the Horizons exhibit available was MGM/UA's – a cornucopia of films, including such all-time favorites as *The Wizard of Oz.* Disney negotiated permission to use these movies, and characters from these movies, in the new park. It also licensed the right to employ the MGM name and trademark in connection with the park. (Later, Disney gained limited access to other libraries, further enhancing the company's ability to capitalize on Hollywood's past.)

In April of 1985, it was officially announced that Disney would build a new $300 million Hollywood theme park on the Florida property. Eventually, this park would include not only a working studio but also reconstructions of Grauman's Chinese Theater and the Sunset Strip, as well as a variety of show biz-oriented entertainments such as innovative special-effects movies conceived and directed by master entertainers George Lucas and Jim Henson. Back in the spring of 1985, however, the Disney-MGM Studio was just a grand idea.

Bob Weis – a senior vice president for creative affairs – was one of those who was called in on the early brainstorming sessions. With a college background in architecture and theater, Weis had gravitated naturally to the Imagineering team and in the early eighties had spent almost two

A reproduction of Grauman's Chinese Theater, leading to The Great Movie Ride, is one of the attractions of the Disney-MGM Studios at Walt Disney World years in Japan during the construction of Tokyo Disneyland (see chapter 18). In the spring of 1985, he had been back in Glendale for some time, working on a master plan for the expansion of the Tokyo park and on EPCOT Center projects.

"After Michael and Frank broached the idea of an arts and entertainment pavilion," he remembers, "it snowballed very quickly from a pavilion to being a self-contained entity. Jeffrey Katzenberg had been brought over to Disney to beef up motion-picture production. He wanted to do many more films a year, and that meant that there was a need for more sound stages. It became one of those ideas that had a life of its own, so that very soon we were working on a whole new park – a Hollywood studio tour."

Weis became the chief designer for the studio tour, and he and his associates found themselves dealing with some unprecedented problems.

"There was the basic matter of what a movie studio should look like, because the public has definite expectations. Forget what the new ones look like. They're much the same as any factory complex. What the visitor is expecting is the kind of studio that was built back in the golden age of Hollywood – something that looks like the Disney lot in Burbank – so we had fun going back to Kem Weber's original drawings for the old Animation Building and his master plan for the studio. We even went back to the furniture he designed for the studio and asked ourselves 'How can we reproduce all this with contemporary materials and stay within a reasonable budget? How do we make this place look like it has this intangible quality that says it's a movie studio?' That was a very exciting process."

Then there was the matter of providing visitors with the opportunity to watch animators at work without making the situation impossibly uncomfortable for the artists themselves.

This New York street is part of the Disney–MGM Studios' back lot

471

The Disney parks have formed a close relationship with George Lucas, which has led to the development of attractions based on his movies such as the Indiana Jones Stunt Spectacular, at the Disney-MGM Studios in Florida (above), with live actors, and the Indiana Jones Adventure at Disneyland Park.

Concept art for the Indiana Jones Adventure

Opened in 1994, the Tower of Terror – located on Sunset Boulevard in the Disney–MGM Studios – has become one of the most popular attractions at Walt Disney World. Its sedate Edwardian architecture and decor belies its raison d'être, a *Twilight Zone* adventure that culminates in a hair-raising ride in a runaway elevator

Concept art for the Tower of Terror

"We had to meet with animators," Weis reports, "and try to understand how they work. What kind of personality quirks do they have? How can you make them feel comfortable when you're about to violate the sanctity of their working environment by bringing guests through to stare over their shoulders?"

The Disney–MGM Studios complex has the advantage of providing a perfect setting for anything connected with the entertainment industry. The Teenage Mutant Ninja Turtles belong there, and so do the Muppets. Other attractions include the Tower of Terror – a major thrill ride that draws on memories of Rod Serling's *Twilight Zone* – and a spectacular Indiana Jones show that continues the Disney organization's fruitful association with George Lucas, which dates back to the mid-eighties (see chapter 18). At the time of this writing, the animation studio tour is in a state of transition due in part to the fact that in 2003 the Florida feature animation operation was closed down. The reasons for this reflected practical business decisions rather than any creative shortcomings on the part of the Florida-based artists. The Florida workshop had in fact been responsible for three successful films – *Mulan, Lilo & Stitch*, and *Brother Bear* – but the restructuring of what had become a bloated feature animation department meant that it made sense to consolidate all future production in California. Top talent from Orlando was offered the opportunity to relocate to the West Coast.

In 1999, Walt Disney World introduced a new and very large attraction in the form of Disney's Animal Kingdom. Almost five times the size of the Magic Kingdom, this is a combined theme park and wildlife park, a place where Disney entertainments (such as a "prehistoric" roller coaster and a Tarzan live show) are available alongside more educational exhibits and safaris through landscapes representing Africa and Asia that permit visitors to see wild animals at close range in near approximations of their native environments.

Like all Disney parks, Disney's Animal Kingdom has a hub, in the form of Discovery Island, which features the Tree of Life, trails with lemurs and kangaroos, and the astonishing 3-D show, *It's Tough to Be a Bug* – based on some characters in Pixar's *A Bug's Life* – an extravaganza that combines startling optical effects with other mind-bending tricks (the senses of hearing, smell, and touch are very much involved). It would be unfair to give away too much in terms of specific incidents, but if you've ever considered how it might feel to be a bug under attack by humans, imagine how it would be if the tables were turned and bugs went on the offensive.

From this hub, visitors can make their way to the safari areas where animals such as lions and elephants can be observed from trucks, and where pedestrian zones such as the Pangani Forest Exploration Trail permit close encounters with gorillas and a host of other animals. The African safari section of the park also features tribal villages, a tropical port, and open-air markets. Other destinations include Rafiki's Planet Watch (devoted to ecology), the Oasis (an exotic garden alive with

Popular destinations in Disney's Animal
Kingdom include the Dinosaur attraction (left)
and the Tree of Life on Discovery Island.

wildlife), Camp Minnie-Mickey (a "mountain" retreat where kids will find the famous characters in an unusual setting), and DinoLand USA.

It is in DinoLand that you will find the Primeval Whirl roller coaster, a modern version of the old "scenic railway" concept (of which the Matterhorn ride is a classic example) in which the cars rush and jolt through a landscaped setting of caves and canyons, in this case dressed to resemble an environment such as might have been inhabited by dinosaurs. Another carnival-type ride is the TriceraTop Spin, in which visitors are sent on a dizzying journey to nowhere in vehicles that resemble triceratops. Most exciting of all is the ride known simply as Dinosaur, in which the whole range of Disney special effects is used to bring visitors face to face with the giant reptiles of the Mesozoic era (and with a meteor shower), while rushing through another prehistoric landscape, this time in "shuttle-craft" cars that feature a technology which allows riders to be systematically jolted and jerked around while traveling at high speed – a trip only for the adventurous.

Nearby is the Fossil Preparation Laboratory, where real life paleontologists can be seen working with fossils. The Boneyard is another attraction, where young would-be paleontologists can engage in a realistic "dig" that features a cast replica of a fossilized dinosaur. Also in DinoLand will be found the Cretaceous Trail, which is a setting for animals descended from creatures that were alive during the age of the dinosaurs.

Like EPCOT, Animal Kingdom provides a blend of education and entertainment, and many families seem to split their time between these two parks. The reality is that there are so many things to do in Walt Disney World that it is almost impossible to experience them all during a single visit, even one lasting several days. Aside from the theme parks proper, for example, there are smaller water parks such as Blizzard Beach and Typhoon Lagoon where bathers can enjoy six-foot breakers produced by a giant wave machine. Add to that golf, tennis, water skiing, and scores of other conventional leisure activities, and it's clear that Walt Disney World is a resort on a scale that has never been seen before, featuring a scope and variety of recreational possibilities that fulfills the vision of its creator, even as it continues to evolve and expand.

20 Renewal

It could be argued that Walt Disney was the archetypal American of his generation – an Everyman of genius – and, while he cherished the values and institutions of Middle America, he also seemed to feel, in a very straightforward way, that America's ethnic plurality permitted him to tap into other cultures and environments from around the world. In his movies he explored British historical legend, European folklore, and the wildlife of Africa, Asia, and Alaska. He did not build his proposed International Street in Disneyland, but Africa was present (in the form of the Jungle Cruise), as was the colorful architecture of the Caribbean, half-timbered cottages out of the Bavarian forests, and even a simulation of one of Europe's natural marvels – the Matterhorn.

EPCOT Center carried the international theme still further. Nor was this a one-way romance. Visitors from overseas loved Disneyland and Walt Disney World. In a typical year, one out of every five visitors to the Florida park is from outside the United States. It was only a matter of time before the question of building a Disney theme park abroad would be placed on the agenda.

The first move came from Japan.

Dreamland – an unlicensed imitation of Disneyland – had been built there in the early sixties, but failed to live up to expectations largely because the entrepreneurs behind it had overlooked the rather obvious fact that a Disney-type park would be less than complete without Disney characters and Disney expertise.

In 1978, a group of executives representing Japan's Keisei Electric Railway Company approached Disney management with an invitation to build an authentic version of the Magic Kingdom on a 201-acre property it owned on the outskirts of Tokyo. Real estate is enormously valuable in Japan. Normally, such a site would have been developed as housing or commercial space. In this case, government regulations forbade that usage, insisting that this tract of landfill on Tokyo Bay be reserved for recreational purposes. Keisei had financial problems at the time and wanted to maximize its profits from the site. It was suggested that building a version of Disneyland – the ultimate recreational facility – on the property would satisfy everyone's requirements.

Disney management was both intrigued by the proposal and worried that the scheme might be flawed. For one thing, Tokyo's climate was very different from that of Anaheim and Orlando. Would people attend the Park in significant numbers during the cold winter season? And what about cultural differences? Surely some of the Magic Kingdom's attractions would have to be replaced with Japanese-oriented shows?

"Don't worry about the climate," Japanese executives reassured them. "If the park is built right, people will come. And don't worry about adapting to Japanese tastes. The reason people will come is precisely because it is so American."

There was also the matter of investment. Disney was pouring much of its resources into building EPCOT Center and did not want to assume additional debt to invest in a Japanese park. But the Japanese entrepreneurs had an answer to this, too. The park would be built, owned, and operated by a new Japanese company named Oriental Land (jointly owned by Keisei and Mitsui Real Estate), which would provide financing. Disney would design the Park and have an ongoing right and

In Tokyo Disneyland, Main Street has been replaced by a covered arcade known as World Bazaar which offers shelter from inclement weather

Most of the rides in Tokyo Disneyland – such as Big Thunder Mountain – would seem to be familiar to anyone who had visited Disneyland in Anaheim or The Magic Kingdom in Orlando

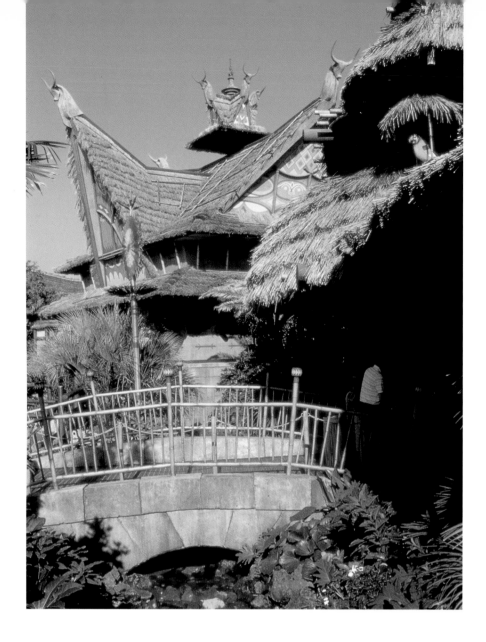

A corner of Adventureland at Tokyo Disneyland

responsibility to advise in its operation, in return for which the company would receive 10 percent of park admissions and 5 percent of revenues from concessions.

This was the arrangement that was agreed to. In retrospect, given the enormous success of Tokyo Disneyland, it might be argued that Disney should have found a way to invest its own capital in the project at the outset. That said, however, the deal proved profitable for everyone concerned, and Tokyo Disneyland demonstrated that the Magic Kingdom concept could indeed be exported to other parts of the globe.

Anyone who has visited Anaheim's Disneyland or the Magic Kingdom in Orlando would find much in Tokyo Disneyland that is very familiar. There is a fairy-tale castle at the hub – Cinderella's, in this case – fronting onto a circular plaza where turn-of-the-century vehicles glide gracefully by. There is a Fantasyland, an Adventureland, and a Tomorrowland; and although Frontierland has been transformed into Westernland, it retains many features of the American parks, such as Big Thunder Mountain, the Country Bear Theater, and the Mark Twain River Boat. Adventureland has a Jungle Cruise, a Swiss Family Treehouse, and its own edition of Pirates of the Caribbean. Tomorrowland has Space Mountain and

The Western River Railroad at Tokyo Disneyland takes its passengers past exotic sights such as this Native American encampment

George Lucas's Star Tours show. The Haunted Mansion has strayed into Fantasyland, where it makes an appropriate neighbor for Cinderella's Golden Carousel and It's a Small World.

But there are some significant differences, too. No railroad circles the park (though a smaller Western River Railroad threads its way around Adventureland and Westernland). Most surprisingly, perhaps, Main Street has been replaced by a cruciform, glass-covered arcade known as World Bazaar. In practice, World Bazaar offers many of Main Street's familiar attractions, boutiques, and cafés, such as the Main Street Cinema and the Disney Emporium, while also affording protection from inclement weather.

As the Japanese investors had predicted, bad weather does little to keep customers away from the Park. One member of the Imagineering team recalls a day when the forecast reported the possibility of the edge of a typhoon brushing the Tokyo area:

"There was talk of closing the Park, for safety reasons, but so many visitors showed up that it would have been more dangerous to try to keep them out. Attendance that day was over fifteen thousand!"

In the first ten years of its existence, total attendance at the Tokyo park was greater than the total population of Japan.

The notion of building a Disney theme park in Europe had been discussed as early as the seventies, but there had been no follow-through at the time because more weight had been given to the myriad problems – site, climate, possible culture clashes, financing – than to the long-term potential of such a project. The success of the Tokyo park began to change the prevailing attitude. Preliminary discussions with the governments of France and Spain were inaugurated in the early eighties, as various sites were investigated by a team led by Dick Nunis, but it was not until after the new management team took over the reins in 1984 that concrete moves were made to realize a European park.

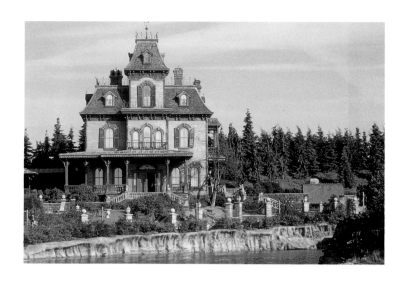

Frontierland in Disneyland Paris: Cottonwood Creek (left) and the Phantom Manor, as the European edition of the Haunted Mansion is called

Spain and Portugal had both campaigned for the Park – the search team had studied other parts of Europe, too – but it was France that was eventually selected as the home for EuroDisney, a name that eventually would be changed to Disneyland Paris in deference to the proximity of the site, Marne-la-Vallée, to the French capital. Michael Eisner had been open to other possibilities, but he was an unabashed champion of the eventual choice, his rationale being that Paris is the hub of Europe.

By the time Eisner signed an agreement with Laurent Fabius, prime minister of France, in December of 1985, Imagineers had been at work on concepts for the Park for some time. One of these Imagineers, Tony Baxter – a senior vice president for creative development – points out that the proximity to Paris brought with it some special considerations.

"This was a new kind of challenge," says Baxter, who grew up in Disneyland's backyard and scooped ice cream on Main Street before becoming an Imagineer. "We had to go into an environment where art and artistry and culture have traditions going back thousands of years. It wasn't like Anaheim or Florida, where there was nothing to judge us against. In France we were going up against fine shopping, historical architecture, and a landscape that defines the words 'charming' and 'pastoral.' We had to go into that environment and redefine Disneyland. What we built had to be recognizable as Disney product, but we had to adjust to a different set of values."

Some decisions, says Baxter, were relatively easy.

"Rethinking the Old West, for example. Walt had visualized it as an idyllic, pastoral Mississippi River landscape, where two boys – Tom and Huck – could run away to an island. It was the perfect escape for consumers who had been sitting in a traffic jam on the Santa Ana Freeway. But Europeans are looking for something completely different. They take serenity and pastoral beauty for granted. When they think of the Old West, they think of the *wild* West. An exciting, energetic place. We realized that our EuroDisney Frontierland would have to reflect that. What we would have to give them was the raucous, roaring atmosphere of the

Main Street Motors (opposite top) is typical of the businesses along Main Street at Disneyland Paris in that it emphasizes Americana to the nth degree. In other parts of Disneyland Paris, however, tribute is paid to European popular culture. In Discoveryland, for example, the submarine *Nautilus* (opposite bottom) pays tribute to the French science-fiction pioneer Jules Verne

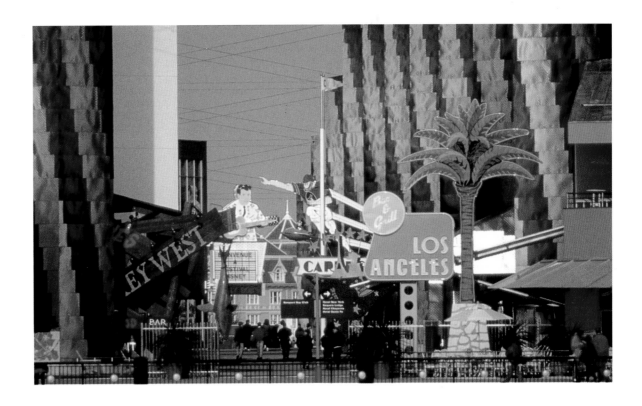

Located on the perimeter of Disneyland Paris is Festival Disney, an area that features American-style entertainment, from jazz to country-and-western music

The Château at the hub of Disneyland Paris is the ultimate storybook castle

1849 Gold Rush – something that had captured the imagination of the whole world – and we would have to cater to their fascination with Native American culture, and to their Hollywood-nurtured love of the rowdy world of the cowboy, including the rustler and the bad guy.

"We even did the Haunted Mansion in a sinister Western land-baron style, like some cattle mogul's palatial spread, and we changed the ride itself so that instead of ending in a gothic graveyard it ends in a California ghost town, with coyotes baying at the moon and ghost riders in the sky.

"That was easy. Far more difficult was deciding what to do with the castle. How do you compete with all those real castles along the Loire? We had to reinvent the castle, and our solution was to make it more like an illustration in a book of fairy tales – an illustration by someone like Arthur Rackham. So it's built on a crag, and part of the second floor is supported by stone trees. The colors are fairy-tale colors and the architecture is deliberately distorted. There's a dragon living in a cavern underneath the castle and Merlin's workshop is in the middle of it all. And we've added a hedge maze, like the one at Hampton Court Palace in England, which is an interactive experience of the most primitive kind. People were predicting that there would be no lines for that, but it's turned out to be a thirty-minute wait."

Unlike the Japanese, Europeans *were* expecting to find reflections of their own world in the Park, and the contract with the French government called for appropriate tributes to French civilization in particular and European culture in general.

"One way we tried to do this," says Baxter, "was to replace Tomorrow-land with something we called Discoveryland, which is based around the idea of Jules Verne's Discovery Bay. Verne's vision of the future had inspired Walt, yet it remains very European, very French, and it gave us the opportunity to come up with something that would let us pay tribute to other visionaries, from Leonardo da Vinci to H. G. Wells to George Lucas."

To a large extent, Discoveryland is about the history of the future, which has the advantage of not going out of date as quickly as the future itself, as represented in the various Tomorrowlands. Even so, it does have the Lucas-inspired Star Tours ride and other concessions to contemporary futurism.

Unlike its Tokyo cousin, Disneyland Paris has a conventional open Main Street, but it is a Main Street that is even more American, if possible, than those in the original Disneyland and Florida's Magic Kingdom.

"Europeans," Baxter theorizes, "are interested in what's behind the storefronts. The facades are not enough. Instead of having Coke Corner, which is just a place where you go for a Coke and a hot dog – something Americans take for granted – we gave European visitors Casey's Corner, which is a kind of vintage soda fountain environment in which visitors are enveloped in American atmosphere and imagery – baseball memorabilia all over the place and baseball songs playing over the speakers."

Disneyland Paris would also feature a huge entertainment center known as Festival Disney. With buildings designed by postmodernist architect Frank Gehry, this area would be home to a wild West show and to streets representing American destinations such as New York, Los Angeles, and Key West, their neon signs luring the visitor into American-style steak-houses, a nightclub, and even a country-and-western bar.

Ownership and management of the entire complex would be primarily European, but this time Disney held onto 49 percent of the stock. Ground was broken in 1990 and the Park was opened in 1992. Almost immediately there were rumors that it was doing poorly, and soon Disney management acknowledged that it was losing money.

One serious problem was that the consortium that built the park sank a great deal of capital into five huge hotels grouped around a lake on the edge of the property. The consortium had not reckoned sufficiently with the fact that Paris, with its vast selection of hotels – from cheap pensions to the finest deluxe establishments – was barely an hour away from the Park by train. Many Park-bound visitors preferred to spend their nights in the city, and the Disneyland Paris hotels remained underbooked to the point where they were operating at a substantial loss. Recession and European habits – like bringing a picnic lunch instead of eating at one of the park's restaurants – also cut into profits.

The theme park itself, however, was a resounding success, attracting more than ten million visitors in its first year. Reports that losses from the resort (as opposed to the theme park) might cause the entire complex to close proved premature when a plan to refinance the enterprise was announced in the spring of 1994. In part, this involved the purchase of 74.6 million shares of EuroDisney s.c.a by Prince Alwaleed of Saudi

Overleaf: sculptural form, dramatic illumination, and the theatrical use of color are made to play crucial roles in the way the theme parks are brought to life. As the evening sky darkens, thousands of lights transform the Orbitron and Space Mountain in Tomorrowland at Walt Disney World, flooding the scene with color that heightens the sense of nocturnal excitement

Arabia, chairman of the United Saudi Commercial Bank, already a major stockholder in the operating company. The Walt Disney Company's financial interest in the enterprise was thereby reduced from 49 percent to 40 percent.

"Europeans love Disneyland Paris," says Michael Eisner. "Some French intellectuals objected to our presence at first, but that's calmed down now and President [François] Mitterrand's recent visit to the Park had considerable symbolic importance. The theme park itself already does wonderful business and I'm convinced the whole complex will be profitable in the near future. To mention just one thing, with the Channel Tunnel open the British are now able to travel from London to Paris in three and a half hours by high-speed train. That alone will make a big difference."

Asked whether he would still pick Paris as his site for the Park if he were starting over today, he says that he has not changed his mind about that.

"As I said when we first launched the idea, Paris is the hub of Europe. . . . It's at the center of three hundred million people living on a landmass the size of the USA east of the Mississippi. And the climate has not been a problem. Not everything has to be done in the sun. Northern Europeans are used to doing things in cold weather. They don't just sit at home. Our attendance figures prove that."

Disney's dedication to the Paris park is apparent in the fact that several new rides have been opened in anticipation of the need for increased capacity, and other attractions, including a version of Space Mountain, are already committed as well. This is only part of a program of updating and expansion that applies to all the parks.

Visitors to the Magic Kingdom at Walt Disney World enjoy the planned scares of Alien Encounter

"The audience changes," says Tony Baxter, "and we have to change with it. That doesn't mean that everything has to be replaced. The Jungle Cruise has stayed the same for decades. It's technologically crude, but it still works because of the rapport the guides build with the visitors. But other things must change because the last thing we want is for Disneyland, or any of the parks, to be like a museum, full of things that have rich associations for people who grew up in the fifties but meaningless to kids who were born in the eighties.

"Even the pace of a ride has to change. When we put together a version of It's a Small World for Europe, we brought the continents closer together to make room for America, which doesn't exist in the other parks. In doing so, we cut the ride from eleven minutes to eight minutes, and the interesting thing is that it seems right at that length. No one feels they're being shortchanged because people expect information to be delivered more quickly these days. That's why commercials run ten seconds now instead of ninety seconds, and our animated features are faster paced than they were in the days of *Snow White*. You have to be aware of these changes in sensibility whether you're making a movie like *Aladdin* or designing an attraction for the parks."

The recent success of special-effects movies – from the *Star Wars* trilogy to *Jurassic Park* – has certainly influenced the way in which Imagineers think about the design of certain rides. *Jurassic Park* is not only set largely in a theme park, but with its shock effects, it is actually very much like an extended theme park ride, the thrills more important than the narrative. The George Lucas *Star Wars* attraction Star Tours, now in the Disney theme parks, derives directly from the films on which it is based. Instead of placing the rider in an actual moving vehicle, as in earlier Disney attractions, Star Tours uses almost purely cinematic means – optical effects and sophisticated sound technology – to create the illusion of travel through deep space and the excitement of intergalactic warfare. The entire cabin is rigged to jolt and vibrate, but beyond that it goes nowhere, though the ride seems to cover thousands of miles. This kind of special-effects ride, dependent upon sensory illusionism, is likely to be encountered more and more often in future parks. It will be seen in the following chapter that this kind of special-effects attraction, dependent to varying degrees upon virtual reality and sensory illusion, has come to play an ever more important role in the theme park developments of the past decade.

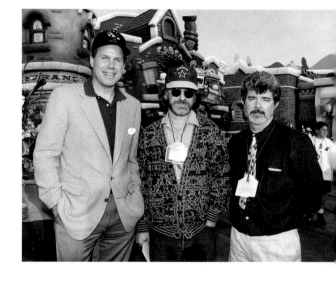

Disney CEO Michael Eisner (left) with Steven Spielberg (center) and George Lucas at the opening of Mickey's Toontown in Anaheim

21 Roots and Branches

Visitors to the Condor Flats section of Disney's California Adventure – the all-new Anaheim theme park which opened at the Disneyland Resort in 2001 – can take a ride named Soarin' Over California, justifiably subtitled an "airborne adventure." It is the epitome of the new kind of special-effects trip, as breathtaking as any roller-coaster ride while at the same time providing a feast for the eyes and other senses that is both exhilarating and absorbing. Before the ride begins, visitors strap into chairlift-type seats suspended from "wings," facing a limpid expanse of pure cerulean. When the lights are doused, the chairs literally take off, sailing forty feet upward inside the dome, which becomes an all-enveloping, wrap-around screen on which images are projected using the latest IMAX technology.

Suddenly the visitor feels as if he is the pilot of a hang glider, soaring through clouds until these part to reveal the Golden Gate Bridge, busy with rush hour traffic, ferries and pleasure craft below in the chilly waters of the bay. The sensation of being there is astonishing, realistic to the extent of feeling the wind blowing in one's hair. The illusion is rooted in the technology that has been used for training pilots in flight simulators, but here it has been carried to new levels of virtual reality that become more evident as the ride carries the visitor to other California landmarks. Banking amongst the cliffs of Yosemite, close to Half Dome, one is presented with a view of the park that no tourist ever sees. Skimming in over a grove of redwoods, one feels as if one's toes are about to touch the treetops, and the sensation is enhanced by the scent of pine needles. Dropping low above a pod of surfers, one smells the ocean and feels – or is it just imagination? – the bracing splash of windblown spray lashed off the breakers.

The journey also visits a whitewater river, the vineyards of Napa Valley, and the snowy peaks of the High Sierras above Lake Tahoe, zooming in so close to skiers that a disaster seems imminent. This is as dramatic as the dizziest drop on any roller coaster, yet no one screams, since everybody is holding his breath, reflexes fooled by the simulated reality, senses dazzled by the sheer spectacle. Finally the visitor finds himself airborne above the nighttime freeways of Southern California, gliding through the high-rise canyons of downtown Los Angeles before arriving above Disneyland just in time to be engulfed by the nightly fireworks.

In one way this ride recalls the early days of cinema when, in order to thrill audiences, it was enough to mount a movie camera on the front of a train and show the landscape it was traveling through as if seen from the point of view of the engineer. In its technical sophistication, however, Soarin' Over California is completely modern, capitalizing on optical tricks and other effects that cannot be found in ordinary movie theaters. It might be argued that this ride typifies California Adventure as a whole, as a mélange of the traditional and the innovative that has managed to strike just the right balance.

At first glance, the idea of building a theme park dedicated to the pleasures and natural wonders of California in the real California seems a little redundant. After all, why not jump in your car and enjoy the authentic thing? On reflection, however, that argument is rather like being in New York and saying, "Why bother to visit a movie theater to see Woody Allen's *Manhattan* when the real Manhattan is right outside the door? Why not just buy a subway pass?" Disney's California

The Paradise Pier section of Disney's California Adventure recaptures the fun of the Golden Age of the state's seaside boardwalks, and adds a few new thrills such as the California Screamin' roller coaster

Grizzly Peak (left) is at the hub of Disney's California Adventure. Nearby is one of the park's most popular attractions, Grizzly River Run, a realistic simulation of a white water run

Adventure does not purport to duplicate California, any more than *Manhattan* pretends to represent the average New Yorker's everyday experience of his city. California Adventure is what it is, a California-themed entertainment – as *Manhattan* is a New York–themed entertainment – that gives some carefully chosen tastes and samples of the real thing in rides such as Soarin'.

The main gate to California Adventure – adjacent to the familiar main gate to Disneyland – gives access to Sunshine Plaza, a retail zone that provides access to the area known as Golden State, the park's central hub, physically dominated by Grizzly Peak, an outcrop of artificial rock that has the appearance of a rampant bear. This hub leads naturally to surrounding themed areas including Paradise Pier and the Hollywood Pictures Backlot. This latter area is a smaller but still spacious version of the Disney-MGM Studios in Orlando, a tribute to the movie industry's golden age. Here are found elements that have been borrowed from the Florida park, such as Jim Henson's MuppetVision 3-D show. The Disney animation display here is not as extensive as its Florida counterpart, but it is impressive nonetheless, with thousands of examples of animation art from all periods, along with films that provide background stories, and a number of imaginative interactive features. The back lot area is also home to some of the park's most lavish live shows.

It could be argued that California has fewer bugs than Minnesota or Mississippi, but it has its fair share nonetheless and this provides the excuse for A Bug's Land, which is in fact a spin-off of the Pixar computer-animated hit *A Bug's Life* (and anyway Pixar is located in California). Much of this area is devoted to Flik's Fun Fair, a cluster of attractions designed for younger patrons who can enjoy rides such as Heimlich's Chew Chew Train, which travels through a landscape of intensely scented food, and Tuck and Roll's Drive'Em Buggies, an updated form of beetle-shaped bumper cars featuring vehicles that talk back when hit. The big show here, however, is the *It's Tough to Be a Bug!* 3-D movie, already such a hit at Disney's Animal Kingdom in Orlando.

Paradise Pier is a celebration of California's world famous beach culture, memorializing the surf and the concrete boardwalks, and especially the great amusement piers that during the first half of the twentieth century were the equivalent of today's theme parks, pushing out into the fringes of the Pacific Ocean from San Diego to Santa Cruz and beyond. Only a couple still survive, and Paradise Pier attempts to make up for those that have vanished. Its atmosphere is less seedy than you would have found on the old Ocean Park Pier in its heyday, but there's plenty of fun to be had with attractions ranging from the gracious Sun Wheel Ferris wheel to the Maliboomer thrill ride. There is an entry-level roller coaster – Mulholland Madness – for the younger crowd, while the bold can pit their courage against California Screamin', a monster coaster that catapults you into your ride as if rocket propelled, its cars looping the loop through a giant representation of Mickey's ears. Nearby are traditional boardwalk games, like Skeeball, and more thrill rides like the Orange Stinger.

Along with Soarin' Over California, the Golden State portion of the park has an open-air thrill ride in the form of Grizzly River Run, a simulated white water trip that leaves everyone wet and wanting more. A loving reproduction of Monterey's Cannery Row, named Pacific Wharf, is home to a number of restaurants. There are places to eat throughout the park, but the Golden State section offers the most, and while on Pacific Wharf you can visit a satellite of Boudin's San Francisco sourdough bakery, seeing how their bread is prepared before eating in their restaurant, or you can watch tortillas being made by hand before dining at the Mission Tortilla Factory. A short walk will bring you to the Golden Vine Winery, where you can learn about winemaking and eat some of the most ambitious food in the entire Disneyland Resort complex.

There was a time when eating at the Disney theme parks tended to come down to a choice between bland sandwiches and bland imitations of regional or ethnic cuisines. There are still examples of that kind of restaurant left for anyone suffering from incurable nostalgia, but all of the parks now boast restaurants that hold their own. At both Walt Disney World and the Disneyland Resort, there is now a supplementary retail and refreshment area known as Downtown Disney where good food is one of the attractions. It is widely recognized that the Disney influence transformed retail shopping areas in America, and in both Downtown Disneys that influence returns to its source in the form of a themed, open-air, village-like mall, to which there is no admission charge.

Disney has been in the hotel business since 1971. Handsome hotels are to be found at Walt Disney World, Disneyland Paris, and the Disney parks in Tokyo, but perhaps the most striking to be built so far is the Grand Californian, which has been slotted snugly into the Disneyland resort campus between California Adventure and Downtown Disney. A lovingly executed tribute to the California craftsman style of the early 1900s, the Grand Californian is a recreation on a huge scale of the kind

California Adventure's Sun Wheel

Soarin' Over California is a state-of-the-art special-effects ride that must be experienced to be appreciated

of hunting lodge/hotel once built for the pleasure of the wealthy in places like Yosemite National Park. Its vast, multi-story lobby is built around a mountainous fireplace constructed from enormous boulders. The design detail recalls the work of famous architects such as Greene & Greene and Frank Lloyd Wright. By any standards, this is an outstanding hotel, conceived to satisfy the tastes and needs of sophisticated travelers. It is another example of how the Disney resort areas have learned to cater to adults over the years.

It was, of course, always Walt Disney's intention to entertain adults as well as children. The American family, however, is no longer governed by the same dynamics as it was in 1955, and in any case visitors to the parks now come from all over the world. Kids remain much the same, at least to the extent that they still get their kicks from riding roller coasters or meeting Mickey Mouse on Main Street, according to age. The adult components of the family package have become more sophisticated, and this is reflected in the more recent parks. California Adventure has plenty to keep both children and teens happy, but with its wine tastings and its appeal to boardwalk nostalgia, it has a great deal to offer well-traveled adult visitors as well.

Much the same could be said of Disney's new Japanese park, the in-elegantly named Tokyo DisneySea. Atmospherically, this park, opened in 2001, benefits greatly from the fact that the Tokyo Disney Resort is located on Tokyo Bay and thus possesses a maritime atmosphere that was built-in from the outset. One section – a nostalgic tribute to American commercial waterfronts of the early 20th century – is adjacent to the ocean, and from the decks of the reproduction ocean liner docked there the visitor can see out over the waters that once provided a favorite subject for artists like Hokusai and Hiroshige.

The American Waterfront also features an antique elevated electric train, such as might have been found in Manhattan a hundred years ago, and this carries passengers to Port Discovery, a science-oriented area where it's possible to experience what it's like to face hurricane force winds and to travel into the eye of a cyclone aboard a flying weather laboratory.

Other areas of the park include Mediterranean Harbor, where can be found a Riviera-like fishing town and a waterfront representing Venice, complete with the inevitable gondolas. The Arabian Coast section is an exercise in orientalism that conjures up the world of *Aladdin* and the Sinbad legends, while Lost River Delta is the Caribbean coast of a Central American rainforest environment furnished with a man-made rocky promontory in which has been installed Tokyo's version of the Indiana Jones Adventure.

Nearby is Mermaid Lagoon, themed around *The Little Mermaid*, and also close by is Mysterious Island in which the principal attractions are based on Jules Vernes' classic stories *20,000 Leagues Under the Sea* and *Journey to the Center of the Earth*. A feature of all these areas is the variety of ships and boats to be found, from yachts and schooners to dhows and river steamers, and, like California Adventure, DisneySea has spawned a shopping and dining adjunct as well as a luxury hostelry in the form of the Mediterranean-inflected Hotel MiraCosta.

In the end, movies, television, stage shows, and theme parks are all expressions of a single philosophy, which can be traced back to the imagination of Walt Disney.

"The Disney name," says Michael Eisner, "conjures up an intellectual response but also an emotional response. It carries with it a certain expectation of quality, and it's been our responsibility…to deliver on the promise that is implicit in the Walt Disney name because of his achievements. But we can't just rest on his laurels. We have to move forward."

In the first decade of the twenty-first century, The Walt Disney Company is stronger than it has ever been and continues to move forward on many fronts. The present management has succeeded in sustaining Walt Disney's legacy while providing the organization with a level of financial security that was seldom enjoyed during the founder's lifetime. There were times when Walt Disney had to mortgage his home in order to realize his next project, and there were few periods when he could afford to finance more than one major project at a time. All that has changed.

Two sections of Tokyo DisneySea include the period American Waterfront (top) and a Mediterranean port (center). Port Discovery is another feature of Tokyo DisneySea that brings visitors into contact with scientific ideas (bottom)

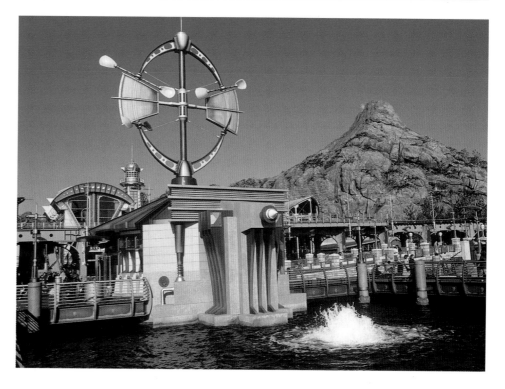

Perhaps the greatest achievement of Michael Eisner and the late Frank Wells has been to build a company in which no creative endeavor need be aborted for lack of available funding. The result has been a flood of creativity that has led to films like *Aladdin* and *Lilo & Stitch,* stage musicals such as *The Lion King,* and innovative theme parks ranging from Disneyland Paris to Disney's California Adventure.

Clearly Eisner is correct in saying that the company must continue to look to the future. At the same time, there is every reason for us to continue to pay tribute to Walt Disney the man, and to his extraordinary achievements. In the end, today's empire is still predicated on those first brief cartoons, featuring Mickey, Donald, Goofy, Pluto and the gang, upon the Silly Symphonies, and on the five amazing animated features released between 1937 and 1942.

Later, Walt Disney went on to build pleasure parks for the millions. It is appropriate that his name has recently been memorialized with a great building, Walt Disney Concert Hall, the widely acclaimed Los Angeles music venue designed by Frank Gehry and opened to the public in 2003. Located a short drive from that first storefront studio, Walt Disney Concert Hall owes its existence chiefly to a generous gift from Walt's widow, Lillian, and to the determination of his daughter Diane who spearheaded the drive to get the building erected when many forces seemed to conspire against its completion.

A question often asked around Hollywood is, "What is the Disney secret?" The answer is, "The persistence of the Disney legacy." It was founded by Walt Disney himself, closely supported by his brother Roy and his close collaborator Ub Iwerks; it was nourished by a generation of gifted artists that included Bill Tytla, Grim Natwick, Fred Moore, Art Babbitt and Norm Ferguson and many others; it was carried on by the Nine Old Men, and they in turn handed it on to the present generation of artists – men like Glen Keane and Andreas Deja – who have enjoyed a boost from Roy E. Disney, a man determined to keep the legacy alive.

It is a legacy that represents more than eight decades of accumulated knowledge – one that is unique in the history of popular culture.

Index

Acknowledgments

The first edition of this book appeared in 1973 and it has never been out of print, in one form or another, since that time. Major updates include the present edition and the edition that appeared in 1995. Over the years, I have interviewed or otherwise received help from many Disney artists, executives, and other employees, past and present, some of whom are no longer with us. For the sake of clarity, I am dividing these acknowledgments into two parts, first thanking those who assisted and encouraged me in this revision and the one that preceded it (there being a number of people whose input contributed to both versions). I will then turn my attention to the men and women whose help and guidance I received while preparing the first edition.

In particular, I would like to offer special thanks to Michael Eisner and Roy E. Disney, who have been generous with their time and provided me with crucial insights into the company's operations and ambitions.

Present and former Disney executives who provided me with wide-ranging assistance include Jeffrey Katzenberg, Peter Schneider, Thomas Schumacher, Gary Krisel, John Dreyer, and David Stainton. Howard Green has always been available to answer my questions, and to guide me to appropriate sources within the organization. Beyond that, he has provided an insider's perspective on the recent history of the company that has been perceptive, objective, and invaluable.

Over the years, I have been fortunate enough to be able to spend a great deal of time with members of the Feature Animation department, conducting interviews, sitting in on meetings, attending in-house screenings, etc., and I would like to extend my gratitude to past and present members of that department, with special thanks to Don Hahn, John Musker, Ron Clements, Jim Pentecost, Don Ernst, Roy Conli, Rob Minkoff, Roger Allers, Gary Trousdale, Kirk Wise, Mike Gabriel, Eric Goldberg, and Hendel Butoy. My gratitude as well to Gretchen Albrecht, Cathy Alexander, Ruben Aquino, Hans Bacher, Doug Ball, James Baxter, Janet Bruce, Hortensia Casagran, Brenda Chapman, Karen Comella, Pam Conklin, Andreas Deja, Alice Dewey, Randy Fullmer, Andy Gaskill, David Goetz, Dee Haramia, Scott Johnston, Glen Keane, Vera Lanpher, Zoe Leader, Tony Meagher, Irene Mecchi, Jonathan Roberts, Robyn Roberts, James Russell, Dan St. Pierre, Chris Sanders, Scott Santoro, Stacy Slossy, and Ann Tucker. From the television animation division, I received valuable assistance from Greg Weisman and Patrick Regan.

I owe many thanks to the splendid team at the Disney Animation Research Library, originally assembled by Kay Salz. My warm thanks to her, to Susie Lee, Doug Engalla, Larry Ishino, and Ariel Levin. Thanks also to Steven M. Rogers and Ed Squair of the Photo Library.

Among the gifted team at Imagineering, I would like to offer my gratitude to Marty Sklar and the late John Hench, as well as Mickey Steinberg, Tony Baxter, Bob Weis, and Joe Lanzisero; also Jill Centeno of WDI visual art services, and Deeanna Willett and Van VanEmon of the Special Services Office attached to the Disneyland Resort.

I would like to reiterate my thanks to all the people who assisted me three decades ago. Among these I must single out Diane Disney Miller, Ron Miller, Card Walker, Tom Jones, Vince Jefferds, and Jim Stewart, and veterans of the Disney talent pool that included Jim Algar, Ken Anderson, Art Babbitt, George Bruns, Les Clark, Jack Cutting, Marc Davis, Al Dempster, Floyd Gottfredson, Don Graham, Don Griffith, Joe Hale, Dick Huemer, Ollie Johnston, Milt Kahl, Ward Kimball, Eric Larson, Jim Macdonald, Lester Novros, Woolie Reitherman, Frank Thomas, Grace Turner, and the greatly under appreciated Bill Walsh.

Other Disney personnel from that period who provided valuable help included Leroy Anderson, Jack Brady, Jan Hedge, Mary Holoboff, Bob King, John Landon, Don MacLaughlin, Jim Matthews, Bob Moore, Frank Reilly, Sue Schwendeman, Dave Spencer, Carol Svendsen, and Bob White.

A crucial figure in the world of Disney scholarship, Dave Smith was on hand to welcome me to the studio in 1972, when I began researching this book, and has remained of incalculable assistance over the decades. I have also received much aid from members of the archive team he has built, notably Robert Tieman, Rebecca Cline, Collette Espino, and Adina Lerner.

Another link to the 1973 edition is my wife Linda, who joined me in my research and found many of the wonderful images that appear in the first eight chapters.

Among the people who were involved in realizing this book, in its various editions, I must single out Margaret Adamic, Chris Boneau, Stephanie Cheek, Allan Frost, Lisa Gerstel, Hunter Heller, Esther Kim, Virginia King, Aaron Meier, Heidi Miller, Russell Schroeder, Ken Shue, Michele Spane, and Krista Swager. Finally, very special thanks to my editors at Abrams, Eric Himmel and Andrea Danese, designer Russell Hassell, photo researcher Samantha Topol, and to the man who originated this entire project, the late Harry N. Abrams.

Christopher Finch